MEMSAHIBS

PRAISE FOR *MEMSAHIBS*

"Railing against 'repetitive and limiting representations' of memsahibs, Nath champions, instead, their colourful personalities, creative output and considerable socio-cultural impact, offering a vibrant alternative lens through which to view British women in the Raj."

—Chandrika Kaul, Professor of Modern History, University of St Andrews

"*Memsahibs* shows through their own writings that British women in the Raj saw their lives as adventurous, within the confines of a colonial world ruled by gender, race, and class, and themselves as heroic, surviving Indian dangers and British tedium."

—Indira Karamcheti, postcolonial literature specialist and Associate Professor of American Studies, Wesleyan University

MEMSAHIBS

BRITISH WOMEN IN COLONIAL INDIA

IPSHITA NATH

HarperCollins *Publishers* India

First published in the United Kingdom in 2022 by C. Hurst & Co. (Publishers) Ltd., New Wing, Somerset House, Strand, London, WC2R 1LA
www.hurstpublishers.com

This edition published in India by HarperCollins *Publishers* 2022
4th Floor, Tower A, Building No. 10, Phase II, DLF Cyber City,
Gurugram, Haryana – 122002
www.harpercollins.co.in

2 4 6 8 10 9 7 5 3 1

P-ISBN: 978-93-5629-008-2
E-ISBN: 978-93-5629-009-9

Printed and bound at
Thomson Press (India) Ltd

MIX
Paper
FSC FSC® C010615

This book is produced from independently certified FSC® paper
to ensure responsible forest management.

To Ma, Babu and Shelly

CONTENTS

ACKNOWLEDGEMENTS

My special thanks are due to Professor Saugata Bhaduri, Professor G. J. V. Prasad, and Professor Anisur Rehman for their valuable advice on my work; Arunava Sinha, translator and friend, for always lending an ear and offering encouragement; my colleagues at work, Professor Kusum Lata, Ms. Kanchan Mohindra, Dr. Seema Mathur, Dr. Mini Gill, Dr. Kalpana Rohit, and Dr. Rajnikant Goswami for their kind consideration and motivation; Professor Douglas E. Haynes at Dartmouth College for his enthusiastic support; and Dr. Jim Clifford and Professor Erika Dyck at the University of Saskatchewan for their relentless help and guidance, as well as confidence in me as I explored my area of study.

Books are written in the mind for years before they are written down, but this one wouldn't have been put to paper without Kanishka Gupta, friend and advisor, who was the first to tell me that I must write these stories about British women in India. My gratitude goes to Michael Dwyer at Hurst for his vision for this book; my wonderful editor, Lara Weisweiller-Wu, for her excellent assessment of and feedback on the manuscript—this book took shape because of her; Olivia Ralphs, who edited this book; and Rahul Soni at HarperCollins for his timely suggestions.

I convey my deepest gratitude to Professor Nishat Zaidi, my mentor and guide through the years, for always helping me see the 'bigger picture' and for always somehow knowing how something should be written, before it is even fully imagined. Last but not least, I am grateful to my friends and family for their love, patience, and kindness during the time I immersed myself in writing this book, especially through the most brutal waves of the pandemic in 2021.

GLOSSARY OF BRITISH-INDIAN TERMS

Aao	Come
Acchi baat	Good job/good thought
Ayah	A lady's maid or wet nurse
Baba log	Young boys
Banghies	Items used for carrying luggage
Bangla	Bungalow
Barha hazri	Breakfast
Barha shikar	Big-game hunting
Bazaar	Marketplace
Bhang	Indigenous intoxicant
Bheestie	Water carrier man
Bibi	Indian lady
Buckshish	Alms
Bursat	Rains
Butteewallah	Lamplighter
Chillum chee	A native contraption used like a pipe
Chota bursat	Pre-monsoon rains
Chota hazri	Meal taken before dawn; snack
Chota peg	A small peg of drink
Chowkidar	Guard
Chunam	Whitewash for walls/chemicals such as lime powder, used to keep away household pests
Churails	Female spirits or demons dwelling in trees, known to be hideous and preying on men
Claishees	Tent-pitchers

GLOSSARY OF BRITISH-INDIAN TERMS

Coolies	Bearers
Dak	Transport by relays of bullock-carriages or postal service
Dakoo/dacoit	Bandit
Dal	Cooked lentils
Dandi	Palanquin
Darzi	Tailor
Dawai	Medicine
Dhai	Midwife
Dhobi	Washerman
Dhurries	Rugs
Doolie	A covered litter
Doonghas	Houseboats, also known as floating houses, used by some locals in Kashmir
Durbar	Royal gathering
Firangees	Foreigners
Ganja	Cannabis
Gharry	Cart or carriage
Ghat	Bank of a river
Ghee	Clarified butter
Hakim	Native healer
Howdahs	Seats on top of an elephant, used during hunts
Hukkah	A smoking instrument that heats and vaporises tobacco, smoked through a long pipe
Hunqahs	Local villagers who helped during hunting
Jaadu	Magic (mostly black magic)
Jaao	Go
Jadoogars	Magicians
Jhampan	A kind of wooden hand-pulled rickshaw with two wheels, or a kind of palanquin common in the hills
Jharuwallah	Sweeper
Jungli	Wild/uncouth/uncivilised
Juwaub	Answer
Kafila	Caravan
Kala jugga	Black 'place'/town

GLOSSARY OF BRITISH-INDIAN TERMS

Kangris	Heated earthen pots
Khansama	Chief table servant
Khedder	Enclosure
Khitmatgar	A manservant or butler, or a servant who waits at table
Khus khus	Sweet grass used to make thin screens/curtains
Kutcha	Raw or temporary/clay
Kutcherries	Court
Lal bhalu/Harpat	Brown bears
Lambardar	Village headman
Loo	Hot winds
Mahout	Elephant driver
Maidans	Fields or gardens
Mali	Gardener
Masjid	Mosque
Mela	Carnival or fair
Missie baba	A young European girl
Mofussils	Rural areas or provincial towns
Munshi	Teacher
Musalchees	Torchbearers
Nautch	Native dance form
Nullah	Stream or channel
Paan	Addictive flavoured betelnut leaves used as stimulants
Palkee	Palanquin
Phansigar	One who kills by strangulation
Pitarrahs	Box cases, suitcases
Pukka	Solid/permanent
Pundit	Male teacher
Punkah	Manual fan
Purdah	A religious-cultural system of keeping women in confinement, in segregated spaces within the household
Rakush	Culturally misappropriated term commonly used to denote a monster or demon
Roomal	Scarf or handkerchief
Salaam	Form of greeting

GLOSSARY OF BRITISH-INDIAN TERMS

Saree	Indian garment for women
Sepoy	Soldier
Serai	Resting houses for travellers, like country inns
Shabash	Bravo
Shikar	Hunting
Shikari	Hunter
Sola topee	Pith helmets
Syces	Horsemen
Takut	Ticket
Tatties	Curtains
Tamasha	Spectacle
Thermantidotes	Devices of revolving fans in a box with *tatties* at the side
Thuggee	The practice of highway robberies and murders by thieves often called 'deceivers'
Thunder box	Toilet basin
Topee	Hat
Verandah	Balcony
Wallah	Man
Zenana	Segregated women's quarters

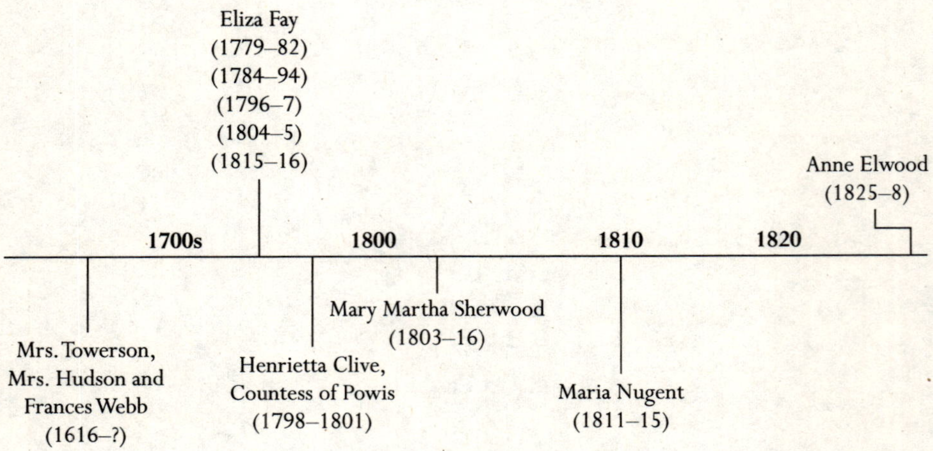
Eliza Fay
(1779–82)
(1784–94)
(1796–7)
(1804–5)
(1815–16)
Anne Elwood
(1825–8)
1700s
1800
1810
1820
Mrs. Towerson,
Mrs. Hudson and
Frances Webb
(1616–?)
Henrietta Clive,
Countess of Powis
(1798–1801)
Mary Martha Sherwood
(1803–16)
Maria Nugent
(1811–15)

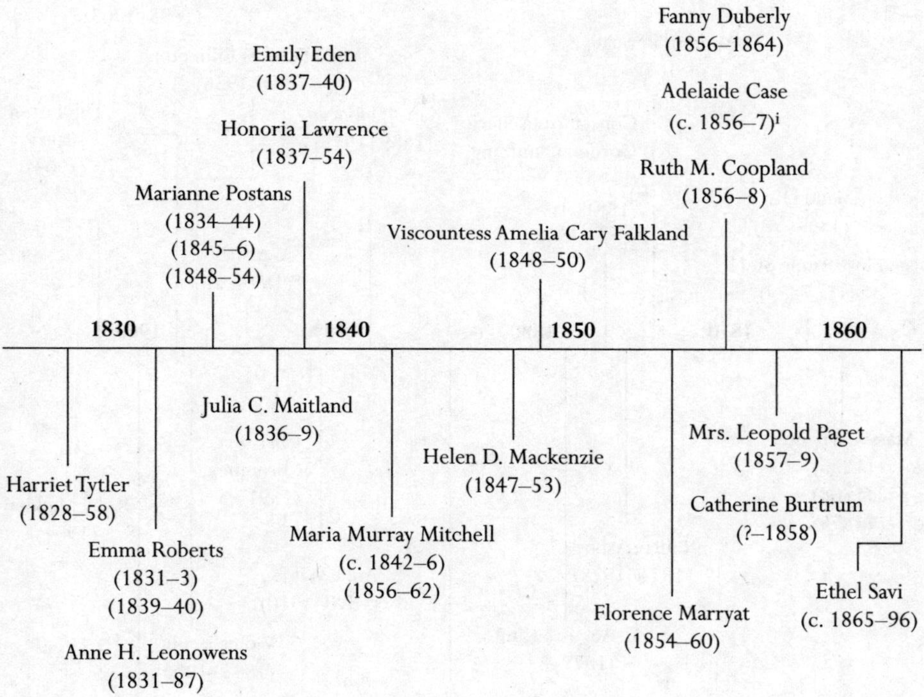

[i] It is unclear when Adelaide Case came to India; however, she was in India during the revolt and left in December 1857. Some recollections of the Rebellion are written by memsahibs who otherwise did not write any other records of their lives in India. Another example is Ruth M. Coopland.

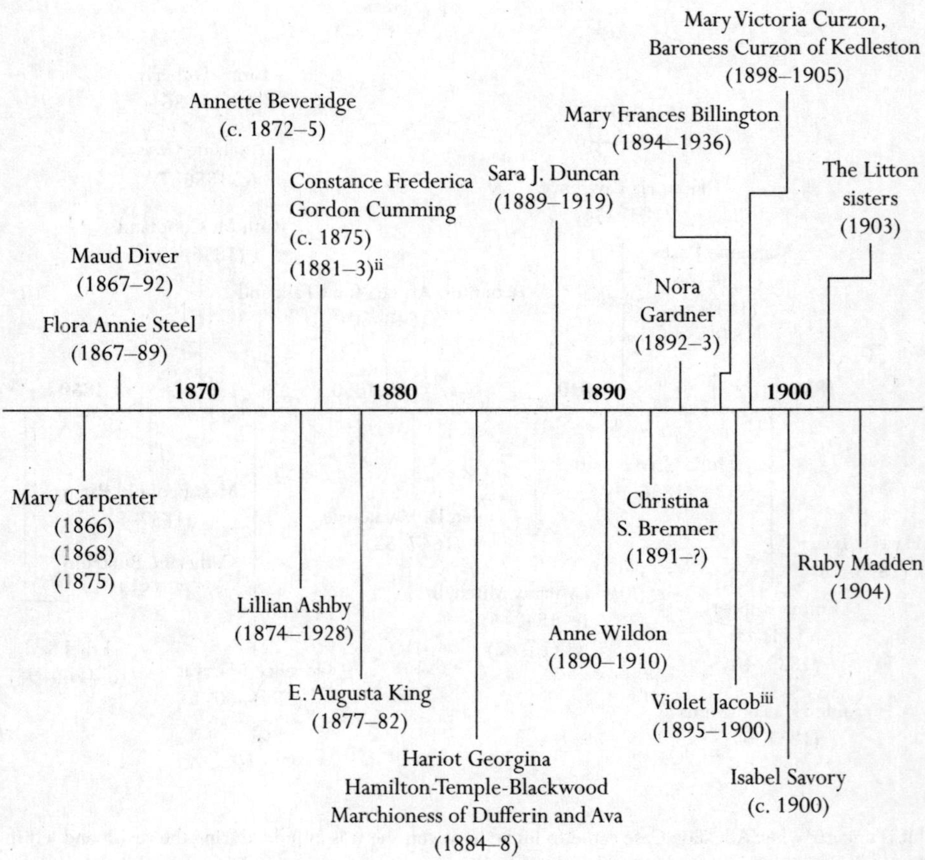

[ii] Constance F. G. Cumming seems to have visited India in the 1870s first, after which she wrote *From the Hebrides to the Himalayas*. She visited again in around 1881 for a period of eighteen months, after which she wrote her better-known work *In the Himalayas and on the Indian Plains*.

[iii] Violet Jacob was Australian and was the daughter of Sir John Madden, Chief Justice and Lieutenant-Governor of Victoria.

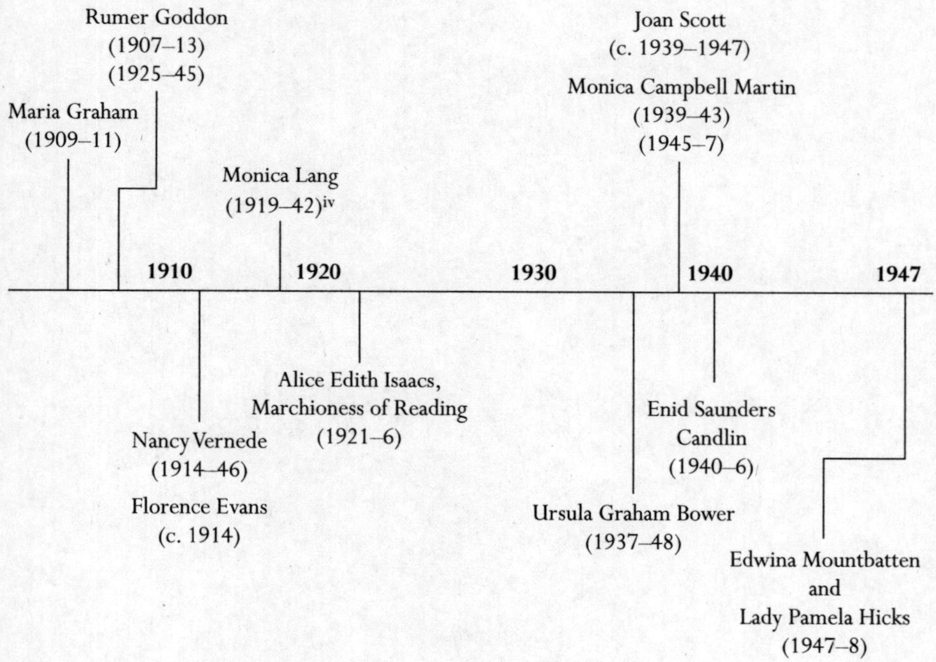

iv Monica Lang did not use exact dates while writing; however, she mentions that she leaves from Calcutta immediately after the Japanese seized Burma and Singapore. Both events occurred in the first two months of 1942, so it is safe to conjecture that she left within a month or two of these events in the same year.

PROLOGUE

One of the earliest memories I have of the word 'memsahib' being used in common conversation is of the time I was given the role of a lady in a school play and had to dress up in my mother's saree. Little did I know that about one and half decades later, I would take up 'memsahibs' as a subject of my doctoral thesis.

Looking back, I am reminded of how the word was frequently bandied about in my Bengali household while I was growing up, used in amusement for girls and ladies who put on airs or threw fits and tantrums. It was mostly tongue-in-cheek and was quite a favourite sobriquet back then, but occasionally it was used to convey genuine appreciation if a woman looked well turned out or dressed up in a 'posh' way. Over the years, the appellation gradually disappeared from common parlance, resurfacing occasionally in films (Bengali classics, which I acquired a taste for because of familial influence, and in mainstream Bollywood as well, although that was rare). By the time I began studying 'memsahibs', the term was no longer used like it was before.

My serious engagement with memsahibs' writings started with a series of coincidences. In 2012, I found a book (tossed into the free books box) at a smallish bookstore near the University of Chicago—a hardback, no less—which was about a British army wife in colonial India—a real 'memsahib', so to speak. At that time, the idea of taking the topic up for research had not struck me. In fact, in 2014, after I completed my Masters, I began courting Urban Studies, certain that it was the subject for me. But like most first loves, it did not work out.

When the idea of studying 'memsahibs' did strike me, just in the nick of time, I should say, because the deadline for the submission of my proposal for Ph.D. research was looming, the familiarity of the term washed over me, making me nostalgic and at once intrigued. Suddenly, the memoirs and letters written by British women in India, which I had been reading casually but steadily since 2012 after finding that free book, made a lot of sense. I still had to come up with a definitive idea of what about memsahibs I was going to study, but given my sporadic trysts with colonial literature, I knew the subject was right for me.

In October 2014, I was accepted into a doctoral programme for a thesis that proposed a study of memsahibs in postcolonial Indian literature, and as I began my research, I realised that I was in familiar territory but still unaware of many things. In December that year, I went to the University of Calcutta for a workshop on Anglo-Indian Studies organised in collaboration with Massey University to present a paper on the theme of *ennui* in Ruskin Bond's representations of memsahibs.

That trip proved to be a lot more valuable than I anticipated. Not only did I get the right exposure through the scholarship, I also felt a kind of alignment taking place. For the first time that year, as I walked through Bow Bazaar (originally the barracks for British troops during the Raj period and now a British-Indian locality), and as I drove through the idyllic colonial railway town while going to the Indian Institute of Technology Kharagpur campus where the workshop took place and meandered through Park Street to sit in Flurry's, a tearoom from the British times, I was truly conscious of the city's colonial past. I realised that somehow, even though I used to go every other year to see my grandparents who lived in a provincial town near Calcutta from where we would take a local train to 'tourist' in the city every time, I had never taken in the history—the crumbling and decaying architecture that was a vestige of an oft-remembered past—as I did during that trip.

Over the next few years, as I doggedly read and reread the works of memsahibs through the eighteenth to early twentieth centuries, I also visited many of the towns and cities that regularly came up in their works, being a bit of a travel enthusiast myself.

PROLOGUE

This was perhaps the best part of my research: living in the places that saw the empire unfold—and eventually come undone. And so I saw Lucknow, Shimla, Landour, Mussoorie, Dehradun, Ladakh, Nainital, Dharamshala, Dalhousie, Poona, Bombay, Pondicherry, and others, and although not deliberately studying history, I certainly absorbed it as I wandered 'in search of the picturesque', quite like the women in the books. Very frequently, my keen eyes sought out some rotting remnant of colonial architecture hidden in plain sight—a dilapidated circuit house here, a broken-down 'British-time' bungalow there—which I fancied was quite invisible to the bustling and apathetic crowd that passed it daily. But obviously, a century is a long time. The landscapes that the memsahibs described have disappeared. The Viceregal Lodge in Shimla is now an institute and a library (although they have preserved the old furniture and decorations in some rooms). I felt the same in London—a city that I had come to know through memsahibs and through the Victorian novels that I had devoured passionately since my schooldays. Naturally, none of it was, nor can be, even a bit as it is in the books. Yet, sometimes, the loss of an era gone by can be disappointing even if you have only lived it vicariously, as readers must.

I must confess here that sometimes a voice in my head asked if, after such a long engagement with the archives, I had been bitten by the 'Raj nostalgia' bug after all. Was it possible? I asked myself. Hadn't it been 'eradicated'? I decided that mine was simply a scholarly inclination given my long-standing obsession with the histories and literatures of the Victorian age. But it made me wonder if the 'nostalgia' did exist, parading around us in disguised forms, as Rushdie suggests—something which is perhaps understandable and inevitable in a nation that has a still developing, and in fact, ballooning, postcolonial psyche.

When it came to my doctoral research, the question before me was: how did the postcolonial imagination conceive the 'memsahib'—an icon of the colonial past—while negotiating historical misrepresentations and inaccuracies, as well as a long-standing tradition of literary stereotyping? Personally, I was also interested in understanding how the term, which was used to refer to British women of superior status in the time of their rule and was part of the colonial vocabulary, came to be used to tease a little girl parading about as a lady half a century later.

I must say that while studying novels by writers such as Ruth Prawer Jhabvala, Ruskin Bond, Nayantara Sahgal, and Kamala Markandaya and watching movies that were about them, I felt as if I had stepped through a 'looking glass', so to speak, and entered the rather topsy-turvy world of memsahibs' special mutation in postcolonial Indian writings. This was a rather investigative point in my thesis-writing, as I doggedly pursued any reference to 'memsahibs' in literature or contemporary and popular culture. What I found was that everything was the same, but different at the same time—these memsahibs were definitely familiar but did not come close to the memsahibs as they were in their own writings, as I had seen them. The discrepancies in representation were too many, the trends in portrayal far too staid, and the voices inadequate.

I saw clearly that in the postcolonial imagination, they had become phantoms of their real selves, and there were too many anomalies and inconsistencies. Even the so-called 'Raj revivalism' lacked critical insights and did not explore the sheer complexity of memsahibs' experiences in India, and the many popular literary and cinematic memsahibs sat uneasily next to the memsahibs that I had come to know. In fact, traits typically associated with memsahibs were almost always inaccurate or partial. It made me wonder if anyone remembered the memsahib at all.

Like most scholars and historians who have attempted to study memsahibs' histories, I was frustrated to see repetitive and limiting representations of these women even in postcolonial fiction. I understood that postcolonial analyses of the memsahib needed to counter the long-standing misrepresentations and fallacies that led to the obfuscation of historical narratives around them. These specimens of the 'memsahib' that came before me required rigorous critique. I am reminded of what Salman Rushdie wrote in his essay "Outside the Whale":

> The British Raj, after three and half decades in retirement, has been making a sort of comeback… It really is necessary to make a fuss about Raj fiction and the zombie-like revival of the defunct

> Empire… propagate a number of notions about history, which must be quarrelled with. (7)

I must mention that memsahibs, and their rather nebulous role in the empire, have been a significant preoccupation of feminist historians because of the steady marginalisation of women's histories and personal narratives. I wanted to know, irrespective of the discourse, 'could the memsahib speak?' Were they heard? And how much weight was given to their literary or cinematic representations as opposed to their own writings?

The potency of stereotypes and cliches was worrisome. It was this that led me to attempt a retrieval of their stories (problematic or contradictory as they might be) aimed purely at reviving and reiterating their narratives in the way feminist historians have advocated for women's writings for so long. No doubt, the larger burden of retrieving the memsahibs' lost and misconstrued voices was borne by feminist scholars advocating for a re-examination of their experiences, but I wanted to also bring their writings to the forefront, and make them heard in their own words, as part of my own engagement with feminist scholarship on women's personal narratives and literature.

To describe memsahibs' archiving practices, I suggest the term 'Epistolary Chronicling', as these diligently written narratives chronicled their varying escapades in British India—in the private and the public—and thus contributed to colonial historicisation. Admirably, by the 1820s they had begun publishing, and many wrote fiction and semi-fictional narratives that had a wide readership. In the absence of sufficient data and records on lives of British women in colonial India, the personal eyewitness accounts are invaluable sources of information about European women's daily lives, private affairs, and socio-political activities in India, and they function as supplements to the hegemonic colonial discourses. The omitted or forgotten histories are crucial because a significant mode of knowledge of the colonial past would otherwise be erased. The entire body of literature produced by them is, therefore, another indispensable source of information on the cultural history of colonial India and British imperial pursuits within it.

Moreover, even though memsahibs did not contribute directly to official work, they did so unofficially by aiding their husbands in dispensing their duties. British society in India was fluid in this manner, and many women were well versed in official matters. As wives, they could influence their husbands' decision-making regarding Raj work and were, in this way, involved with the imperial work, albeit in a mediated manner. These contributions and interventions are mostly unrecorded and untraceable because of their private and unofficial nature. However, one husband pointed out how indispensable his wife was to him: "Time after time she raised points which I had overlooked and showed me aspects of a problem under discussion which I could not have seen myself" (Procida, 49). Sometimes, memsahibs even worked as stand-ins for their husbands if they happened to be away, dealing with official documents and making decisions for them. Sir Edward Blunt dedicated his book, *I.C.S.: The Indian Civil Service*, to his wife, who knew "as much about the I.C.S as I do".

When it comes to scrutinising memsahibs' part in the colonial process, it must be kept in mind that they were not direct agents of the Crown but were co-opted into it, mainly through the institution of marriage. They were 'outsiders' as they were outside the ambit of actual imperial mechanics, but at the same time they had sufficient insider knowledge because of their relationships with the sahibs. The typical notion that memsahibs were merely 'trailing spouses' can therefore be contested even though they did mostly rely on the status and power of their husbands for establishing their place in the Raj society. Their unofficial positions even allowed them a kind of unique insider-outsider position that helped them cultivate an alternative perspective to mainstream colonial discourses and ideologies.

Indeed, as the memsahibs wrote copiously about India, mostly only for private consumption, they did not hesitate to include sundry details or even write critically with considerable impunity. Some who were passionately invested in their male counterparts' official work also commented on it in their writings. There is no doubt that their intimate relationships with the sahibs helped them access sensitive official matters and become contributors to imperial work. It is noticeable that their writings are often replete with a sense of anxiety because of their liminal position, but it was this in-betweenness that helped them candidly express their often unorthodox opinions on imperial activities. Very often, they managed to transcend the barriers of race, class, and gender and ended up going against the dominant stance, contradicting official records altogether.

What is to be considered is that even though memsahibs' perspectives can sometimes be inconsistent, they are organic in most cases. They demonstrate how these women became ensconced in colonial India through their own ways of documentation. Those of their accounts that were published even influenced colonial understandings of the subcontinent abroad by providing vivid images of life in the Raj. Thus, the marginalisation of their writings from. histories only suppressed their voices and disparaged their reputation.

No doubt, the question of authenticity comes up given the personal and uncorroborated nature of their written works. More important than tracing the facts and accurate depictions of real life in their works, it is crucial to trace the motive of such depictions, which was often rooted in colonialist agendas. Memsahibs were possibly motivated by a racial imperative, in addition to the desire to witness the 'unseen' and 'undiscovered', like their male counterparts. Needless to say, such motivations were in tandem with the nineteenth-century expansionist aims of the Empire. It is likely, therefore, that memsahibs were building themselves up to be participants in the colonial process, modelling themselves on the male orientalists.

Indeed, highlighting memsahibs' imperialist attitudes (despite them not being direct employees of the government) is necessary, especially since the idea is not to glamourise them or paint them as innocent and blameless through romanticisation. Apart from their occasional lapses into counter-colonial or anti-hegemonic discourses, their collusion and compliance in the process of imperial domination and exploitation, wherever present, cannot be overlooked. On the whole, they benefitted majorly from the spoils of imperial activities, and some frequently revelled in the glory of grand Britannia.

However, as someone who had been too invested in Kipling's memsahibs and John Masters's British-Indian heroines for years, it shocked and interested me to see that many of the memsahibs effectively exploded many debilitating traits associated with them. Their marginalisation from official and mainstream histories has also effaced the counter-imperial voices that were contained in their writings. I realised that to understand and 'unveil' memsahibs, I had to first understand how they were misunderstood. For this, it was imperative to resuscitate their own writings and study their subjectivities to gain fuller understanding of the gendered histories of the empire in order to make a study of their representations in postcolonial cultures.

I suppose that brings this book close to my doctoral study, which was also, in some ways, revisionist and rehabilitative. In fact, my thesis work helped me to see that while in colonial India the memsahib was hardly ever the hapless heroine in need of rescuing, in the postcolonial era she was stuck in a matrix of nostalgia which led to her utter mythification. And for once, she had to be rescued.

While researching for this book, I was forced to see both the good and bad. I cannot deny that there were some memsahibs' writings that were plain odious; one can easily find records, personal and published, replete with prejudices and racial arrogance, and smacking of selective historical amnesia, including different forms of 'othering', which seemed to have the deliberate intention of projecting the East as 'barbaric' and sub-human. A number of writings were run of the mill, generic works with stuffy narratorial voices. I found a few that verged on hyperbole with woefully obvious dramatisation and exaggeration of the 'white woman's' so-called adventures in the jungles, based very evidently on stories figuring the sahib as a discoverer, explorer, and conqueror.

The pretentious style may be blamed on the popular narrative techniques of pro-imperialist literature that became widespread during the Victorian period, but that was not all. There were recurrent references to incidents of imperial violence and justifications for the overall colonial project, and various other 'civilising' methods.

Nonetheless, occasionally I came across some voices that were delightfully eccentric, countercultural, and so utterly unadulterated that they took me by surprise. Take, for example, Veronica Bamfield, who was posted in India in 1838 with her husband. Unlike most army wives who languished in India, she knew with absolute certainty that the country knew her as she knew it, and she embraced the sights, smells, and scenes with utmost relish. In her accounts of army wives in India, which she wrote later to commemorate her years as a memsahib, she confessed that "nowhere else in the world have so many opportunities been missed as were missed by the army wives of India". In fact, she was quite critical of the women who took the trouble of lugging enormous quantities of British items from back home, purchased European furniture, and hankered after the newest English books and European fashions without ever trying to actually learn anything about the country they were living in. She said that they had retained their arrogance for too long, for which they did not have the excuses their grandmothers did in the late eighteenth or early nineteenth century. She wrote caustically:

> The army wife never really acclimatised herself to India and there is no doubt that boredom, though often unrecognised, crippled her character in all sorts of ways. She wasted her time and her often not inconsiderable talents. She learnt nothing and contributed nothing. We should be ashamed. All of us.

But of course, if there was one Veronica, able to appreciate rather than look down on Indian society, there were others too. Many times, by harbouring their own interests in understanding India, which stemmed from motivations which may or may not be imperialistic, memsahibs became significant 'chroniclers', at times accidentally and at times deliberately. Lady Amelia Falkland, who was married to Lord Falkland, Governor of Bombay (1848–53), noted her observations in *Chow-chow; Being Selections from a Journal Kept in India, Egypt, and Syria* (1857), albeit with an orientalist eye but with genuine interest in Indian culture and religious custom.

Maria Murray Mitchell's book about India, *In India: Sketches of Indian Life and Travels from Letters and Journals* (1876), is invaluable for insights into India from a woman's perspective, and it devotes a whole chapter to '*zenana* life' (*zenana* meaning segregated women's quarters). The literary women like Maud Diver, Flora Annie

Steel, and Ethel Savi wrote a great number of novels and short stories in which they expressed their interest in Indian society.

British India was considerably liberating to memsahibs, in an unlikely way. The Raj was largely unregulated, and women, quite by accident, enjoyed more liberties here than they did in the morally rigid society back home. In the absence of most societal restrictions in comparison to England, the Raj became a place to discard conventions and undertake adventures. Nonetheless, taking up professional work, or doing anything out of the ordinary for that matter, could be risky in its own way as it could mean inviting scrutiny and public ire. Yet some British women were not averse to bending the rules in order to pursue their ambitions and did deviate from the standard figure of wife or mother, irrespective of the risk to their reputation. The comparatively freer space of India was liberating—if they chose for it to be. Many persevered in their attempts to pursue their goals and ambitions and are remembered for their admirable quality of staying resolute in the face of the most crippling ennui.

Moreover, there were a number of British women who invested themselves in India, especially some women from privileged and aristocratic backgrounds. Annette Ackroyd, married to Henry Beveridge, was a college-educated woman who set out for India in 1872 and discovered that most Indian educational reformers were limited because of their own prejudices and did not do substantial work to educate women. She wanted to rectify this and so initiated the establishment of separate schools for young women. She also tried to understand the culture of India and learnt Bengali, and even though she was somewhat (and typically) averse to India, she occupied herself in various intellectual pursuits. Her translation of the diaries of the Mughal Emperor Babur, titled *Baburnama*, which she published between 1912 and 1922, was one of the first, and remains well known today.

Violet Jacob, married to a Lieutenant, came to India towards the end of the nineteenth century, and was quite a daring wayfarer. She travelled far and wide by train and horseback, and delighted in exploring what she called "this country outside the watertight little world of the cantonment", visiting many historic cities and never tiring of India (as memsahibs supposedly did). Similar to her, Fanny Parkes—the nineteenth-century equivalent of the 'solo traveller'—never got bored in India and travelled through the country in search of adventure. Far from doing needlepoint or sipping tea and gossiping with other memsahibs, Parkes unabashedly went "in search of the picturesque", as she called it, and became a self-styled ethnographer. The image of the bored and insipid memsahib truly falls short in the case of such women.

Sara Jeannette Duncan, who was a journalist before coming to India, wanted to be more than an ordinary memsahib like so many others and shunned the dull day-to-day existence of India. She was a talented writer and wrote novels to keep herself occupied. She sometimes struggled to find suitable engagements matching her skills and intelligence, which was natural because at times the clever and hardworking memsahibs had a tough time reconciling themselves with some of the limitations of life in India.

Another maverick, Mary Frances Billington, was also a writer and journalist working for the *Daily Graphic*. She had a wonderful career in newspaper reporting, and became known for several of her publications, one of which was her book, *Woman in India* (1895).

It must be mentioned that amongst the feisty memsahibs who broke norms in India, there were also those who had come to India specifically to earn a livelihood. These women were not 'memsahibs' *per se* and wanted jobs that could sustain them. A number of women began to take up jobs as secretaries, while some came in and found employment in royal Indian families as companions of the daughters, but perhaps the most common and acceptable professions for women at that time were those of teacher, governess, and nanny. Teaching, especially teaching Indian women and girls, was considered the British women's forte, and initially, missionaries doubled up as tutors. With the renewal of the Company charter in 1833, women were welcomed to come in as 'secular' teachers. There was also a great demand for them amongst the British families who wanted to give a proper English upbringing to their children.

Some, however, took up teaching simply because it was their passion. Mary Martha Sherwood, an army wife who became a children's writer, employed her time in the instruction of children as she felt "a religious obligation resting on her to be useful in the land of ignorance and degradation, where her lot was thrown". In Dinapore, she gathered many children of soldiers, and at one point had forty children including local Indian children. Her little school was soon broken up because of her husband's new posting, but she began afresh, with a new batch of pupils. Although she had a definite colonialist perspective, Mrs. Sherwood was quite an atypical memsahib and did not believe in whiling away time at home or engaging in endless social affairs to stave off boredom like the other Raj women. She was hardworking, industrious, and quite determined to engage herself in productive work even though it could be quite challenging for a memsahib to work consistently given their mobile lifestyle.

Those who came for evangelical work either came as 'help meet' for their missionary husbands or became associated with missionary societies and worked for the European community in India. In the latter half of the nineteenth century, British missionary women appointed by Ladies' Missionary Societies began arriving in India with the specific goal of proselytising the women in *zenana*, which they believed could be achieved by educating the women and then easing them into Christianity. Women from various Christian denominations, such as the Baptist Missionary Society, London Missionary Society, and Church Missionary Society, came to India aiming to convert women (Dutta 6). The work by missionaries such as Elizabeth Sale, Marianne Sale, and Dorothy Carey became prominent.

It must be noted that even taking up God's work involved a great level of rule breaking for women because becoming missionaries, travelling to distant lands, and moving amongst natives, which involved rubbing shoulders with men, was not a wholly acceptable profession for British women. Moreover, these missionary women were mostly single women amongst the surplus of genteel women in England who would have had few prospects back home. The professionalisation of missionary work for women in the colonies took a long time, and it was only after 1861 that the work began proactively. This gave British women greater mobility and agency, enabling them to alleviate the suffering of their Indian sisters, while also emancipating themselves.

Flora Annie Steel, who began teaching children from her home, went many steps further and advocated reforms in the whole system of education. She established several small schools and was later appointed as the Inspectress of Government and Aided Schools in Punjab. She was energetic and proactive, and the challenging work attracted her. She wrote:

> When inspecting, I began work at 7 AM, coming back at 11 for a lunch break fast, resting and correcting exercises during the hot hours and so to work again till late dinner time; and sometimes after that at work again till the small hours of the morning. For I was always in a hurry to get home as swiftly as possible. And I was very strong; in mission inspections there was even a joke that I required three relays of ladies to keep up with my speed.

After 1860, there was a surge of documentation on the interactions between British women and Indian women, as the former were exceedingly curious to know about their 'eastern sisters' (even though they mostly eschewed friendships with them). This pursuit sometimes stemmed from the absence of British families to mingle with or sometimes from their husbands' work, which took them to various palaces of the Indian nobility. And so, while the memsahibs' husbands engaged in imperial work, they engaged in their own 'diplomatic relations' with Indian women of rank. Afterwards, they left behind detailed sagas about their encounters in *zenanas*. It is to be noted that since men were not allowed into the women's quarters, memsahibs' easy access to Indian women in their *zenanas* gave them an uncommon insight into the private and intimate lives of their subjects.

Most memsahibs who visited royal or aristocratic Indian women in *zenanas* found that they lived abysmally cloistered lives as they were kept in constant confinement within their homes. Marianne Postans wrote, "Surrounded by slave girls, all chatting merrily together, and some with their infants in their arms, we proceeded through a suite of several apartments to the Beebee's sitting room". This was the '*purdah*' system, which entailed the restriction of Hindu and Muslim women to the inner quarters of their homes, unable to venture beyond the verandas, and even there they had to remain concealed from the eyes of passers-by. According to the then prevalent Hindu customs, women who flouted this rigid system were met with shame and disgrace. It was the norm of the time and did not change for several decades.

British women, nonetheless, marvelled at Indian women's magnificent and elaborate attire as they would always stay decked up because of their social position and rank, but they found them to be bashful and not very forthcoming, although they were hospitable to the foreigner ladies who visited them inside their chambers. E. Augusta King was curious about a particular Bengali lady who was learning Roman characters and wanted to eventually learn English. She wanted to know if the Bengali lady was married or not but found that Indian women were not open to discussing their domestic matters openly. Due to certain experiences, she felt that there was a "gulf between the two races", which seemed to be irreconcilable.

Undoubtedly, therefore, despite the apparent keenness to learning about Indian customs and curiosity to know Indian women, memsahibs' writings display a 'Eurocentric gaze' in their discoveries about *zenana* women and other aspects and customs of Indian life such as marriage. They believed these women to be abominably suppressed and were disappointed by the insulated lives they seemed to live. They also wrote that Indian women remained voiceless and thoroughly subjugated, and almost always, they showed disdain and pity for their 'inferior' sisters in the East. Although replete with stereotypes, these memsahibs' encounters in *zenanas* provided a rich body of work on Indian women's position and *zenana* life, especially for readers back home in England. There were even deliberate attempts to Westernise the *zenana* ladies, as most wanted to educate them and help in 'improving' their condition. Indeed, memsahibs' 'gentle imperialism' (as I call it) was along the lines of the imperialist agenda of 'civilising' the Indian masses, and they were instrumental in buttressing the view that non-Christians were 'heathens' who needed uplifting—and needed their help for it.

However, some radical British women in India tackled the 'women's question' out of genuine concern and compassion. They were also interested in the politics of the country, and began networking with Indian political individuals, artists, and freedom fighters. Some committed themselves to bringing about social change, and some engaged in charitable and philanthropic work.

Margaret Elizabeth Noble, better known as 'Sister Nivedita', is perhaps a fitting name in a discussion regarding radical British women in India. She came to India in 1898 to learn about its culture and values and to educate Indian women who had long been deprived of intellectual engagement. She also wanted to gain spiritual insights into Hinduism through her association with her guru, Swami Vivekananda (who, simply put, was a Hindu monk, mystic, intellectual, and reformer), to understand the complex social structure of the country, and to effectively advocate for reforms. Besides, at that time, reformation was the mood of the era, aided by Indian thinkers and intellectuals, such as Ram Mohan Roy and Debendranath Tagore. The Brahmo Samaj—a monotheistic reformist movement—was already attempting to do away with rigid anachronistic religious and social evils in Hinduism such as child marriage and *Sati* practice (a practice in which widows were burnt—alive and conscious—at the pier with their husband's bodies, which was outlawed in 1829 by then Governor-General of India, Lord William Bentick).

Nivedita was also determined to achieve her goals of India's amelioration. She was sympathetic to the Indian freedom struggle and was drawn into the movement. She began associating with important political leaders and nationalists of the age, such as Sri Aurobindo Ghosh and Gopal Krishna Gokhale. A forward thinker, she believed in encouraging Indian artists to turn to their own cultural and literary traditions for inspiration and supported scientific development by patronising the work of the knighted Bengali scientist Jagadish Chandra Bose. She remained steadfast in her beliefs, and in a world dominated by men and divided by deep racial, religious, and political conflicts, she emerged as an icon of British women in India.

Another woman who was deeply committed to the women's question in India was Hariot Hamilton-Temple-Blackwood, Marchioness of Dufferin and Ava, who came to India with her husband, Lord Frederick Dufferin, when he became the Viceroy in 1884. She worked in the area of women's healthcare, and in 1885, established the National Association for Supplying Female Medical Aid to the Women of India, known as the 'Countess of Dufferin Fund'. This fund helped build a proper medical support network in India by funding medical education and training for Indian women to help them become nurses, doctors, and midwives. It also facilitated the establishment of clinics, dispensaries, female wards, and female hospitals. The idea was to initiate change in Indian society so that women could overcome social and religious limitations and seek proper medical facilities. More significantly, the fund offered a chance at emancipation for Indian women and offered scholarships to acquire a degree in medicine. Kadambini Basu was one of the first Indian female doctors who benefitted from this fund, alongside Anandabai Joshi, both of whom trained in the medical field despite heated opposition from conservative quarters. Lady Dufferin was awarded the Imperial Order of the Crown of India for her extraordinary efforts.

However, not all women received awards and laurels for their efforts. And not all women who wanted to benefit Indian society were from privileged backgrounds. British women across ranks frequently took up voluntary work, such as at schools for teaching Indian children, or at hospitals nursing the sick and injured, often without proper returns. The Birch sisters, for instance, worked diligently at the Residency Hospital in Lucknow, nursing the wounded and dying despite the stench, flies, and scarcity of disinfectants and anaesthetics.

There is no dearth of examples to disprove the notion that memsahibs were merely spiritless trailing wives. Such notions arise from gross generalisation, which led to historical misrepresentation, and which perpetuated sexist depictions in popular culture. Memsahibs, in actuality, were resourceful, self-willed, and driven women whose unconventional attitudes and sheer zest for life allowed them to break, or at least stretch, many social codes that had formerly restricted British women. Many times, they discarded typical feminine behaviour when it became too oppressive, and were not hesitant in working by themselves without the support of their male counterparts. Even though the avenues for them were limited, they were undaunted in the face of harsh conditions and challenges, and carved a way for themselves to pursue their goals.

1

"DAYS ALL GOLD AND NIGHTS ALL SILVER"

JOURNEY TO THE 'LAND OF THE OPEN DOOR'

> *When we first started our idea of travelling to India by the way of Egypt, our project was treated as visionary by several, and numbers considered it as impracticable for a Lady. Some kind friends sought to deter us by magnifying the dangers of the expedition… But though we were fully aware this was a route hitherto but little frequented even by gentlemen, and that no lady had ever attempted the outward overland journey to Bombay, we were not to be deterred by imaginary difficulties… On the 6th of October, 1825, we left Windmill Hill for New Susans, at EastBourne, which latter place we quitted on the 8th, and proceeded along the coast to Dover, our first day's journey on our route to India!*
>
> – Anne Katherine Curteis Elwood, 1830

By the time the Raj era began, British women had a fair notion of what to expect in India. They were not overzealous and dreamy travellers who wanted to experience the romance of life in the East with its unlimited wealth and luxuries. They were practical women who knew that the glint and glamour of British society in the distant colonies was mostly a myth, and that they must be prepared for all contingencies in a harsh, unpredictable, and unforgiving land. Everything was going to be unfamiliar and extreme, and they very well knew that only the toughest of them would survive.

However, unlike what most had anticipated, the adventure began even before landing on the shores of India, from the moment they set foot on the vessels bound for the East. Most of these women had never been to India before, and the voyage was going to be just the prelude to the shocks and surprises that lay in wait for them. They also knew that they would probably not see their loved ones for several years or even decades. India was too remote, and if they were successful in their mission of 'settling down', visiting home even once could be unlikely.

While the idea of separating from their homeland and leaving behind their families was painful, these India-bound women were not able to dwell on it for long. At the bustling ports of England where they stood with their luggage, the farewell celebrations all around lifted their spirits considerably. These were like mass going-away parties, and the families of the passengers cheered loudly as the ships left the docks (de Courcy, 30).

Maria Nugent had mixed feelings when she embarked on the *Baring*, a three-decker East Indiaman, and wrote in her journals, "I wish to forget all I felt on that day".

By mid-century, the vessels coming into India were mostly steamers, and were comprised of a mix of people, ranging from missionaries to women adventurers, husband-hunters, and professionals, as well as civil and military officers serving the Company. Some of the women on-board were born in India and were returning to their families after completing their education back home in England. For them, returning to India brought back heady emotions of nostalgia and awe for the strange but familiar place. For those who were coming into India for the first time, the long journey across the seas itself was a great trial.

Minnie Blane, who was a newly wedded bride at the time of her first journey to India, was quite nervous about sea-travel so soon after her honeymoon in 1856, even though she had very little idea of the actual trials that lay ahead of her as a wife of an army officer. It was a surprise to her that even securing a passage to India on a suitable ship was a great challenge. Her husband, Captain Archibald

Wood, had to spend the day at the East India Docks looking for vessels bound for Calcutta. They wanted to sail in the *Blenheim*, but it was full: every cabin had been reserved a month or two before, as there were too many passengers going out. They took tickets for the *Southampton* ship instead, and embarked at Portsmouth, avoiding the Straits of Dover, which could be quite perilous.

The transition from sail to steam vessels was an important one for traders and travellers because of the increase in speed. When the Suez Canal opened in 1869, ocean liners from England took passengers to India directly without the Cairo stopover. Before that, from the sixteenth century and even up to the beginning of the nineteenth century, voyages were made from England around the Cape of Good Hope at the southern tip of Africa, such as on the *Reliance* (an 1815 ship). This route was used especially for trade, but the journey was long and perilous. It took about six months to a year in the days of the sail.

From the mid-1830s, the 'Overland Route' was used by Peninsular and Orient (P&O) steamships, which reduced the travel time significantly. Post and passengers were now transported to Bombay in India via Egypt. The passengers would deboard at Alexandria and travel to Cairo via the Nile. Cairo had several famous hotels for passengers wanting to stay in Egypt for touring or resting. From Cairo, the passengers went in small batches to Port Said, which was a distance of 84 miles, with six desert-way stations on the way where food and drinks would be available. From Suez, passengers took a steamer to reach Bombay, through the Red Sea, occasionally anchoring in different coasts along the way. Small steamboats went between the Suez and Bombay through the Indian Ocean.

Eliza Fay, who travelled to India during the eighteenth century, wrote a letter in 1779 that described the desert journey between Cairo and Suez as "a journey of three days over a most dreadful desert, where every night we slept under the great canopy of heaven, and where we were every hour in danger of being destroyed by troops of Arabian robbers" (Fay, 49). The infamous carriage ride through the desert was the toughest part of the journey for many like her. The threat remained for many years as passengers in carriages or caravans on those passages could easily be targeted.

When Harriet Tytler, born in India in 1828, was sent back to Britain with her siblings for her education, the Suez Canal had not yet been opened. When she returned to India in the 1840s, she too had to take the overland route, travelling by train from London to Southampton from where she took a steamer. During that time, it was customary for young women to travel with someone even though it was not always feasible. The travel guide for the journey to India, *Messrs. Waghorn & Co.: Overland Guide to India by Three Routes to Egypt*, clearly stated that the P&O steamers that departed from Southampton at 2 pm twice a month and landed alternatively at Gibraltar and Malta required "experienced and respected female's attendants for the ladies' cabins" (Waghorn, 8). Tytler did not have attendants or guardians, but fortunately for her, she met an acquaintance travelling with her 16-year-old daughter, who agreed to take her under her charge for the duration of the journey. As was a trend with most passengers, their group toured Malta, Alexandria, and Cairo and took a carriage to cross the desert before taking a steamer to Bombay.

Even at the time Harriet made the journey, crossing the desert was risky and exceedingly arduous. The rickety carriages would seat six people at one time and had extremely uncomfortable seating. They had no springs, and the passengers were completely bruised because of the bumping. Sometimes, the horses died on the way because of heat and exhaustion, adding to the piles of skeletons littered through the way. The passengers would then have to wait for a change of animals, which delayed their journeys. After the journey, Harriet's feet had become so swollen that she was not able to walk properly for several days.

Upon reaching Suez, they went into the Shepheard's Hotel and waited for the rest of the steamer's passengers. The P&O steamers at that time ran only once a month carrying mail. Later, there would be weekly steamers to Bombay and even up to Calcutta. When Harriet made her journey, it took 7 weeks to reach India, whereas some years later it was possible to get there within 16 days via Brindisi at a cheaper price (if on chose second-class). She wrote miserably, "the heat was unbearable in the Red Sea".

The previous routes of travel from Britain to India involved immense loss of life and property, and yet the opening of the Suez Canal in 1869 was met with dismay by the P&O Company as they had large sums invested in wharves, officers, and warehouses in Alexandria and Cairo. Nonetheless, the Suez project, within a decade, became finalised, after which the journey became a matter of a few safe weeks.

"Champagne flowed like water"

No matter which route passengers took, it was a long voyage to India.

Very soon after embarking on the journey, the need for socialising began to be felt on-board. Passengers had to devise ways to spend time pleasantly or surrender to the trials of living in the confines of a ship, without good company. Even if they tried their best to keep occupied, mingling with the others and making new friends was needed to keep up the good spirits as the long months at sea could bring on terrible anxiety. Moreover, people often made important contacts while journeying on the ship. Socialising was particularly important for women because the acquaintances they made on the ship could often help them upon landing in India.

A lot depended on the crowd they found on-board. Sometimes there would be great activity, but on ordinary days, they spent time reading books borrowed from the ship's library, seated on their deck chairs, breathing in the warm, moist air, or walking around for some exercise. Every now and then, there would be some excitement on the ship if whales had been spotted cruising alongside it, spraying jets of water over their heads. If the passengers were in a jovial mood, they would get together and plan shark hunting. Flying fish whizzing about disturbed people on the deck and caused a cacophony of squeals and laughter. The passengers on the ship with Julia Charlotte Maitland caught four albatrosses with a fishing line and bait.

Such activities changed the oft gloomy and monotonous days when there would be no land in sight. Sometimes, a fiddler would enliven the mood in the evenings. Men played at quoits while women sat idly, watching them. The more riotous men engaged in 'Sling the Monkey', in which a gentleman would strike a suspended man's bottom with knotted handkerchiefs. During such times, the atmosphere of the ship would lift, and passengers would venture out of their cabins, looking merry. If the weather were temperate, they would go around greeting each other and participating in group activities.

The social interactions on-board, however, were subject to various social behavioural codes. Victorian society had strict conventions, and flouting rules, even during sea voyages, could be problematic. Women, especially, had to be on their best behaviour, and drinking, loud talking, dancing, merry-making, and free mingling with the gentlemen were looked down on. Young and unmarried women on the ships were considered particularly vulnerable, given the absence of their parents and sometimes even chaperones who could protect their honour at sea. Usually, they were the most conspicuous on-board and could be the subject of great speculation.

Edwina Mountbatten, née Ashley, had no one to accompany her on the ship to India, and asked a random acquaintance to be her formal chaperone. Her desperate measure was not without just cause. Women had to remain conscious of their image to avoid gossip around their character. Even before they landed in India, their conduct was monitored strictly not just by their chaperones but also by the self-styled custodians of morality, such as matrons, missionaries, and even the captain of the ship. This was mainly because most male passengers on-board usually had little concern about manners and propriety. Because of this, most women faced extreme sexism and prejudice on-board and were often even barred officially, or forbidden by family, from using common spaces. Some memsahibs even wrote about their encounters with tyrannical captains who would not allow them to be on the deck because of the drunken revelries and frequent brawls between the male passengers. Even in cases where there was no formal restriction, women were often restricted inside their cuddies and even forced to eat inside because the men aboard could become rowdy after drinking. Such impositions severely curtailed their activities on the ships, rendering them highly oppressive and unfriendly segregated spaces.

The rigorous monitoring of young women's behaviour on the vessels is not surprising given the sexual mores of Victorian England wherein sexual repression was prevalent. The more or less conservative mood of the time demanded a strict adherence to prevalent gender codes irrespective of the situation. Parents of young women wanted to ensure that their daughters' conduct during the long days of the sail was never improper and sent them with strict instructions. Their main concern was that young and middle-aged gentlemen, mostly officers of the Raj, were prone to conversing indelicately with ladies, often flirting with them, and initiating affairs. The latter was deemed particularly risky because even a slight rumour could taint a woman's reputation and ruin her chances of finding a suitable husband after landing in India.

Sometimes, the ships stopped at ports on the way to India, allowing passengers to disembark. While most women preferred not to leave the vessel, which they were advised not to do, some did visit the shores for sightseeing. This was believed to be quite precarious as the ports had a mixed crowd of foreigners with unknown backgrounds and because it gave too much exposure and freedom to the 'virginal' eyes. Very often, the ports were sites of excessive debaucheries as men and women shed their moral and social inhibitions to enjoy the gay ambience of whichever place they landed in. Port Said in Egypt was notorious for such philandering.

Despite the restrictive atmosphere of ships, most codes of conduct were very frequently nullified as there was no option for men and women but to coexist and commingle in the face of terrible boredom. Besides, the vessels were not very large, and passengers would begin to recognise each other very quickly. It is to be expected that despite all attempts to curtail the 'fun and frolic' on-board, dinners, parties, and dances on the deck were altogether common. Moreover, even though these were deemed to be a threat to propriety, heavy drinking was a custom as most of the men who were serving the Raj were used to the '*chota peg*' and sundowner, which were the popular drinks amongst the British in the Raj. Women drank a little as well, and it was said that on the regular Indiaman, "champagne flowed like water".

Indeed, women regularly took part in recreational activities and socialised with the men on-board, dancing reels, gavottes, and quadrilles to the songs played by the bands on the deck (Hickman, 158). If they were spirited enough, they enjoyed themselves to the fullest, playing cards and chess, and reading books in the common spaces. They also accompanied the gentlemen in singing duets, despite the glares of judgemental genteel women.

It could be either the lack of activity or the freedom of the sea, but the on-board activities could sometimes become extremely scandalous. It was an open secret that the relatively free and unmonitored intermingling between the sexes in the small space of the vessel regularly led to 'mischief', which the moral authorities futilely attempted to curtail. Indeed, the moral climate of ships remained dubious and was a major cause of discomfort to the self-righteous passengers who did not approve of the daily flirting and riotous behaviour of men and women around their cabins. Perhaps because of this, married ladies, some of whom were seasoned memsahibs returning to their husbands from a vacation back home, had a great curiosity about the goings-on around them. Some revelled in the salacious and entertaining gossip on-board as it was a good source of entertainment, and in the absence of anything productive to do all day, keeping an eye on the activities of young girls and bachelors was a good pastime for the meddling sort as it distracted them from the idleness and nausea.

There is no doubt that there was plenty of gossip to go around. Even the stench of the ship and motion sickness did not deter romance on-board. In fact, the ships could be extremely sexually charged spaces; after all, the journeys were long, the nights balmy, and there were too many handsome officers returning to India, who were unmarried and desperate for female companionship. For this reason, women were advised to stay well-dressed on-board in all circumstances. They would often traipse around on the deck in groups, showing off their lovely dresses and handkerchiefs as the men cheered after them. Most women, in any case, were going to India to find a man to marry, and the ships presented a great opportunity for gaining suitors and securing proposals even before landing.

Moreover, there were no prying eyes on the deck after hours, giving lovers the perfect cover under the starry skies. Infatuations developed, and several shipboard dalliances sprung up within the journey's short span of a few months. It seems that the dangers of the sea, combined with the absence of normal rules of society, heightened the excitement of affairs. And despite all the restrictions, there were no concerns about decorum amongst the young because the passengers might never meet again in India. Most of the time, both parties mutually agreed that the affairs would end the moment they reached India, and the complete lack of obligation added to the fun of such flings.

Sometimes, serious entanglements took place on-board, which became quite public. Couples who openly got involved in shipboard romances would be stalked and teased to no end. Enid Shillingford managed to fall in love twice on her two journeys to India (de Courcy, 52). The first man turned out to be married, which forced her to return midway. Years later when she set out to India, determined this time to find true love, she fell in love with an honourable man and had a happy marriage after all.

It was not uncommon for women to get engaged during the journey itself. A lady who was coming into India for her widowed father, to keep house for him in some remote inland province in Guzerat (Gujrat), got betrothed to a young officer on board, and was anxious because she was afraid how her father would react to her accepting the man's proposal without his knowledge. Caroline Baker met her husband, a military officer called Captain Legatt, on the ship bound for India (Hickman, 159). A lady who was already engaged to a Lieutenant met a Captain on-board, and a great intimacy formed between them, so that when they stopped at the Cape, she returned as a married woman (Nevile, 163).

However, some affairs were questionable and ended badly, bringing dishonour upon the woman before she had even set foot in India. A certain Miss Moresby had a whirlwind of an affair with a man who was nearly always 'three sheets to the wind'—Mr. Traherne—who proposed to her, and she accepted. However, the very next day, he was nowhere to be found and she looked for him for several days. It later emerged that after sobering, he had confided to one of his friends saying, "What am I to do? I don't want to marry the girl!", after which he began to ignore her, causing the young lady much mortification.

Long sea voyages could be quite a test of character and revealed people's true nature. While women did not break out in physical fights like men did, some women engaged in equally deplorable mischief, accusing each other of being 'half-castes', or bad-mouthing the other passengers and making a row on-board until everyone became irritated and suspicious. This kind of atmosphere could be quite detrimental to unmarried women who were travelling alone as they would always be slandered by scandalmongers.

Ships, Wrecks, Hurricanes, and the Sea Voyage to India

We were in great peril, and bade adieu to the sea at the hazard of our lives, the bar of Nile being exceedingly dangerous. Fourteen persons were lost there the day before we crossed it… and which was told to me just before I closed my last letter… Our only alternative to this hazardous passage was crossing a desert notorious for the robbers and murders committed on it; while we could not have hope for escape and, from the smallness of our number, had no chance of superiority in case of attack. The night after we had congratulated ourselves on being out of danger from the bar, we were alarmed by perceiving a boat making after us, as the people said to plunder and, perhaps, to murder us …

On the 29th we reached Bulac, the point of Grand Cairo, and within two miles of that city, to my great Joy, for on this river there is either little wind or else it comes in squalls so suddenly that the boats are often in danger overset, as they carry only, what I believe is called a shoulder of mutton sail, which turns on a sort of swivel and is very difficult to manage when the wind takes the wrong way. It seems indeed miraculous how we escaped…

– Eliza Fay, 1908

Despite various infrastructural and maritime developments, sea voyages in the Victorian period were exceedingly uncomfortable. The South Atlantic and Indian Oceans were prone to swell frequently, and the perennial storms made the journeys rough and dangerous in some parts. Wooden vessels that conveyed the people from England to India were not sufficiently sturdy or stable, and even during ordinary weather conditions, hardly anything stayed on the tables. While eating, dishes rolled about in all directions, and great streaks of gravy streamed. Passengers had to clutch their plates and gobble down the food before it was tossed off.

Passengers knew that the sea conditions could change at any time and had to stay alert all the times. If the skies looked murky or there were signs of a storm, the entire ship would hasten to secure everything as tempests could cause great damage. The cabin windows would be closed up and the deadlights would be lit in anticipation of the choppy seas, especially in the Indian Ocean. The cannons and other heavy objects would be taken down and sent below, so that they did not roll around and crash against anyone. The animals would be tied with extra strong posts to prevent them from flying around. The ladies would cram into the more secure cabins, depending on the chivalry of the other passengers. Everyone had to be extremely cautious because sudden gusts of wind could easily send people tumbling inside their cabins, or worse, throw them off board. Frances Isabella Duberly (née Locke) was aboard the magnificent steam ship *Great Britain*, in the year 1857, when a man fell overboard and had to be hauled up with the life buoy.

Apart from the few perilous routes and uneven waters, passing through the straits at night was particularly risky. The captain of the ship would always be apprehensive when it happened, making everyone on-board nervous. Most of the storms were life-threatening if ships were caught in the middle of them and would invariably cause hysteria amongst passengers if they were on deck. They would rush around trying to secure their belongings or to find cover, grabbing railings and objects as they staggered during the violent tossing. The shrieking gales, the deafening crashing of waves against the ships, and the din of objects smashing everywhere added to the chaos. The cabins could easily be flooded, much to the panic of women who would take to praying. Sometimes, passengers would be so terrified that they would refuse to go into their cabins, certain that they would drown in their beds. This worsened matters because the danger of someone being injured or washed off was even more if they stayed on the deck during storms. This was also the reason that accidents on-board were common. Minnie Blane wrote in her letter: "My dear Archie had the most narrow escape the day we came on board. The boom of the cutter which took us to this vessel gave way and fell on his head. Luckily for him he had his tall hat on, or it *must* have killed him".

When Harriet Tytler, having completed her English education, sailed back to India in her adolescence, she witnessed a woman sliding backwards and forwards on the deck as the ship lurched precariously from one side to the other during a storm near Ceylon. In another instance, a lifeboat got loosened, and instead of falling into the sea, flew up as the ship almost keeled, and got stuck in the rigging, threatening to fall down on the cabins below.

It was also quite common during severe hurricanes for waters to rise in waves and crash down on the livestock that were usually tied on the deck, carrying them off-board if the ropes gave way. Once, a cow went flying off-board, before the eyes of the passengers who could do nothing but watch in amazement.

During storms, nobody knew when the danger would pass. Sometimes, the threat lasted some hours; sometimes it went on for longer. Afterwards, the passengers would slowly emerge from their cabins to examine the damages, and salvage whatever they could. The sight of broken furniture and miscellaneous personal items from women's trousseaus or men's luggage would wring their hearts. But damage and loss of personal property was something that they always knew was likely during sea voyages.

The dangers of the sea were unavoidable, but the pathetic state of the vessels made the experience of the long voyages to India all the more unpleasant. The poor facilities on-board were a major inconvenience, particularly to women, as the cabins and communal bathrooms were usually ill-fitted and insanitary. Very often, the ships carried men, women, animals, livestock, poultry, and baggage, crammed in very limited space.

Mary Martha Sherwood and her husband Captain Henry Sherwood, who was promoted to the post of Paymaster in India, were travelling to India in the *Devonshire* in 1805, leaving their child to the care of Mary's mother in England. Her cabin was next to the pumps, and every other hour, putrid water rose up outside their cabin door. The walls were of canvas, and their bunk was slung crossways over the gun, shared with a thankless lady who was perennially sick. Fiercely evangelical and pregnant at the time, Mary was puzzled by the goings-on of the ship and angry at everyone on-board. Given the circumstances, she could hardly be blamed for her ill temper.

In 1856, the newlyweds Minnie and Archie Wood found the *Southampton* cramped and insanitary, and completely unlike what they had imagined. Minnie, pregnant at the time, was horrified at first seeing the appalling condition of the vessel, even though that was its maiden voyage. It had a dining area which was too small to accommodate all the diners, and the eighteen passenger cabins were completely sparse. In fact, even at the time when the Woods made the journey, most vessels did not have furnished cabins and passengers had to furnish them at their own expense or undergo immense discomfort for weeks, since it took up to four months to reach Calcutta.

However, even after such troubles, the journey could be uncomfortable. The cabin that Minnie was given was hot and airless and she felt suffocated inside at all times. This is not surprising as facilities and provisions on most vessels were known to be poor. Trooper ships were worse; they were described as 'rotten tubs' and entering them felt like entering one's own coffin. The post-Crimean reforms brought about the construction of new army transports for the India run, and by 1863, five new ships were functional. With that, the standard on-board was improved to include proper cabins, nick-named 'dovecotes' for women, while mothers with families shared larger cabins called nurseries. Husbands slept in the dormitory cabins and had to help their wives with chores because of the absence of stewardesses. One deck cabin was allotted to the officers' families by rota, but there would always be squabbles about it.

Cabins could also become extremely crammed, and sometimes travellers put hammocks under the cots of other passengers, because there would be nowhere else to sleep. The memsahibs, although inclined to take up lodging in the lower cabins, would be awakened by the din in the wee hours of the morning. Still, it was not uncommon for the ladies to sleep on the deck because the cabins could get intensely humid. But even that was inconvenient because at night there would be drinking on the deck, and the sailors hollered and sang while tackling the sails. In the morning, the riotous menagerie on-board began making noises even before daybreak, and when everything else was quiet, the shrieks of babies wailing disturbed the quiet of the seas.

Julia Charlotte Maitland, who was travelling to Madras via the Cape route in the 1830s, tried to be calm and patient during the entire sea journey, but it was impossible. She wrote:

> certainly, the first morning, when I woke, there did seem to be as quaint a combination and succession of noises as could well be imagined... the nursery noises: Major O'Brien twittering to his baby—the baby squealing—the nurse singing and squalling to it—the mamma cooing to it. Then the cuddy noises: all the servants quarrelling for their clothes, &c. &c. So on until breakfast-time. I was too sick to laugh then, and I am used to it now.

Indeed, the cacophony could be a great nuisance, particularly to the women who seldom had engaging activities to participate in and lay about in their cabins suffering from seasickness. Minnie Blane, who was soon to be a mother herself, was so tired of the babies bawling morning, noon, and night, that she wrote in her letters that she wanted to pitch all of them overboard.

Women faced the added problem of poor sanitary provisions on-board. Most vessels did not have private bathrooms, and this put them in a rather precarious situation since Victorian society demanded stringent forms of modesty. Rushing back and forth between the baths and their cabins in nothing but their gowns and shower caps could be mortifying, but it was not something that could be helped. Their servants prepared the bath for them in advance, placing their prized rose, honey, and glycerine marine soap (especially purchased for the voyage from outfitting warehouses), which smelled sweet and lathered well even with salt water, next to the tub, and they rushed through the process for fear of keeping others waiting or being barged in on. Washing stands had to be procured for the cabins, some with swinging basins and looking glasses, others with folding tops made in iron.

Foot-tubs and small baths with cans could be a necessity due to the common bathrooms.

But even simple tasks like washing clothes were extremely difficult because ships often ran low on fresh water, and the salt water could ruin fabrics. It was commonly known that most of the travel clothing would not last for long. It was recommended in the manuals on packing for the voyage that a lady keep four dozen day chemises, four dozen night chemises, three dozen gauze flannel or thin merino vests, four dozen pairs of drawers, and so on. These were to be made from the finest long cloth, not linen. Flannel and coloured petticoats were needed, along with some woollen stockings for winter. Soiled clothing had to be dried carefully after washing, because damp cloth could develop mildew and turn to rags. These garments would become so tattered by the end of the four-month journey that women would usually discard their worn-out clothes, especially undergarments, right before reaching the harbours. Sometimes, you could see a long trail of ladies' underclothes floating on the seas, much to the amusement of the male passengers (de Courcy, 27).

Perhaps the worst and most common hardship on-board was seasickness. The constant rocking and rolling brought on severe nausea, and many women would feel sick almost immediately after commencing on the journey, especially due to the cloistered and crowded condition of the ships. But when the cabins became suffocating during hot weather, even the worst cases of seasickness would have to emerge from their rooms and come up to the deck despite the incessant rocking. Even passengers who found their sea legs succumbed to illnesses brought on by exhaustion and the oppressive atmosphere of the cabins. Women had to take chloroform mixed in water, or homeopathic medicines, to stay sedated. The desperate ones resorted to heavy drinking to stay in a state of stupor. Alcohol was, in fact, recommended as a tonic for seasickness, and for bolstering immunity against infections. In fact, a little bit of 'Dutch courage' was considered the best antidote for melancholy and anxiety on long voyages.

Given the cloistered spaces and insanitary conditions of vessels, maintaining health and hygiene was a great challenge for the passengers. The dingy accommodations with poor ventilation in the lower cabins, the effluvia from the animals, and severe overcrowding could lead to spread of infections, sometimes resulting in epidemic outbreaks that could take their toll quickly. Florence Evans was making the journey to India in the early 1900s, and the steamer she was on, *SS Nubia*, was so crowded that disease spread suddenly and rapidly. She and her companions had been given a clean bill of health before being allowed on-board where they were allotted beds and quarters, but they later heard that scarlatina had spread amongst the children on the vessel. There were two small hospitals on-board for the sick (de Courcy, 23).

Another reason for infectious outbreaks was the lack of cleanliness, which caused the breeding of various unpleasant insects inside the cabins. Women had no choice but to take jars of chloride and of lime and packets of Allnut's fumigating paper. Putting a few drops of camphor and camphorated spirits of wine on clothes kept off insects, and the corrosive sublimate dissolved in turpentine that was put inside the cracks of walls or the bedstead with a brush was most useful, although it was poisonous and inflammable.

Stale or ill-prepared food exacerbated people's health ailments on ships. Although meals were mostly sumptuous, menus depended purely on the provisions and supplies. At the start of the 4-month journeys, there would be fresh meat and vegetables, but when the supplies began dwindling, the preserved foods developed mould. Sugar and eggs went bad within three months, and biscuits, figs, and Ratafia was crawling with maggots, which, unfortunately, the partaker often discovered after taking a bite. The butter would be too salted, and sugar would run out quickly. Sometimes, the food would be completely rotten and taste foul but was still served because there would be nothing else to prepare. Even if the food had not gone bad, the quality of meals deteriorated as there were no means of replenishing the stock. Passengers had to survive on the same menu of hardened food for weeks, which was injurious to digestive tracts; sometimes, there would be only pork, boiled, roasted, curried, or fried and always with too much garlic. This frequently caused dysentery and dyspepsia amongst the passengers. Minnie Blane was acutely irritated with the pathetic menu and wrote about it in her letters to her mother.

Harsh weather conditions intensified the passengers' ordeals at sea. In some regions, it could get intensely hot during the day, and sometimes, the temperatures went higher in the night, especially if they were in the tropical areas, making the men 'rig tropical' with their collars turned down because of the heat and humidity. Around Africa, the heat could be unbearable, and women stayed in their cabins wearing only their sheerest of muslin gowns, sweating and moaning in discomfort as if they were in a vapour bath. Flies buzzed around at all times, not giving them a moment's peace.

The harsh weather inevitably affected the passengers' emotional and physical wellbeing. The heat was one of the reasons why tempers would flare suddenly and erupt in squabbles over petty conflicts. Minnie wrote about a man who had stabbed someone on the deck because of some trivial argument—but at least it gave the ladies some excitement and something to talk about in the next few days! After all, the monotony took a toll on people just as the heat could. The sameness of the scenery—of rolling waves and no land in sight—could drive anyone mad. Some women chose to spend their daytime listening to sermons, which helped them stay calm despite the unrest in their hearts, and the unrest of the seas.

Heat was not the only weather extremity. In cold regions, snow would make the passengers miserable, and the ladies would shiver under multiple layers of overcoats. Sometimes, pleasant winds around the Arabian Gulf provided temporary respite to the seafarers when even the cockroaches and ants disappeared as the winds cooled the inner cabins. But the seas were always treacherous and could change moods unpredictably. If there had been a hurricane in the surrounding waters, the winds would change direction, and this could cause problems to sailing ships by taking them completely off course. Changes in wind direction were a major problem before steamers and could cause significant delays in the journeys. The lack of wind could even slow down the pace of the vessel—down to one knot an hour—making everyone impatient and ill-tempered. Sometimes, ships sat listless for hours.

Delays and detours significantly elongated the already cumbersome journeys; however, they seemed to be unavoidable. Sometimes, there would even be unexpected stopovers, such as at the Cape of Good Hope (if that was the route), and the ships would stay docked for days. This could be a relief sometimes, if all passengers had the inclination to explore the towns that were filled with a mixture of settlers ranging from Dutch to Malayas to Parsees. But at times, the ships docked for several days without warning, at places where there was not anything to explore, leaving the passengers—in the words of Christina Sinclair Bremner—to "grill under the Egyptian sky in a bleak desert of burning sand".

Unfortunately, while sailing in the vast oceans there were greater fears in the hearts of the female voyagers than dirty toilets and sultry climates. The risks of being captured by enemy ships, being fired at, or shipwrecked were quite real in the open seas, and the India-bound ships were particularly vulnerable as they were prime targets for hijackers. This was a terrifying possibility, especially for women on-board, and whenever there was danger of enemy ships, the passengers were instructed on how to act in case they were attacked. Everyone was to have a weapon of some kind or other.

Sometimes, accidents also took place on the ships. The *Eastern Monarch*, which was known to be one of the finest sailing ships that went between Great Britain and India, had a bad voyage because of a persistent east wind that caused it to run out of provisions. An explosion occurred one night on the same ship in June 1859; everyone rushed onto the deck in their night things, and all women scrambled into the lifeboats, although there was not enough room for all of them. Another ship, the *Sarah Sands*, caught fire after an explosion some way off Mauritius.

If a ship got wrecked, the passengers would try to get onto the next vessel that came by. *Alma*, a Calcutta steamer, was wrecked in the Red Sea, and all the passengers returned to Aden and were put on another full ship, causing severe overcrowding. Emily Polehampton and Lady Julia Inglis were wrecked off the coast of Ceylon while returning to England in 1858.

In the spring of 1815, the *Arniston* foundered on Lagullas Reef, the southernmost tip of Africa, after a journey of 2 months, with a loss of all but a few of the crew and passengers. Six women and twenty-six children were among the passengers. Some of the bodies were washed ashore, locked in each other's arms. The small town Arniston was named after the disaster.

The *Birkenhead* was a ship that had been modified for troops, and the modifications had deprived her of watertight bulkheads. In December 1851, she sailed from Spithead for South Africa, with soldiers of different regiments, and in February of the following year, she floundered on a reef while approaching Port Elizabeth. Water gushed in because of the absence of the bulkheads. The women and the children were ordered into the cutters, and the men were left to organise everything on deck. The whole scene was horrific as the women clung to their husbands for the last time before their deaths. The men then swung into action, and tried to arrange matters, such as leading the horses blindfolded into the sea. When the *Birkenhead* broke in two and orders were given to abandon ship, it was impossible for all but a few to survive the dense seaweed and sharks circling them. Miraculously, all women and children were saved, because of the heroic attempts of the men on-board.

The *Charlotte* floundered near the Algoa Bay in 1854. Women and children were screaming for help in the darkness of the December night, but the lifeboat could only rescue a few because of the choppy sea.

The Mediterranean and the Gulf of Persia were particularly risky zones. In 1846, Helen D. Mackenzie, who became the wife of a Scottish army officer in the British East India Company and was the author of *Mission, the Camp, and the Zenana; Or, Six Years in India* (1853), was travelling to India when the captain of her ship told her that some years ago a big ship called *The Morning Star*, which was 300 tons, was nearing St Helena when a pirate brig came into sight. The captain of the ship wanted to fight but a Major on the ship recommended they submit. The captain and some men who went on board the pirate brig were slaughtered, and the mate of the pirate ship came on board the *Morning Star* with his crew. They tied up all the passengers and placed casks upon them. Then they ransacked and plundered everything, drank the wine, and ate as much as they could in the cuddy, in which they also kept five or six European ladies. However, most of the passengers were spared as the pirates left soon after, which was a massive stroke of luck for them because the pirates usually killed every passenger after plundering a ship.

Anne Katherine Elwood, British traveller, writer, and avid photographer, who was said to be the first English woman to travel the 'Overland Route' in the early decades of the nineteenth century, was also lucky in the same way, managing to escape a great calamity. It was the year 1825, and the ship, *Eliza*, was near Crete, when the winds suddenly changed direction, and they passed into an unfavourable quarter. The passengers on the ship were extremely tense when pirate ships were spotted, and telescopes were passed around. The women were filled with dread—they had all heard the horrific stories of what pirates did to passengers, especially women. No one on-board had a weapon. To their immense relief, the ships passed on without attacking them.

Mrs. Sherwood wrote, "Those who have not been at sea can never fully conceive the hundredth part of the horrors of a long voyage to a female in a sailing vessel". She was travelling in the year 1805 in the *Devonshire*, and the packet, an English Indiaman, had been converted for trooping. She passed time reading and teaching a soldier's boy to read. Britain and France were at war with each other, and the fleet was prepared for battle. After 3 months at sea, three French ships approached the British fleet, and two of them began to fire. The *Devonshire* was the nearest and three shots passed through the rigging. The women were sent to the lower hold of the ship. There were six ladies of the families of the officers, nine soldiers' wives, two or three female servants, and children. The place was dark, and the ladder was taken away, meaning they were left in the darkness while the cannoning and general confusion of battle went on above their heads. Fortunately for them, the battle passed without serious damage, and they made it to India by August.

Indeed, it was no exaggeration that passengers—men, women, or children—who made it to India unscathed were considered immensely lucky.

Landing in India

The approach to the City of Palaces from the river is exceedingly fine; the Hooghly at all periods of the year presents a broad surface of spar-

kling water, and as it winds through a richly wooded country, clothed with eternal verdure, and interspersed with stately buildings, the stranger feels that banishment may be endured amid scenes of so much picturesque beauty, attended by so many luxurious accompaniments... The houses... are either entirely detached from each other, or connected only by long ranges of terraces, surmounted... with balustrades. The greater number of these mansions have pillared verandas extending the whole way up... long colonnades, and lofty gateways, have a very imposing effect, especially when intermingled with forest trees and flowering shrubs... These are the characteristics of the fashionable part of Calcutta; but even here... a certain want of keeping and consistency, common to everything relating to India, injures the effect of the scene. A mud hut, or rows of native hovels, constructed of mats, thatch, and bamboos, not superior to the rudest wigwam, often rest against the outer walls of palaces, while there are avenues opening from the principal streets, intersected in all directions by native bazaars, filled with unsightly articles of every description.

– Emma Roberts, 1835

As soon as the vessels drew close to the ports of India, the memsahibs felt the change of air. From their cabin windows, they could see the ruins of chapels erected by the Portuguese conquerors, combined with a lush tropical foliage, and the silhouettes of temples with their distinct architecture, which appeared amidst thick clouds like a fantastic apparition.

Many thoughts rushed to their minds as they saw the first glimpses of the mighty *ghats*, the landing shores, leading up to the dazzling mainland. Were the stories they had heard about the 'exotic' East true? What were their lives as memsahibs going to be like? How would they adjust to such a different culture and environment? Would India change them, as they so often had been told?

One of the first things memsahibs struggled with, even before landing on the shores, was the steadily rising temperatures as they neared the subcontinent. During summer months, the intensity of heat would be unbearable. Sometimes, the ships would have to be anchored before reaching the shores because of the high tides, causing protracted discomfort. Helen D. Mackenzie's ship was delayed for two nights before it could reach the Diamond Harbour in Bengal. The passengers were all on the deck and were extremely impatient about disembarking and finally exploring the country after a long voyage. When they finally went to shore in a boat, they enthusiastically cried "*shabash*, bravo!" to the rowers.

If they reached the ports in daytime, they would be bathed in the unforgiving tropical sun, sweating under their *sola topees* (lightweight pith helmets commonly used by the Europeans in India) as they disembarked from their ships, dressed in their proper British paraphernalia. These rather overwhelmed ladies, holding onto their dear birdcages, were then carried over the mud on a wooden seat, and quickly taken to the carriages waiting for them.

Nothing the memsahibs had read or heard about India had really prepared them for the scenes of 'Asiatic life' that they beheld. Amidst the chaos, they gazed around in wonderment at the kaleidoscope of colours. If they happened to disembark at night, the land looked ethereal as the harbours would be bathed in cool moonlight.

India was a world like no other, and women who chose to land on the other side of India, in Bombay, were awestruck by the scenes of 'oriental' splendour as they drove to the fort and town of Bombay. The town was situated within the fort and was a mile in length from the Apollo Gate (part of the Bombay Fort) to the *bazaar*. Fort George and the two gateways facing the harbour were remarkable to behold. Passing through these gates, they visited the famous Bombay Castle. The dockyard was immensely fascinating, and they passed by several cotton-presses, which were striking because of the enormous mountains of cotton piled up to be packed for transportation to Europe, China, and other countries. On the Bunder Pier, there would be palanquins waiting for them to convey them from the shore. The palanquin-bearers were called *hamauls*, and their simple white loincloths greatly shocked the newcomers' unaccustomed eyes.

As they were carted into the towns, they were suddenly faced with a myriad of striking views yet again. In fact, whichever port they landed in, the scenes of day-to-day commerce shocked and awed them at the same time. All of a sudden, England seemed like a distant reality, and they somehow felt exhilarated and terrified at the same time. The heady sights and smells of India, new as it was to them, were dizzying; they passed by the eclectic crowd of turbaned men (as some described them) smoking their *hukkahs*, merchants dressed in flowy robes and looking sombre as they waited for customers, native women dressed in curious attires, beggars asking for alms, *coolies* in nothing but loincloths slaving under the burden on their backs, hawkers displaying their wares, bullock carriages ambling along the roads, and so on. Viscountess Amelia Cary Falkland came to India after Lord Falkland became Governor of Bombay in 1848, and wrote in *Chow-Chow: Being Selections from a Journal Kept in India, Egypt, and Syria* (1857):

> We drove through the native town and bazaar of Bombay. Here I was quite bewildered with the novelty of the scenes around me—too much so, indeed—as we passed rather quickly through the streets, to note separately the endless variety of groups and pictures that presented themselves, in all directions: still, I saw a great deal.

Not all memsahibs, however, were pleased with Indian scenes. Indian-born British woman Anna Harriette Leonowens wrote, "Everywhere there is more filth and dirt than is possible to conceive at first sight; odors of *ghee*, or clarified butter, and fish in every stage of decomposition, assail you amid all manner of deafening sounds". She was also aware of the sinister goings-on at the ports of Bombay as ships came in. Secret robber societies would bring in their cargo consisting of stolen goods from merchant ships, which they dropped into the water to retrieve later or directly from merchant ships into their own, and then surreptitiously brought them to the shores as if they belonged to them. Sometimes, beautiful girls could be seen being brought into the ports, no doubt to fill the harems of the rich merchants.

As travellers to Bengal made their way into the main city, into the segregated quarters meant for Europeans, the scenes around them changed. These spaces were pleasing to the eyes and built keeping in mind the needs of the sahibs and memsahibs. The developed parts had beautiful architecture, and the memsahibs delighted at the sight of the Government House with its lush *maidans* (gardens), the lovely St Andrew's Church, and the sprawling area next to it called Chowringhee with its picturesque houses surrounded by gardens. Calcutta lived up to its name of the 'City of Palaces', and women who settled there were glad about the spatial segregation between their manicured localities and the rather squalid areas of *kutcha* (clay) buildings called the '*Kala Jugga*' or the 'Black Town', where Indians lived.

Not everything in India was as dreamy and fantastic as they had imagined. The European enclaves were lovely; however, homes for British families in barracks could be completely unlike the regular government bungalows. Zoe Proctor, who initially went to live with a British couple, visited beautiful sights such as the Royal Palace in utmost luxury and enjoyed the scenic landscapes of the Valley of Kashmir as she drifted on a *shikara* (a canopied boat) on the lake, but she saw the real face of India only when she entered the crowded streets of smaller towns much later.

Indeed, more often than not, the series of rude shocks, challenges, and hurdles for memsahibs had only just begun when they landed in India. In fact, landing on the shores of India did not even mean an end to their journey. They had to travel up the country, to their husband's posts, or to whichever place they were lodging in, which could be several hundred miles away. For instance, Minnie and Archie made a journey from Calcutta to Lahore, now in Pakistan, when they landed in 1856, which was 1,300 miles. Those who were in no rush could take a boat and go up the Hooghly river to join the mainstream of the Ganges after 10 days and continue to proceed slowly up the river. This could be quite comfortable and idyllic in a two-storey boat with an awning on the top deck and fourteen oars and a steersman to propel it, with a smaller boat in tow carrying the servants. But Minnie and Archie had to take the harder route. They travelled by railway to Raniganj, from where they continued up-country by Government *dak-gharry*, a box-like vehicle that jolted terribly on the *kutcha* roads. The horses galloped and the *gharry* lurched and jerked on the Grand Trunk Road until every one of Minnie's bones ached. She was six months pregnant at that time.

Thus, whether the British women had married back in Britain and arrived in India with their new husbands, or married after coming to India, they soon discovered that building a life in the colony was not an oriental fairy tale. The challenges before the memsahibs were innumerable, and they realised their theoretical preparation was going to be inadequate when it came down to the actual cold realities of life in India. Becoming good wives and mothers was considered the 'white woman's burden' in the Raj, but housekeeping in India was very different from housekeeping back home and presented several unforeseen challenges, so that the years of training in domestic aspects of life in England proved to be utterly futile. The empire ran like clockwork, and they had to quickly adapt. This could become quite overwhelming, and the newcomers—'griffins', as they were called—often suffered because of the pressure.

Indeed, some women were able to adjust quickly, blending in with the culture and climate organically, some took longer, while some simply gave up and left. If they chose to stay on, they had to adjust to everything against all odds. Sometimes, grave mishaps occurred and became a great cause of suffering. But they had to adapt quickly. Some like Delia Brown had to adapt quickly. She had moved to India with her husband soon after marriage, and when he died within a year, she remarried a soldier to be able to survive in the foreign land. Some memsahibs, however, grew disillusioned over time and lived miserably, tolerating adversities as best as they could until they grew stoic in the face of them. Maria Murray Mitchell wrote,

> among the many delusions which are obtained among you folks at home regarding this wonderful land, a favourite one is that it abounds in luxury. Now the greatest luxuries I know are this rather doubtful one of a night *punkah* [fan] and a glass of really cold water, which of course means that it is iced.

It might then be asked: what induced British women to undertake such risky and expensive trips across the seas just to lead difficult lives in India?

The answer perhaps lies in the composition of the 'Fishing Fleet'. It is little known that not all the women who came to India to find husbands were strictly 'lady-like', even if they belonged to good and affluent families. During the nineteenth century, as India became a sought-after destination for settling down, it was not uncommon for women to be sent out there to evade persecution or ill repute back home. Families of 'trouble-making' women frequently shipped off their daughters to distant colonies to get them off their hands, because such women were unlikely to find suitable men to marry in the places where they belonged and needed to have a fresh start away from those who knew about their questionable past.

Intellectual and learned women, as well as women who wanted to be financially independent, faced similar problems in securing husbands in the conservative spaces of Victorian society, making India a viable alternative for them. Although the sahibs in India did not particularly want a bluestocking for a wife either, the perennial shortage of women in the outposts compelled everyone to make exceptions. Women who were divorced or had passed the normal marriageable age were also sent out in the hopes that they might still find someone willing to overlook these matters. Iris James, who had a polio-ridden leg, had slim chances of marrying in England, and was shipped to India in the hopes that she would be able to get proposals from the multitude of (often desperate) bachelors in the Raj. India, for such women, was an escape, as well as a chance for redemption.

Whatever the case, marriage was on the mind of every woman who had come as part of the 'Fishing Fleet'. Some were able to mask their desperation to find husbands, whereas some did not bother to. Mrs. Leopold Paget, who wrote a journal of her journey through India and life in camp and cantonment in the late 1850s, mentioned a young lady "of most objectionable manners" who was on the same vessel as her while returning home. Having failed in her enterprise of '*la chasse aux maris*' (the hunt for a husband), she made desperate attempts to seduce any on-board soldier she could, laughing and giggling coyly at all men at odd hours, much to the alarm of her cabin mates, one of whom took chloroform to sleep to avoid listening to the tawdriness.

However, most young women of the 'Fishing Fleet' had better luck than Mrs. Paget's cabin mate. The marriage-market was far better in India than back home because of the abundance of lonely and young imperial officers, and marriageable women could get proposals quickly. In fact, women had scores of affluent government officials to choose from, and it was said that even the least pretty woman with moderate means could find several proposals easily. Patience Winifred Horne was engaged to her husband within 6 months of landing in Calcutta. She was immensely successful in gaining the attention of the officers and received several proposals in quick succession. Indeed, memsahibs thoroughly enjoyed the attention lavished upon them by the sahibs, young to middle-aged, and across all ranks, even after marriage. Lilah Wingfield wrote about dances in India: “India being a country full of men, the few women find themselves very popular”.

Most women who came to India dealt with marriages in a practical manner, deciding on a man only after weighing all their options in the typical Victorian fashion of fixing alliances. Marriage was in fact like a business transaction, and it was advised that a woman not commit too quickly just in case better suitors came by later, which was almost guaranteed in most cases. Financial considerations were of utmost importance, and happiness in matrimonial life was possible only if the sahib had enough finances to keep his wife in a good house.

It must be kept in mind that in the nineteenth century the need to marry was a compelling one, particularly for women who belonged to the middle classes and had little hope of finding husbands who could provide adequate financial support. Without marriage, it was not possible for women to sustain themselves since they had little or no scope for acquiring jobs. They were expected to marry soon after they became adults, and an unmarried woman was not treated with dignity in patriarchal British society. Spinsters, widows, and divorcees were considered anomalies, and life without a husband could be not just socially transgressive but also financially untenable.

At the time when the empire was at its height, Britain was undergoing rapid industrialisation and urbanisation. A new bourgeoisie class was emerging, and various occupations were available now. This provided some avenues to women and allowed them to gain financial independence if they acquired the skills. However, the moral climate of Victorian society remained conservative, and it was believed that women stepping into the public space and earning a living went against the proper codes of conduct for the female sex and severely compromised women's virtues.

Victorian social mores therefore consistently excluded women from the public space, and acceptance of women in the workforce was mostly absent. Education for women was undesirable and careers were scandalising. Social attitudes were extremely conservative, and great importance was given to a woman marrying before passing the marriageable age. The ages were not fixed, but an 'old maid' was any woman over the age of 30, and spinsters were just under it, although the term was used for women who still had a chance of finding a husband (Phegley, 150). Still, spinsterhood was abhorred, and such women were almost like social pariahs. In fact, unmarried women, unless they had a large fortune or inheritance, found it difficult to survive without the charity of family members, and led ignominious lives. They were deemed to be burdensome and were derogatorily called 'redundant'. Sometimes, batches of spinsters were shipped off to distant lands including America, in the hope that they might find husbands there.

Moreover, the demographics in Britain were completely unfavourable to a common woman who had come of age. According to statistics in 1840, 52 per cent of married women wedded between the ages of twenty and twenty-five. By 1851, an alarming census revealed that 30 per cent of women between the ages of 20 and 40 were unmarried (Phegley, 151). There were spinsters and widows everywhere, and hardly any eligible bachelors left back home for even the most accomplished lady.

Middle-class women faced worse conditions, as they either had to find an occupation to support themselves or survive on the charity of affluent benefactors or relations, both of which were deemed undesirable. In the early half of the nineteenth century, it was known that spinsters in India were of different categories. The first consisted of the daughters of civil and military servants, merchants, and others settled in India, who returned from England after completing their education. The second comprised the sisters and relatives of those women who had successfully found husbands in India and were now settled. These women often did not have adequate fortunes or prospects back home. The third category was made up of the orphan daughters, legitimate and illegitimate, of Indian residents. This category of 'dark beauties' was great in number and these women had little chance of finding suitable proposals. Still, India was their only hope.

The fear of never getting married was all too real. At times, women who did not expect to get married easily gladly accepted the first proposal for fear of becoming a burden to their families or of facing poverty. Those who crossed a certain age acquired the reputation of not receiving offers or of having turned down too many. The 'returned empties', like Mrs. Leopold Paget's thwarted young friend from the ship, were ridiculed for not being able to secure a husband even in a land where men were plenty and women too few. Those who remained unmarried were usually bandied about between relatives, living on their charity.

There is no doubt that the system was cruel and unrelenting. But while memsahibs were single-minded in finding a catch, bachelors were also anxious. Competition amongst the best-ranking men was high, and low-ranking officials had little chance when their senior, middle-aged superiors were competing for the same women. It can be seen that men were also practical in matters relating to matrimony and did not wait to find the 'woman of their dreams'. As soon as they heard that there were new arrivals, they proposed to meet at the port or the road so that they may avoid competition from the many other suitors. Naturally, given the number of options a lady had, the forlorn and rejected suitors returning home, still wifeless, were jokingly referred to as the members of the '*Juwaub* Club'—men looking for a 'yes' from a woman. Sometimes, money matters influenced men's decisions as well. A young Lieutenant, Thomas Bacon, who wanted to find an heiress posed as a Captain to win over a wealthy widow in the hopes of profiting by the match, but it turned out the lady was as broke as he was.

What is striking is that courtships were brief, and once engaged, couples could marry at express speed. The hastiness with which young people committed to marriage could sometimes result in ridiculous fiascos. Florence Marryat, a close observer of British-Indian society and wife of a British officer in

Madras, knew of an engaged gentleman who, in a drunken state, proposed to a lady who was considerably senior to him, then proceeded to quarrel with his betrothed, and even wrote to his family to announce his broken engagement.

Such romantic debacles were common in India. Marryat recounted how once a young lady fell so desperately in love with a man that when her parents did not approve, she eloped with him after a ball, determined to have her way. However, there was nowhere to run to in a cantonment and no clergyman was willing to marry her without the consent of her father. The couple went to a hotel, where the lady was found the next day, dressed in her ball gown as the night before. For fear of scandal, her parents relented, and she was finally married to the man.

Another incident narrated by Marryat was a similar 'comedy of errors' involving a pretty lady who had newly arrived from England and was much discussed in the British circles. It was known that because of her beauty and charm, she had quickly found many suitors. One day, two officers who were staying at the club were eating together and began discussing their love interests casually. Both were determined to marry their respective beloveds as soon as possible, and fearing rivals, wanted to hasten the proposal. It was sometime during that conversation that, to their utmost shock, they realised that they were both courting the same girl and were about to propose to her on the same day!

A British officer, Walter Yeldham, writing under the pseudonym 'Aliph Cheem', satirised the questionable love affairs of British India in *Lays of Ind* in 1901:

Colonel White was over forty;
Jane, his bride, was seventeen;
She was also very naughty,
For she loved a Captain Green!

Every evening, at dinner,
Colonel White would tipple deep,
And that pretty little sinner
Let her Johnny fall asleep.

Then beyond the dark verandah,
In a shady nook unseen,

> She would folly and philander
> With the wicked Captain Green (52–3).

Nonetheless, the caricature of the memsahib as frivolous and capricious reveals the double standards and gendered expectations of British-Indian society. Although the Raj was a comparatively free society in which to find a husband, where women had a greater degree of agency and choice, they were subject to restrictive rules and expected to cultivate the required merits to be the ideal wives of sahibs in India. In this, Raj society was not very different from Victorian England, where feminine qualities like sobriety, chastity, and subservience were valued. Intellect was not of great importance; instead, a woman's domestic skills were deemed accomplishments. Playing the piano, singing, sewing, knitting, sketching, riding horses, and playing polo were some suitable hobbies for them both back home and in India. In fact, in India, in addition to those qualities, they had to have the capacity to adapt quickly to different tropical environments, and have tremendous endurance, resilience, and tenacity not only in marriage but in all other aspects of life as well.

As it turned out, the most valuable asset for memsahibs in India was their indomitable spirit of adventure. These women were the ultimate risk-takers of the empire, brave before anything else, facing the dangers of the sea, determined as they were to find a better life in the East. They cried, complained, appreciated India, and denounced it, all at the same time, and though they were often tempted to leave, India captivated them no matter how they resisted.

2

"MY IGNORANCE OF MOST THINGS USEFUL WAS A DISGRACE"

BECOMING A MEMSAHIB

The centre of the cantonment is occupied by a large green parade ground, which looks like a well-kept common, and lined by rows of white houses, each standing, cottage-like, in its own garden, does strike the eye at first sight as might an English village on a large scale…

The Europeans who have permanent appointments in Bangalore take pains, of course, to make the surroundings as comfortable as they can, but the officers of regiments liable to be ordered off at a moment's notice have no such inducements to spend their money. Bare necessities are all they aspire to, and very bare their houses look in consequence… I learnt that it is possible for human nature to exist in a house so much more scantily furnished than the first one of which I was mistress…

– Florence Marryat, 1868

When the initial excitement of the whirlwind courtship and nuptials abated, the memsahibs travelled through the country to their new residences to at last begin their new lives.

To their great disappointment, their rudimentary government bungalows sat in bleak *mofussils* (provincial districts or rural towns) or in remote cantonments. Far from the fantasies of picturesque homes in romantic corners of the outposts, they found the rural posts to be mostly dismal and secluded, and in stark contrast to the vibrant Presidency towns of Calcutta and Bombay. Even the accommodations meant for the families of the British officers turned out to be worse than they had ever imagined.

If memsahibs had married soon after coming into India, as was the case with many, the wedding itself would have been a bit of a disappointment. Bridal tours were also not always possible unless they could afford to spend a significant amount of cash, and they generally went straight to their residences. Upon arrival, these newcomer women had to immediately take on multiple responsibilities within the domestic space.

Memsahibs often found the sights and smells of the Indian bungalow, in the middle of a sprawling nothingness, difficult to deal with. During the day, they would mostly be left alone for long periods as their husbands travelled for official Company work. Provincial areas usually had only one or two British families, so their social lives were restricted; there was hardly any good company and barely any mode of recreation. Even if they wanted to go somewhere by themselves, the heat made venturing out impossible. Much of their time was spent indoors, idling in great discomfort.

Little did these unsuspecting memsahibs know that daily existence itself would be perilous. For most, the initial charm of novelty quickly gave way to sheer horror as they discovered that the serene countryside, which had seemed soothing at first, was a hotbed of strange events and untoward occurrences. They would be seized with terror at finding a stray snake coiling languidly behind the basins or be awakened by tropical lizards making unearthly sounds in the middle of the night right next to their heads. It also took them a long time to get used to the large and spacious rooms with the constantly rippling curtains, which could be eerie in the long soporific afternoons because of the constant shifting of shadows as the servants came and went, whispering amongst themselves. What were they talking about? Were they watching from the shadowy corners, concealed by the darkness cast by the *chik* (woven bamboo) curtains? The memsahibs had no choice but to stay occupied with reading or sewing, uneasy in the dim corners of their chambers as the horizon darkened in the evenings. Sometimes, they would wander through the verandas, or sit outside as dusk fell about them, pondering upon the amazing possibilities of life beyond their compounds. But even the open windows and verandas, next to which they sat, could be strangely unsettling when various denizens of the night began calling from the wilderness.

If nothing else, memsahibs knew that cantonment life was going to be extremely difficult and came prepared as if for battle. Victorians were sticklers for detail when it came to travel, and the variety of information was staggering back in the day. Advice and warnings on life in India were readily available to the soon-to-be memsahibs, and a number of guidebooks provided stratagems on dealing with the practical details of life in the far outposts. Even before setting sail, they were bombarded with guidelines on how to furnish and maintain the household, supervise the servants, ensure a proper diet, and so on.

Extensive clothing was considered necessary for anyone going on a long sea voyage. Most manuals on proper packing listed hundreds of items, and memsahibs packed a staggering amount of luggage, in addition to their wedding trousseau. Flora Annie Steel and Grace Gardiner wrote *The Complete Indian Housekeeper and Cook* in 1888 for women who had no prior experience of coming to India. This widely popular and meticulously detailed domestic manual explained the items of clothing, shoes, hats, and so on that had to be included in baggage.

Packing for India was no mean task. Memsahibs had to pay special attention to the necessities for the sea voyage and also invest a great deal of energy and resources in purchasing special garments and items for use in India. Some of the rules of British attire were impractical in India and were discarded because the climate was hardly compatible with Victorian fashion. Wearing heavy European fabrics in the sweltering heat of tropical zones was ludicrous, and they were traded for cottons, muslins, and linen. Even stays were made of special lightweight material suitable to the warm climate. Leather shoes were sturdy and preferred by memsahibs, white dresses were more durable and easier to maintain than coloured or patterned ones, and rich silks were required for the balls and parties (but needed to be lined with flannel to avoid perspiration marks when worn). They had to carry a great number of items such as bonnets, pairs of gloves, and handkerchiefs because these sundry items were often not available in provincial towns, putting them in awkward situations. Sanitary napkins were not easily found in India, and women were advised to bring a good stock.

In fact, memsahibs packed as many of their garments as they could because the Indian climate was sultry and required several changes during the day. Ordinary wear and tear happened too frequently for their comfort, and their beloved dresses would change colour within weeks because of sweat and the vigorous washing by their *dhobi* (washerman). Sometimes even their newest dresses developed yellow spots, blue garments became stained, and lilac and mauve gowns simply looked dreadful in the light of oil lamps. This could be extremely frustrating to the newcomers since finding European fabrics and clothes was difficult, and there were hardly any *darzis* (tailors) who could stitch European designs. Moreover, packing these items also required extra care to make them last longer: the boxes would have to be lined with tin or zinc, and carefully soldered to preserve the material within.

Women who were setting out for India must have found the enormous range of advice intimidating, but upon arriving, they were glad that they had read and prepared beforehand. For instance, all those extra silk stockings and the multiple boots, cambric calico petticoats, and so on turned out to be necessary because European items in India, particularly women's garments, cost a lot, if they were available at all. A woman's cotton stockings in India cost almost as much as silk stockings back home, and stays could cost between 30 shillings and 2 pounds. Carrying multiple stays was also useful because they could not be reused as they were back home because of excessive perspiration.

In addition to personal items, medicines such as quinine, chloroform, magnesia, ammonia, laudanum, James's Powders, and *Eau de Luce* had to be brought in for emergencies, and memsahibs, fastidious as they seemed to be, even brought their guns and pistols from home.

Much to the relief of inexperienced memsahibs, the bungalows meant for the families of civilians were sometimes furnished according to European standards, but not everyone was as fortunate. Many wrote home of their disappointment with the non-European appearance of their homes, which were mostly spartan, albeit spacious. The structures were stuccoed on the outside, and usually built of stone. If the walls were not whitewashed, it could give the interiors a ramshackle and dilapidated appearance, especially because there would be no wallpaper like in their own homes back in England. The kitchens could be especially disappointing because of the grubbiness, and the primitive appliances and fixtures. The bathrooms were particularly appalling.

Flushing toilet systems had become common in Victorian homes by the second half of the nineteenth century. Before the 1870s, sponge bathing and 'hip baths' were common, and even portable showers were used sometimes. After the 1870s, plumbing technology was been developed which allowed for the installation of a fixed-pipe hot water system. Bathrooms had become a permanent feature in many homes in Britain by then, and by 1900, only the smallest of homes in London did not have them. Towards the end of the nineteenth century, the washdown toilet pan was developed. However, in India, all they had was a tin bath and a washstand. The bath would be on a raised platform, with built-up sides, and a drain. Hot water was poured in from vessels by the servants, and they added cold water from a large Ali Baba jar. The dirty water was tipped onto the platform by the sweeper later and ran outside the bathroom through a pipe or hole. But perhaps the oddest bathroom fitting in the Indian bungalow was the 'thunder box', which was a large and uncomfortable commode with massive arms and a removable bucket. The user of the thunder box was required to do their business, and when they were done, to holler to the servant outside to come and empty the contents. The box was then returned with cresol solution. To go with the thunder box, there was the 'Bromo', which was lavatory paper put inside a black and yellow container with a label detailing the benefits of said toilet paper. It warned the user that if it was not used, the most painful and humiliating anal infection and inflammation, 'piles' (quite common in the country), was guaranteed.

At least the toilets were out of sight, but the dreary drawing rooms and bedrooms could not be ignored. Memsahibs disliked the furniture in the sparse government houses, and couples often liked to purchase suitable items after marriage according to their budget. Nostalgia for English scenery made women passionately decorate the interiors of their homes in as much of a European fashion as possible, and they purchased items in the markets in Calcutta, specifically at the shop of M. de Bast where they could find a great variety of marble tables, luxurious settees, and large gilded mirrors. They also brought with them as much of their own homes as possible since table covers, Axminster and Brussels carpets, curtains, and other such items could be transported easily, while chintz furniture was picked up in India whenever possible. The piano, like other musical instruments, was carried from home and specially packed for travel in the tropics, even though India was considered a bad country for it. They also brought table ornaments, dinner and breakfast sets, and ironstone china, which were not available in India.

Whether the furnishings were to their taste or not, memsahibs did appreciate the basic architecture of the bungalows, which were constructed in accordance with the hot climate. The breeze flowed inside the inner quarters even on the hottest of days, and the roofs, which were made of *khus khus* (fragrant dried grass), kept the temperature low inside and provided a great respite during peak summer. The floors would be entirely covered with matting, cooling the interiors further. And the windows and doors, beyond which were fine-looking Venetian windows, would always be flung open to permit ventilation. The rooms were lofty and spacious, and opened into one another, through large folding doors with bolts, for better air circulation. Curtains hung everywhere, blocking out the sun.

However, during the summer months in coastal cities like Calcutta, the climate was unbearably sultry. Hot winds called '*loo*' rolled in throughout the day, and the interiors of the bungalows would become extremely suffocating. From the end of March to June, winds would blow ceaselessly night and day, and all the *khus* curtains were kept wet at all times. The *thermantidotes*—devices of revolving fans in a box with tatties (*khus* curtains) at the sides—were kept turning to enable circulation. The *punkahs*, which were huge wooden fans suspended from the ceilings, were moved to and fro by a man outside by means of ropes and pulleys, and these provided some comfort. They looked magnificent, as they were usually gilded and painted in brilliant hues, but they did not help in the peak summer months as they only churned the hot air inside. Nonetheless, these fans were suspended above the bed during the night, for the comfort of the memsahibs, although they had to get up periodically through the night to wake up the servants operating them because they invariably stopped as soon as they saw that their mistresses had fallen asleep. Sometimes, memsahibs kept a basin of water by their side, and soaked their head and hair before trying to go to sleep, repeating the process if they woke up in the middle of the night by the calls of jackals outside their window.

Throughout the day, the memsahibs did not stir from their homes, trying to stay in the coolest of the corners and exerting themselves as little as possible to stay cool. A hot blast of wind would greet them whenever they dared to open the doors or windows in the hopes of getting a cool draught. The intense heat and ubiquitous dust seemed to permeate their skin and caused several illnesses, apart from acute emotional distress. Many complained that they got up in the morning rather more tired than they were when they lay down to sleep at night.

Several memsahibs avidly recorded their struggles with the climate in their letters back home, even after years of living in India. They wrote how just before the monsoon, the days grew steadily hotter as the clouds piled overhead. Monica Campbell Martin, who came to India with her husband, Peter Martin, in the year 1923, wrote that no woman could look well in that heat: "You long to take off your skin and sit in your bones. You are a slab of melted butter."

The Martins were established in Domchanch in Koderma (in modern-day Jharkhand state), which was one of the largest mica-mining areas and where Peter served as Assistant Mines Manager and Zamindar Manager. The colony consisted of a few other European families whose male members were likewise employed in the management of mining in the area. Monica was fortunate to have the guidance of the only other lady in the *mofussil*, otherwise she would have found it extremely difficult to settle in. Their bungalow consisted of whitewashed rooms, screened windows and verandas, and large dim bedrooms with their own bathrooms. They had a golf course nearby, which was a good thing because golf and tennis were the only games that could be played after sundown, in the small window between dusk and twilight. Monica made an order for a customised brassie, a mashie, and a putter for a woman as soon as she settled in. She was quite forbearing in the face of difficult postings, and wrote in her memoirs:

> At our new destination there was a bungalow into which we could not move because the roof was broken. There was a well from which we could not drink. While fresh tiles were being brought to mend the roof, Peter lived in a tent. As soon as the roof was on, he moved in, and I joined him. While the well was being hurriedly deepened for our use, the water in it was a dark tea colour. In this we washed, bathed, and cooked. I could face up to the bathing part, but to brush my teeth I decided to use soda water. The result was surprising: I frothed like an epileptic.

Like Monica, one of the first things a memsahib saw as they began their new lives in the far outposts was that some of the most ordinary and day-to-day things, to which they had never given much thought before, could be extremely exhausting in India. In Monica's time, many British families had automobiles at their disposal, which allowed them to transport their luggage and travel much faster. Several other facilities were easily available even in *mofussils*; however, Monica still encountered many challenges in Domchanch. She was an inexperienced memsahib new to India. Back home, she had always been surrounded by women who were adept at domestic skills, but now she was on her own, a mistress of a house with four servants who spoke a different language and could hardly work in the way she liked. She communicated with them with the help of signs and gestures, and over time, learnt a handful of words and phrases.

Furthermore, the changing weather in India presented a whole different challenge to memsahibs as it could be quite unpredictable.

Although the afternoons were undoubtedly sweltering, after sundown the memsahibs enjoyed riding in the twilight, with fireflies hovering around them and twinkling in the wilderness as they rode through the countryside. However, sometimes the north-westerly winds crashed through the apartments, flinging all the doors and windows open. Lightning and thunder rolls were frequent when the air got dry and static.

The tropical climate also meant heavy rains and frequent thunderstorms during monsoons. Damp winds would sweep through the surrounding forests, making the trees swish around with the force. The *chota bursat* (pre-monsoon showers) would arrive ahead of the monsoon and burst upon the memsahibs without warning. Rains brightened up the landscape, and the colours seemed more vivid during the monsoons. The 'prickly heat' would be relieved, and the skin would stop burning. But almost too soon, the heat would return and stay on for days, until once again the clouds would gather in a dark beauty, and everything would smell dank and heavy like wet earth. There would be deathly quiet all around just before the rain poured down with heavy thunder, sometimes continuously for months, pinning everybody indoors.

In the more flood-prone areas, continuous rain could result in severe waterlogging. Memsahibs would wade through knee-deep water in their gardens, fending off nine-inch centipedes and black scorpions to get to their front door. When Monica Campbell Martin was in Bagaha, the surrounding villages were submerged. She quickly began evacuation efforts with the help of her servants, punting down the village streets in dugout canoes and helping people off the roofs. Then she opened her house up to the locals who needed shelter because their thatched houses were damaged, so that her entire compound housed several families, as well as livestock and poultry. That time in Bagaha, large areas were submerged, and families were camped in empty goods trucks. The bungalows that were on the low-lying lands were flooded due to the river overflowing. When Martin and her husband went out on a rescue expedition, they reached an Englishwoman's bungalow and found her balanced on the top of a table, lost in thought about how she would sleep that night.

That year, there was a deluge of rain, and Monica and her husband decided to move to a house in Turkaulia, which had not been impacted by the floods. Since the roads everywhere had turned to slush, they decided to paddle down by boat. Inside that house, the bed smelled of mildew, but it was better than a water-logged bungalow.

To add to the peril, earthquakes could cause extensive damage in the hills, where the ground was soft or where water was close to the surface. Low-lying places with alluvial soil could be badly impacted. When the Martins were in Bihar, there was a devastating earthquake that occurred right after the monsoons. Monica was in the garden at the time and heard a distant rumble, which suddenly became like the roar of a train travelling underground. The earth seemed to heave, and her house swayed before her eyes. Then suddenly, there was a crash of windows breaking, as the lawn ripped underneath her. The dogs were barking loudly as she ran towards the bungalow. The hills and trees seemed to be dipping, and one hill dropped from view before her eyes. Hundreds of birds flew up in alarm. She was catapulted headlong into the ground but was miraculously unhurt.

Even when floods and earthquakes did not occur, all sorts of troubles accompanied *bursat* (rains). Just after the showers, there would be a sudden onslaught of insects and reptiles. Memsahibs could be smothered by thousands of white ants that cascaded out from a crack in the wall next to their heads in the veranda without warning. When lamps were lit, moths arrived in millions. Green flies flew in swarms in places like Calcutta and were called 'Diwali flies'. They piled around the bases of lamp posts in small hillocks. The spider lick was like an earwig, and although it did not sting it would crawl over the skin and the area would become a burning pus-filled blister the next day. It got into towels and even shaving brushes and could cause masses of blisters on the face and body. Insects like the Bengal lancer left a fearful stink. Another stinkbug was the black shield bug, which had a pungent cloying odour that could permeate a whole room. People became so familiar with the smell that when they got a whiff, everyone yelled in unison that it was "stink bug night again!" and set about putting out lamps. If a bug landed in someone's clothes and got crushed, the person was 'scented' and everyone within range suffered. Almost every day, the floor would be carpeted with them as they dropped in thousands, saturating the air with the abominable stink.

Lizards were a common household pest in tropical cities, and memsahibs would be disgusted when they saw them crawling all over the walls and ceilings looking as though they might drop on their heads while they were having their meals. Eventually, they became used to them gliding around trying to catch insects with furtive darts of their long tongues. E. Augusta King wrote, "Sometimes at dinner our forks remain poised in the air while we watch with a positive fascination the tactics of a lizard stalking a moth".

Leaping frogs took refuge in shoes and sailed through the air every now and then, landing anywhere. Sometimes, they would hide in hats, making them jump off the heads of sahibs, startling everyone.

Moths were also very common in the plains, and memsahibs would be dismayed to find their lovely dresses eaten away to shreds. After the monsoon season, Monica Campbell Martin's clothes smelled of mildew—no one had warned her about that! She decided to air her expensive clothes out only to find that her meticulously sealed fur coat, which was a wedding present from her husband, came apart in tufts. She realised to her dismay that Indian insects could not be fooled with mothballs (and her entire closet continued to smell musty, no matter what she did).

In fact, the rains brought all kinds of creatures swarming out of their burrows. Black beetles and centipedes would be in abundance. Memsahibs used leaves of a plant called butch, which they spread around the room to drive the insects away, and sprinkled *chunam* (lime powder) generously to get rid of termites. There was no cure for cockroaches and crickets, and memsahibs just surrendered to them.

If the bungalows were located in the hills or damp valleys where it rained frequently, there was the certainty of finding spiders of the strangest species. Mother scorpions carrying several baby scorpions on their backs were a frequent occurrence in the bathrooms. Leeches in tubs were very common, and memsahibs had to make a thorough inspection every time they went for a bath. Snakes of four to eight feet could strike the unknowing traveller, and the poison would slowly consume the insides of the person over the next few hours. The hooded cobras regularly entered homes, and all of a sudden, a menacing hiss, perhaps from underneath the bed, would draw conversations to an unpleasant halt. Lillian Ashby, who grew up in Bengal and Bihar between 1874 and 1895, recalled one incident from her childhood when she was playing her mouth organ one afternoon inside her bungalow: two cobras crept up to her and began to dance a serpentine love dance to the music. She was terrified, but somehow kept playing until her grandfather finally came to her rescue.

In fact, Lillian Ashby had the most terrifying encounter as a baby right within her own home. Her mother had dozed off on the veranda while Lillian was in her bassinet, and a female ape whose baby had recently died came up and snatched Lillian. Her cries roused her mother, but it was too late because the ape had already climbed up a tree some way off. Their neighbours came running to help, hearing her mother's hysterical shrieks.

Lillian was rescued that day, but upon growing up, she would have to face the challenges of life in India by herself. Unlike many others, her Indian upbringing would be to her advantage, and she was likely to be better equipped to handle the practical realities of day-to-day life as a memsahib.

Tenderfooted Memsahibs and their Housekeepers

A very useful but expensive person in an establishment is a sircar; the man attends every morning early to receive orders, he then proceeds to the bazaars, or to the Europe shops, and brings back for inspection and approval, furniture, books, dresses, or whatever may have been ordered: his profit is a heavy percentage on all he purchases for the family… This man's language was a strong specimen of Eastern hyperbole: one day he said to me, "You are my mother, and my father, and my God!" With great disgust, I reproved him severely for using such terms… they dress themselves with the utmost care and most scrupulous neatness in white muslin… his reed pen is behind his ear, and the roll of paper in his hand is in readiness for the orders of the sahib… The servants hold him in great respect, as he is generally the person who answers for their characters, and places them in service.

– Fanny Parkes, 1850

Given the range of challenges memsahibs faced in their own homes, it was fortunate for them that there was an abundance of domestic help in India. Servants, in fact, were one of the chief highlights of the Raj lifestyle. Struggling memsahibs trying to grasp the rudiments of cooking and housekeeping in India gladly employed battalions of servants to take care of their every need.

Memsahibs wrote that the obsequiousness of Indian servants was much greater than that of English servants, who could be quite arrogant and unrelenting. They were particularly delighted by the attentive butlers and maids who seemed to always be waiting to be summoned, greeting memsahibs with ample *salaams* (a form of greeting) and dutifully abiding by '*jaao*' (leave), '*aao*' (come), and '*acchi baat*' (very good) directions. This was probably owing to the high competition because there were many contenders for one post within a British household in India. Anna H. Leonowens wrote of: "silent barefooted domestics, robed in pure white, who are seen gliding noiselessly to and fro, which lend a powerful magic charm, a flavour of the Arabian Nights, to the interior of even the most ordinary of British homes in the East".

Not all memsahibs revelled in the luxury of domestic help simply because of the convenience it provided. Many of them lauded the virtues of their help and struck great bonds with them. The Bamfields' head servant, Mahomed Yusef, was such a responsible and reliable man that they handed him all the cash, and he dispensed with the household expenses on his own. He even took decisions about the management of the house, and the family, well aware that they were living under Yusef's spell, were glad to comply.

Yet, despite the presence of good domestic help, there could be multitudinous problems in 'making home' in India which the memsahibs did not foresee. Usually, Indian servants were designated a single specialised domestic job: the *khansama* was the leader of the other servants of the house, the *butteewallah* was the lamplighter, the *ayahs* were lady's maids, the *dhobi* took care of the laundry, the *bheesties* were employed to bring water into the bathrooms and kitchens, the *jharuwallah* (sweeper) swept the premises, the *syces* (horsemen) took care of the horses, the *darzi* was the tailor hired for sewing and mending clothes, and so on. However, maintaining the division of labour amongst the servants required great skill and practice on the part of the memsahib.

It was also a common misperception back home that life in India was economical. Even servants, who were thought to be cheap, were actually not affordable by all. In fact, an entire army of servants was required to do the kind of work that a smaller number of servants could achieve back home, simply because every servant had a fixed job and did not do any work other than what they had been employed for. As a result, the expenses mounted considerably. Thus, economising domestic expenses and budgeting the upkeep of the household was not always possible in India. In the Presidency towns, rents could vary, and could be exorbitant for middle-class families, although up the country small houses were available cheaply, and good ones in most stations were well within the budget of an average household. The houses in Chowringhee, Calcutta, could be extremely expensive because of the architecture of the buildings. Flora Annie Steel and Grace Gardiner gave estimates for memsahibs planning to migrate to India in 1909 in order to help them plan their finances better. However, expenses increased with the rank of the sahibs and memsahibs.

For instance, the Viceroyalty were supposed to maintain a certain level of lifestyle and usually had many expenses to take care of. The Curzons had financial problems in just maintaining their home in India during their viceregal tenure between 1899 and 1905. Lord Curzon did not have a private fortune, and the income from his marriage settlement was not much. Mary Curzon only had 5,000 dollars, on which she received interest. The Viceregal salary at that time was 25,000 pounds, but all of it went to maintaining the staff at Calcutta and Shimla. The Curzons had difficulty in meeting the initial expenses of his office. To add to it, they realised that they had to buy from the outgoing Viceroy all his plates, horses, and carriages, along with the contents of his wine cellar, and even purchase their own fares and freight for the voyage out, which came to 9,717 pounds, to which the government made little contribution.

Moreover, the multitude of servants could be extremely difficult to manage and supervise, and memsahibs from the most ignorant to the most skilled found it a great challenge to keep them in order, especially because of the language differences. Sometimes, the servants outright refused to behave decently, getting drunk at the parties or refusing to work. If the memsahibs became too harsh with them, they would cause a commotion, while other servants would add to the hysterics by shouting in their broken English: "Sar! Master boy, cry Sar!" If they tried to dismiss someone, then the whole lot of the servants would disappear together. This shows that Indian servants did act collectively without unionising. One memsahib realised that her *ayah* was the head of a sort of council (*panchayat*) for *ayahs*, and if a particular family had mistreated their servants, they would spread the news amongst each other.

Finding domestic workers was indeed quite a cumbersome process. When a vacancy in a household arose, news spread like wildfire. Multiple men and women came to ask for the job, and memsahibs interviewed them one by one. Sometimes, they carried superlative 'chits' of recommendation, but would not know more than how to boil rice. These would be written in English, which they would not be able to read. One such chit carried by a man and given to Monica Campbell Martin read:

> TO WHOM IT MAY CONCERN:
>
> Mittoo Ram, the bearer of this letter, has worked for me for three months. His bazaar bills are double those of any servant I have ever employed. He is the biggest liar I have met and he has lost most of my shirts.

Managing the help could prove to be quite tricky, and memsahibs were warned that if they were too soft, there would be regular insubordination from male servants in particular. They were told to train their servants well and be firm in their treatment. They were also constantly warned of the 'skulking' servant who was sure to complain when given work and cut corners when not watched. Memsahibs also frequently complained in their writing of how their workers were liable to make excuses not to work or how they would go to their families for several days on end, which left their employers quite incapacitated within their homes. Many of the memsahibs never learnt any domestic work or were simply out of practice. How much of this is true and how much is rooted in racist ideas is not possible to tell, but such advice did prejudice the memsahibs who were setting up home in India and influenced their treatment of help.

The complexity of managing servants could sometimes increase because of religious and caste restrictions. Memsahibs were wary of their workers' perception of them as they often felt that the servants did not respect them because they were women and believed that only the sahibs deserved their best service. For this reason, many of the memsahibs expended a tremendous amount of time and energy on looking for help because they wanted to employ the correct person for each task. Despite their labour, however, there could be great confusion, often because of the socio-cultural and linguistic differences.

Interestingly, the management of the home and domestic help was the primary reason that memsahibs were inclined to learn Indian languages. Although this was not the only reason they made an effort to learn 'Hindustani' (Hindi), they did find it useful to learn a handful of local words for names of ordinary domestic items, or 'kitchen Hindustani', in order to give proper instructions about the house. Books containing such lessons in everyday communication with domestic help, which also gave detailed equivalents for English words, were understood to be a household necessity. However, there were some who preferred to never learn any native words to avoid any kind of conversation with the servants. One lady arrogantly declared: "thank goodness, I know nothing at all about them!".

Unfortunately, not knowing anything about them was a formula that was bound to fail. Even if a memsahib was not haughty, it could take them several months to learn the intricacies of the social structures in order to understand the Indians' social behaviour. For instance, they had to learn the nuances of the caste system, along which the division of domestic work was arranged. Most learnt quickly that the cook could not be asked to wipe a spot on the floor because the sweeper must do it and so on, but caste codes were particularly complex, and memsahibs had to be accepting of the local practices to avoid conflicts and fiascos. Once, Anna H. Leonowens was going to host a party, and it slipped her mind that her cook, who was Hindu, would not concede to cooking meat. She prepared dinner by herself, along with some Christian servants. When the cook returned, he insisted on taking over but fell asleep on the kitchen floor so that the dinner was burnt.

Apart from such complexities in assigning cooking tasks, food was an important aspect of domestic management that memsahibs had to supervise quite diligently. Diet was an important issue for the British in India as various ailments were linked to an improper diet, which were only made worse by extreme weather conditions. The heat could worsen health conditions, and rich foods, which were standard in the Raj, could often worsen matters. For instance, they were used to consuming more meat in Europe because of the cool climate, but in India, they had to take it in moderation due to the heat.

Moreover, hygiene was a great concern. Memsahibs were particularly concerned about cleanliness, and in most cases, it was a matter of life and death due to the prevalence of contagious diseases such as cholera. The health and hygiene of the *khansamas* and *khitmatgars* was therefore a priority because the cooks would often use their dirty hands to cook and clean. The servants usually had separate quarters, but if they were not cleaning their hands well or grooming themselves, it could directly affect the families they were serving. It was almost taken for granted that the *khitmatgar* might be prone to using his toes as toast-racks or soiled clothes for straining soup just because it was quicker and easier. In this, some of the memsahibs were brainwashed by gossip or popular books while some actually had unpleasant experiences, which they then wrote about at length.

Keeping the kitchen and storage clean was also of utmost importance because the surroundings were often insanitary. Memsahibs kept an eye on the stored provisions in the larder, particularly meats which had to be stored in a special manner to ensure that insects did not get to them. Still, ensuring cleanliness was difficult. The tropical climate, the dense foliage, the dust, and the enormous variety of house pests and strays meant that hygiene within the house, especially the kitchen, could not always be maintained.

Monica Campbell Martin recounted how she had once ordered fowl to be cooked on the veranda by her cook, and the situation quickly spiralled out of control in the most ludicrous manner. It had been several days since they had eaten anything but vegetables, so even the house pets were drawn by the smells. What she did not know was that there was a kite infestation in the area, and the open verandas allowed all sorts of birds and creatures to come in at any time. No sooner was the fowl brought out to be prepared, than a kite dove down and was immediately attacked by the dogs, who nipped its wings. Immediately, all the crows in the vicinity erupted in loud screeches, and the cook began yelling, trying to keep the dogs from carrying away the meat. Somehow, the cook beat all the contenders and brought back the chicken triumphantly. They ate that for tiffin. After that incident, whenever the cook prepared chicken, she stood guard outside the kitchen and shot at the kites circling above with her gun.

While preparing meals was usually not as perilous as this, memsahibs were still required to be alert. If they were suspicious of the quality of the groceries, they taught their cooks to make fresh bread and churn their own butter. Sometimes, they had their cows milked before their eyes on the verandas because milk contamination was a common cause of diseases. Memsahibs were aware that it depended entirely on them to keep up the high English standard in the maintenance of their homes. Sometimes, they liked to cook for themselves in the proper European fashion, but their servants did not like that and hastened to take over the chores. Martin, for instance, struggled in the kitchen like most other memsahibs, who tried, often in vain, to train their cooks to prepare English dishes. This endeavour was not always successful, mainly because of the cultural differences in culinary experiences, so that the memsahib and her cook often learnt cooking at the same time. Ultimately, memsahibs had to reconcile themselves to the idea that their meals, like everything else about their identity, would always have a distinctive mark of India.

Monica, like most other memsahibs, found it challenging to train her domestic help in matters of personal hygiene and sanitariness. She even employed a *dhobi* and had him wash their clothes in their premises to prevent the skin disease common in India known as '*dhobi's* itch'. It is to her credit that she learnt quickly and even eagerly several domestic lessons for life in India and wrote in her accounts of the knowledge she had gained. She described how it was necessary for the doors to the house not to be left open during the day, but for the house to be well ventilated with *chik* doors. Keeping milk next to a drain, or not changing the water in the pot frequently, could cause poisoning due to contamination. It was necessary to see if the servants were boiling the water well or not, and if they had washed the fruits and vegetables before serving them.

The Martins' cheeriness in the face of most challenges, and their ability to take things in their stride, were well demonstrated by one example when Monica, perceiving contamination of the water, devised an elaborate homemade filter for ensuring clean drinking water. The contraption she created was made with earthen pots fashioned to her requirement by the local potter. Several jars were put into tripods made with bamboo. In the topmost jug they poured boiling water which flowed into the next pot filled with charcoal to clean it and finally dripped out through a hole at the bottom into the pot underneath. The next jug was filled with sand, and the water dripped through this too, filtering for a second time before trickling into the last jar at the bottom; this water was then safe to drink.

Memsahibs also had to oversee how the servants were behaving around the house at all times. Intoxication was quite prevalent amongst some Indians as many were addicted to smoking *ganja* and consuming *bhang* (a sweet potion made with cannabis), and memsahibs had to learn to tackle this problem since opium, which was known as a major mood-altering drug, made the workers lethargic. It must be noted that notions around drug usage vary according to cultures. Addictive substances and intoxicants like tobacco and *bhang* were culturally acceptable in India, but the British were averse to them. Moreover, in the nineteenth century, India was a major site of poppy cultivation, and opium was one of the most valuable exports. Consuming opium was quite common amongst the Indian population—perhaps it was the exertion of the work, the poverty, and, often, even hunger that had led to such addictions. There is no doubt that such cases of drug dependency require a more complex examination of the British-Indian government's massive drug economy. And in the absence of any accounts of the memsahibs' servants consuming drugs while on duty to induce torpors throughout the day, it is difficult to trust the colonialist's perception that servants were derelicts; focus should instead be on the absence of the subjectivities of the subalterns in question.

Still, memsahibs were told to keep a vigilant eye on the servants, not just by word of mouth but through published domestic manuals that advocated stringent domestic management. Some of the manuals which offered advice on tackling servants were highly problematic. For instance, Steel and Gardiner's *The Complete Indian Housekeeper and Cook* said that the secret to good housekeeping was to treat the Indian servant as a child, with kindness but firmness: "the laws of the household should be those of the Medes and Persians, and first faults should never go unpunished. By overlooking a first offence, we lose the only opportunity we have of preventing it becoming a habit".

Furthermore, no matter how trustworthy their servants were, since there was little security in place, memsahibs were told to be alert at all times. Helen Douglas (Mrs. Colin) Mackenzie wrote about the time she was out on a walk when she was faced by a gentleman's servant who was carrying a huge axe with a red handle. The sight of an armed Indian servant strolling in the gardens took her aback, but upon enquiry she found that the man was carrying it as protection against thieves. This showed that despite living in close quarters with servants, the British were constantly wary of them and, particularly as the servants greatly outnumbered them within the house, stayed alert about the goings-on around them.

British families even hired a guard called the *chowkidar*, who was supposed to keep guard against thieves. Every night, memsahibs would be roused from their sleep by calls of the guard announcing to possible intruders that he was awake and on the lookout. This security system did not ensure complete safety, especially if the servants themselves conspired to loot their employees, as many memsahibs wrote in their accounts. Emily Eden was in Calcutta in the winter of 1823 when her friend who was staying with her found that his desk containing gold and valuables had been carried off from his room, along with his clothes and military cloak. They suspected that the *khansama* himself had plotted with the *chowkidars* to commit this burglary.

Anna H. Leonowens recorded her own encounter with a mischievous though not cunning servant. During the incident, she was living in Bombay in one of the beautiful airy bungalows that epitomised the luxurious lifestyle of the sahibs and memsahibs. There was nothing to suggest any untoward activity, but one morning when Anna, having woken up early, stepped out onto the veranda to take in the scenic sunrise beyond the trees, she suddenly caught sight of her *darzi*, Tom, making off in her husband's clothes. He had on her husband's best dress-coat and embroidered vest, pointed shoes, her stockings, a frill that was six inches deep, and a huge cocked hat on his head over which he held one of her favourite parasols!

Comical as this incident was, most memsahibs did not adopt a humorous tone while relaying such incidents. Several wrote about the threat of burglars and intruders around their bungalows. Once, Julia Maitland's *darzi* purloined a pair of sheets from her home in order to make his own jackets.

Indeed, the more experienced memsahibs warned the newcomers to be mindful of their possessions in case of any thieves in the household, avidly circulating their personal stories of thieving servants. Some even claimed that though servants were lacklustre and indolent in dispensing their household duties, they could be quite shrewd and cunning when it came to pilfering from their employers.

For the British, particularly women, safety and security were a major concern in households so densely populated by Indian servants, whom they could sometimes hardly keep track of or communicate with. Keeping out intruders was always tricky because there were so many servants and their family members around that it was not possible to keep track at all times. Julia Maitland was once awakened in the middle of the night by the most horrible yelling and screaming, and she scolded her servants for not keeping out what she called "hobgoblins". Then again, one afternoon, she caught a girl she had never seen before, creeping up the back stairs outside her house, which made Maitland suspect her even though it was quite common for the children of servants to enter the house when their mothers or fathers were working.

Such accounts of the perceived threat from servants need direct scrutiny. There was a general fear and distrust towards Indian servants, and even though many memsahibs regularly praised their hardworking disposition, their writings constantly brought up instances of servants and underlings causing confusion within their homes due to behaviour that was seen as careless or shrewd. Younger memsahibs were advised by senior memsahibs to be careful in employing someone and to get background checks to ensure safety. Once, E. Augusta King was approached by a native Christian convert for a job as an *ayah* but had been warned against Indian Christians and therefore turned her away. This is possibly symptomatic of the coloniser's desire for gaining control and maintaining 'discipline' in the colonial space. In the microcosm of the home, the female 'colonisers' adopted strict measures wherever possible. Accounts about neglectful servants are therefore unreliable, although plentiful.

Moreover, memsahibs were apprehensive of their male servants because they would regularly be alone with them in remote locations for long stretches of time. Even though accounts of perceived sexual threat are sparse, many memsahibs recorded how the presence of male servants was inconvenient simply because they would have to stay fully dressed in layered outfits throughout the day. However, too frequently, the troubles of the heat triumphed over any concerns of propriety, and even the most modest ladies learnt to ignore the gaze of half a dozen male servants even inside their sleeping apartments. After all, it was always too hot, and sweating under layers of clothing was simply not feasible. Neither was getting rid of the help, who fetched them iced lemonade and filled their washbasins for them to wash their hair in. Moreover, as many memsahibs noted about their domestic help, the servants seemed to blend into the surroundings, barefooted and quiet as they always were, coming in and going without being noticed. Most women eventually grew comfortable staying in their dressing gowns and flimsy flannel clothing. In fact, memsahibs sometimes dressed and undressed in the presence of their male *darzi* without scruples, since there was no knowing how much they had seen or heard anyway.

Ultimately, memsahibs accepted the fact that the Raj lifestyle that came with the luxuries of multitudes of domestic help also took away privacy. It was inevitable that the servants would be privy to the most intimate affairs of the households they worked in, and the memsahibs knew that there were no secrets in the house: whether it was an affair or a domestic quarrel, the servants were silent spectators, blending into the background, but always watchful, and all-knowing. They were even aware of their masters' bodily functions, as they were the ones who cleaned the bathrooms and emptied the thunder boxes!

Sometimes, the realisation of how exposed they were made the memsahibs uncomfortable, but they had come to believe that servants were an integral part of the domestic space, which inevitably caused the memsahibs to dehumanise them and view them in terms of their utility rather than their humanity. Nonetheless, the memsahibs knew that they could never dispense with the servants because they would not be able to fend for themselves in a country like India. It is quite a paradox that due to their woeful dependency, the memsahibs were slaves to their own servants.

Clubs, Calling Cards, and the Indian *Dastur*

My programme filled almost at once, and when people went to supper one could have some lovely turns, so I hadn't any fear of being a wallflower... I was a country cousin coming to see the sights and I intended to see them... Lady Curzon, who looked perfectly lovely, was dressed to carry out the idea in an entire dress of cloth of gold embroidered in tiny peacocks' feathers with an emerald sewn on for the eye; all her diamonds and crown and some real creamy lace about the shoulders. You can't conceive what a dream she looked... How good it was of Pap and you to let me come, and it was a chance of a lifetime and I am so grateful to think I have got it. Everyone I knew was there, so from a social point of view as well it was a great success... I didn't get to bed till 3.30 and was tired out with so much excitement.

– Ruby Madden, circa 1903

While the perils faced by a memsahib were numerous, the flipside was the gay social life of the Raj.

The fresh batches of memsahibs arriving in India were immediately taken into the fold of British society. For those who landed in India to get married, life was initially all about parties, flirtations, and affairs. And away from remote rural areas, in most ports, hill stations, and cities, memsahibs enjoyed an exuberant social life. There were brunches, luncheons, and dinners, and dances, theatre, and other gay congregations. Katherine Welford wrote giddily, "Every night there was dancing after dinner, to which one was escorted by some chap". Betsy Anderson had been to some big dances at home, but in India, at the Yacht Club, "life became a glamorous fairy-tale... Everything was perfection—gorgeous evening dress, the men in uniform, and we danced on a superbly sprung floor. The gardens, which were discreetly lit, had well-watered smooth green lawns looking across the harbour to the ships twinkling with lights—all very romantic and unreal".

One of the basic unwritten rules in India was that every family was supposed to have regular home engagements, and periodically host parties and gatherings. What this meant was that there was always a party happening somewhere, so that the 'Fishing Fleet' girls, especially, were swept into the flurry of social engagements immediately upon arrival. Those living in garrison towns more than welcomed the party culture. Nobody minded being a 'garrison hack', as such party-going women were called, when there was so much fun to be had. A sort of speed dating system was also practised by the twentieth century, whereby young single women were positioned in strategic spots in a ballroom, sometimes in the Government House, and bachelors were brought in after which the women had 10 minutes with each young man. This was convenient because the women knew they would not be stuck with any uninteresting man for too long ("The Lost World of the Raj", Ep. 2, 14.00–15.50).

However, these women had much to learn even about the art of partying in the Raj. The machinations of British society in India were complex and multi-layered, and they had to adapt quickly or end up inadvertently flouting the written and unwritten rules of proper social behaviour and be penalised mercilessly. Not only was the Raj society complex, but the obligations were too many and all too demanding. Moreover, basic events such as hosting guests were very different from what they were used to and tested their patience all the time. Memsahibs sometimes learnt the hard way that no matter what the situation, they would have to develop a high tolerance for all kinds of unexpected events—even in the face of the most excruciating company. After all, in the Raj, hospitality and sociability were prized qualities in a lady, and apart from good housekeeping, the wife of a sahib was expected to be an impeccable hostess.

Another facet of life in India was that the empire existed based on a fastidiously maintained categorisation between levels. A formal and clearly demarcated pecking order was firmly established. This rule of precedence was etched in stone, and there was no scope for concessions. Naturally, in a society that was so stratified, there would be an enormous respect for hierarchy. Prestige and power were in direct accordance with rank and position: at the top of the list was the Viceroy, with more than sixty ranks under him, ending with the tax collector. Everything, from seating arrangements at dinner tables to other social formalities, was governed with this scale.

It is noteworthy that the rules of British society in India were inviolable because their patrons were rigid and unrelenting. They did not want to make any concessions lest their carefully constructed world shattered to pieces. For instance, the British fraternised only with their fellow 'exiles', and transgressing such rules could have severe repercussions.

No doubt, in Raj society, class exclusivity was common. Emma Roberts recounted how people from the lower ranks wanted to destroy all distinctions of rank and gain unlimited entry into the Government House. But hypocrisy ran high: those who were anxious to get admission to the higher ranks' gatherings were the people who wanted to exclude those immediately beneath them.

Just as officers of the Indian Civil Service and the army had their respective ranks and a proper institution to subscribe to, memsahibs formulated a similar system for their own organisation in social situations. Memsahibs realised that there was a neat categorisation even amongst the new arrivals of women in India, as they could be accepted into the social circles based on recommendations only. In this, Calcutta was no different from London in its "exactions of certain passports and credentials for admission into the best society", as Emma Roberts mentioned. The 'griffins' had to quickly establish their position. But their reception in suitable circles, as well as future social interactions, depended on their class and social stature, and the higher the rank, the higher their position in the social pyramid. Thus, women of viceregal families enjoyed the best privileges and epitomised the glitz and glamour of Raj society in India. The Lytton sisters, Elizabeth Edith (Betty) and Constance (Connie), gushed about the attention lavished upon them when they accompanied their father and mother, the Viceroy and Vicereine, to India during the Imperial *Durbar* of 1877. They were accompanied by aides-de-camp and detachments of cavalry, and followed by a retinue of Indian rajas and maharajas as well as magnificent animals and weaponry.

In fact, newcomer women discovered that the title of the 'memsahib' itself was exclusive and jealously guarded in the nineteenth century, granted to only those women who could 'make it'—that is, find suitable husbands or in some other way establish their position in British circles. Women who wanted to be recognised as a '*pukka*' (recognisable) memsahib had to abide by the Raj customs and practices. The pressure to conform was exceedingly high, and lapses in fulfilling the proper social roles and duties were not taken too kindly. The 'griffins' often found it surprising to see just how rigid and formal social etiquettes and protocols were. Those who defaulted became social pariahs. The British circles in India were close-knit and ruthless in this way, and word got around quickly. Sometimes, the misdemeanours of a lady also reflected poorly on the entire community of the British, who fought hard to maintain an image of superiority (racial as well as moral) before the subjects of the empire. Effectively, a memsahib's business was everyone's business.

It must be kept in mind that the Raj wives' own identity barely had anything to do with their actual rank and position. Their status was dependent entirely on their male counterparts, and personal merit did not matter most of the time, especially if they were in India primarily as 'trailing spouses'. If they were daughters to important officials, they had easy access to prestige from the start, and if they married a high-ranking officer then it enabled them to secure and sustain a position amongst the more socially superior memsahibs.

When Mary Victoria Curzon arrived in India in 1898, she experienced for the first time the extraordinary distinction, and indeed isolation, that was afforded to her and her husband because of their position. Even though she belonged to a privileged class and was highly educated and well-travelled, her sudden initiation into Viceroyalty was quite bewildering. She wrote, "We might as well be monarchs", and was mildly surprised by the reception they received, which was attended by more than 1,400. A gold carpet was laid out for them, the guests bowed as they walked, and she was pleased by the attention given to her. She was also grateful to see that the decorations featured stars and stripes alternating with the Union Jack, acknowledging her American roots, and responded to the gesture with bows and waves of genuine gratitude. The crowds immediately saw that she was a natural at being a Vicereine. Indeed, disorienting as all the furore was, Mary had no difficulty understanding the complicated protocol of imperial India and seemed completely self-assured. She was described by Nigel Nicholson in *Mary Curzon* (1977) as:

> A tall stately woman with blue eyes, masses of dark hair, and a face that could be described as a picture. Her self-possession of manner was evident as her beauty, and during the half-hour that the proceedings (at the landing-stage) lasted, she was pre-eminently the most self possessed individual under the white and yellow stripes of the manlap. As she leaned with crossed hands on the twisted silver handle of a parasol that matched her dress one could detect no suggestion of nervousness in a single twitch of her fingers (Nicholson, 112).

The social dynamics in the Raj era were complex and diverse, and a stratified society meant that ordinary memsahibs, unlike Mary, had to function under the power of the '*burra*' (senior-most) memsahib, wherever they were posted. The common rule was that the senior memsahib's authority had to be acknowledged, and their rank honoured, at all times. The junior memsahibs had to win the good graces of their seniors, and rally for their patronage. This was an important system, and although unrecognised by the colonial administration, was as crucial to the careers of the new memsahibs as any Raj work was for an officer serving the empire.

The importance given to outward appearances and the performance of graces was evident when two officers and their wives were dining with their hosts Florence Marryat and her husband. Florence's husband escorted the older lady in for dinner instead of the wife of the officer of the higher rank. This was taken as a serious affront, and the indignant husband came in the next day to reprimand them for this supposedly gross oversight. In another example, a memsahib was surprised to find that when she declined an invitation to attend a *levée* (a reception in honour of someone), the lady who was hosting was thrown into a fit of temper at her audacity. She received a lecture about her 'duty' to attend such gatherings and had to concede helplessly in the interest of her husband's reputation.

Indeed, the tyranny of the senior memsahibs was widely dreaded as they were known to use the power of their husbands' position to interfere in other families' private affairs. There were many cases where the senior ladies habitually bullied the wives of officers of inferior rank, knowing that the junior memsahibs would compulsorily act with *savoir faire* and always be placatory. Indeed, due to the pyramid structure, women were acutely conscious of the rank distinctions and often would not even socialise with wives of officers who belonged to an inferior post. Fathers who had risen in the ranks would not wed their daughters to men who were of a lower rank than a Sergeant Major.

Inevitably, pretentiousness was fashionable amongst the memsahibs, and a lady was judged by the clothes she wore, how she did her hair, and how beautiful she was in general, because such things reflected her social standing. No matter the weather, women were inclined towards silks and velvet gowns for the evening parties and balls. They ensured that they had their elegant gloves, silk stockings, and heels for dances. Their hair was done in the proper British way, curled and styled fashionably, and sometimes adorned with fresh flowers. Outward appearances were always crucial, and memsahibs expended a great deal of energy on maintaining a certain social status. One afternoon, a lady visited Julia Maitland while she was in the middle of some household chores and was quite covered in dust. The lady had her best clothes on, and wore muslin and yellow gloves, and it made Maitland feel ashamed of her own appearance, even though she was just sorting her bookshelf.

Memsahibs expended such tremendous effort in constructing a social system because they had built a duplicate England in India and were willing to do everything to maintain it. Moreover, in the absence of a social life, society in India was dull. It was always difficult to make and maintain contacts given the highly mobile lives of the British officials. Therefore, as the Raj progressed, various conventions evolved, keeping in mind these logistical matters. Some of the rules and trends necessarily had to be followed by all. Regimental entertaining, for instance, became a common practice, and wives of colonels in particular had the responsibility for hosting many gatherings, which then brought into place a strict code of conduct for socialising.

Moreover, at stations, regiments would frequently come through, and they would make passing visits; sometimes, many of them would turn out to be old acquaintances. Lady Anne Campbell Wilson wrote, "There is hardly an official in any one of the two hundred rural districts of India who does not hold himself responsible for the comfort of every stranger, official or non-official, who enters it. Who they are and what they are is a matter of quite secondary importance: they must be looked after in any case".

One of the ingenious methods of maintaining social connections was the system of 'calling cards'—a ritualised practice that polite society subscribed to—which became firmly established as a legitimate means of making acquaintances in India. For the new memsahibs, these calling cards were a public announcement of their arrival, to declare that they were open to invitations and prepared for entering society. Every newcomer had to have her own calling cards and was supposed to leave them at everyone's houses to procure invitations for dinner. If a newcomer woman was staying with her relatives, young men would drop by to leave their cards, and then she would invite them to parties or dinners.

Lady Anne Campbell Wilson, who published a collection of her letters she wrote from India in 1911, noticed how outside every bungalow there were boxes labelled 'Not at Home', so that if someone came by to leave their cards, and the hosts were not available to receive them, they could simply drop them into the boxes. This was quite convenient as the ladies of the houses would often find it tedious to greet every person who came by to drop off their cards. Sometimes, they sent their servants to answer the door, make excuses to the visitors, and politely turn them away with a plain, 'not at home'.

Signing the books at the house of the Divisional Commander or near the gate of the Governor's house, in order to be invited to any of the good gatherings, was also a much-liked practice. The business of meeting and inviting was so important that people took offence if so-and-so did not call upon them but did on the others in the given circle. They would go to the lengths of exchanging notes to keep track of the activities of the people they mingled with and always found out if someone had neglected them.

Stressful as such rigid conventions may have been, one of the chief delights of social life in the Raj was the endless string of balls. These were highly celebrated and lavish affairs, and ballrooms in Cawnpore (Kanpur) would be completely lit up during such events. Several memsahibs looked forward to such grand dances, when the guests would be directed inside the houses by the illuminations in the neighbourhood. In some places, the floors would be boarded, and the memsahibs found it easier to dance the quadrille on them rather than on whitewashed floors. When proper music could not be procured, they would have drums and fifes. Although this music was less pleasant, these *belles* were determined to dance and enjoy their balls.

In cantonments, parties were not so lavish, but there would be games for the soldiers, attended by women, several dances, and theatre, which would provide some sort of recreation to all. The theatre opened in some places once a month and would be elegantly decorated. Most of the time, it would secure full audiences. Outside the theatres in Calcutta, the carriages and servants would wait for the show to finish so that they could carry the sahibs and memsahibs to the next location. There would also be palanquins, buggies, and automobiles. After the play, there would be supper and a ball at the neighbouring assembly rooms. The tables would be laid out and the head servants would supervise the arrangements.

The 'Indian breakfast' was another extremely popular social activity amongst the Europeans. It would be the most scenic repast, brought to perfection in the middle of a desert or in sprawling and meticulously pruned lawns. There would be fish of every variety, fresh, dried, pickled, or preserved, delicate fricassee, resoles, croquettes, omelettes, and curries of all kinds. Cold meats and game were popular, and pâtés, jellies, and jams brought in from London were also served. There would be china, cut glass, and silver, and the guests would be thoroughly entranced by the presentation.

In Peshawar, it was common for memsahibs and sahibs to gather under trees with iced drinks, discussing their activities over the season. Towards teatime, they would stroll down to the club for tennis and racquets, loafing, and coffee. The bands would play (mostly "God save the Queen") as the parties would sit together and gossip. Clubs had been established by the British in various parts of the Raj and were also used for entertainment, games, and social events. Some of the clubs were very '*pukka*'—exclusive for the British. There were often band stand gardens in cantonments where gentlemen loitered, enjoying the evening air and the walk. The men would also go around greeting and conversing with women, often flirting with them. This sometimes led to scandals—once a lady's bonnet and a quantity of empty bottles were found in a garden where music was played.

The party atmosphere in India could be so extreme that the 'Fishing Fleet' girls would sometimes have to shunt between multiple parties in one single evening. A young Australian girl, Ruby Madden, daughter of Sir John Madden, Chief Justice and Lieutenant-Governor of Victoria who came to India in 1903 to attend the Delhi Durbar held for the coronation of Edward VII, was so occupied with attending balls and parties that it was days before she could write to her mother. In a single letter, she wrote about how she went riding with Captain Cameron, how Rose Price was sorry he could not come to see her as he was ordered away to Quetta, how Captain Clarke (a bachelor) had promised to take her to Madras, how she went lunching with Mr. Landon and met Mr. H. V. Cobb who invited her to Bombay for *shikar* (hunting), how Mr. Lombard called for them in his carriage, and how they went to see Captains Templar and Clarke, who knew Harry and Pat, and so on.

Newcomer memsahibs were especially conscious about marking their presence in all the gatherings they were invited to, going to great lengths to ensure that they did not miss any if they could help it. Very often, this was a cause for great anxiety as they were often unable to procure the proper transportation to go to their parties, particularly in army stations where carriages were not easily available to them. Some unfortunate memsahibs had to bicycle their way to their hosts' residence after hitching up their skirts. Sometimes, they got confused about the invitations, went to the wrong one, and then had to go home and change for the one they were originally meant to go to. These women knew that no excuse of illness, tiredness, or even a little baby at home was good enough to skip a party, much less leave a dinner table early. Even if there was a bad *ayah* at home who did not pay attention to their children or if the road by which they came could become dangerous after dark, they simply persevered through the entire duration of the party without attempting to explain to the hostess why they wanted to leave early. Most of the time, they could not decide what was worse: the wild animals in the dark or the ire of senior memsahibs who did not care for the concerns of the junior ones.

It would be accurate to say that attending social events was deemed to be a memsahib's public duty as much as an officer's imperial work was his. In fact, dinners and parties were taken so seriously that women who missed a few were accused of being careless and were looked down upon. Thus, despite their innermost psychological and emotional struggles, most memsahibs built and maintained their image and reputation carefully. However, this endless show of politeness felt burdensome even to the most obsessive memsahibs, and the pressure of social events afflicted women across the ranks.

Lady Curzon, during her stay of 3 months in Calcutta every year, had to host dinners and parties regularly with her husband. They were expected to give a state evening party, a garden party, and a fortnightly dance, provide two levées for men only and a drawing room for ladies, give official dinners of up to 120 people once a week, and give lunches and dinners every other day. The couple dined with important dignitaries on other occasions, and the Vicereine's attendance was obligatory and compulsory. She did not enjoy all the events, and the perpetual obligations caused her severe mental and physical exhaustion. She wrote in her personal accounts about how she would have headaches because of attending parties, in spite of which she smiled when she could have sobbed because of tiredness. After one particular party, she was so tired that she could not walk and had to be carried upstairs, and the doctor advised her against such strenuous activities in the future. Yet, the social events went on ceaselessly. During one instance, she had to dine at the Lieutenant-Governor's house despite being severely fatigued because seventy people had been invited in their honour. That evening, she fainted twice while dressing and was carried to the carriage. Then she had to shake hands with seventy people and talk through dinner, and afterwards she had to chat with each lady. She only ate some biscuits and drank some brandy and collapsed in the carriage back home (Nicholson, 118).

Undoubtedly, even though social events made the memsahibs' lives cheery and brought variety to the humdrum of their daily existence, several ladies expressed their dissatisfaction with such an exacting lifestyle. Memsahibs like Isabel Savory found that parties and clubs could entail "paralysing ennui" as meeting the same kind of people over and over again could become extremely tedious. It was sometimes downright dreadful to ride with them at breakfast and then meet them again in the evening. They would feel silly to sit for tea and snacks, then meet for tennis and games, play cards together, indulge in the same gossip, and even discuss the same matters, repeatedly. In fact, even gossip got boring after a while as everyone was aware of the intentions of every man in regard to the woman he was pursuing. The dinner parties had the same guests, the same courses, and the same chit chat, and it could become unbearably tiresome. There was often a dearth of good conversation because of the monotony, and even the liveliest of gatherings could feel mundane. This caused ill tempers, spite, and slander, and sometimes, so anxious were the memsahibs for a diversion, anything new—even a hat on someone—could trigger heated chatter.

For the memsahibs of the middle classes, perhaps the greatest challenge in their social life was not the stupefying monotony but that throwing parties or receiving invitations required finances and other resources. It was possible for the rich couples to host frequent dinners and luncheons; however, the people with limited income were not able to meet frequently over food and drinks. Servants of the Company, particularly from the Upper Provinces, could not afford European goods to supply to their guests readily as they were quite expensive and liquor was a luxury. These subaltern soldiers and officers were not able to mingle in an unrestricted way, limiting women's social interactions as well.

Even if they went out of their way to make such events happen, the station dinners could be lacklustre because the parties were usually small, comprising eight to ten people; the bungalows could only accommodate about twenty people at a dinner table at best. One family tried to invite a regiment that was passing through for dinner, in addition to their own circle, but found it to be a difficult task. They had to be selective about who to invite from the regiment, meaning the married couples were asked and the bachelors were left in the tents. Such selective invitations were considered insulting, and the uninvited bachelors were unlikely to attend even if they were later asked in.

Indeed, it is not surprising that even inviting guests to parties required art. The best host and hostess could unwittingly offend their guests, and to their embarrassment chairs at the dinner table would go empty. In addition, when such gatherings took place with empty spots at the table, the mood and ambience would automatically deteriorate. The other guests would be annoyed at having so few people to meet and would grudgingly receive the apologies of the hosts. In fact, sometimes, such dinners and parties became causes for *ennui*, even though they were supposed to dispel it. Emma Roberts found parties a colossal waste of time as they only involved sitting and waiting for guests to arrive, only to be faced with insipid company and futile conversation.

Sometimes, it was difficult just getting the station together in a sociable way as people became unused to common courtesies and decencies, having become accustomed to lounging about their houses in their dishabille. Still, it was common for families to be willing to sacrifice their family's budget and comfort for the sake of socialising because there were few other opportunities for proper indulgence for memsahibs in India. Options were limited, and apart from dinners and parties, gambling became a common pastime in the Raj, though it was deemed an evil result of 'Indian life' because it led to debts, difficulties, and social disgraces. In places like Cawnpore, where gambling was quite common, it resulted in dangerous outcomes for heedless young men who, for want of proper social events such as balls and dinners, chose to spend their leisure hours in games of cards and dice. There was simply nothing else to do.

In this way, parties came to be hated and loved at the same time, and the 'party culture' in India ultimately became inextinguishable no matter the circumstances. In places where there were few Brits, there would still be regular gatherings of some form or other as these events were important to feeling part of a community. Moreover, the memsahibs seemed to have been fixated on the idea of maintaining a social life, particularly for fear of becoming too insulated. They worried it would make them lapse into periods of gloom, or worse. Parties and gatherings were also the only way in which they could hope to find any new friendships, or even topics for discussion.

In all this, society life in the Raj was at least amenable to a certain degree to free hobnobbing, as memsahibs were sure of obtaining admittance to the houses they visited if they followed the rules. This was useful since memsahibs were not able to climb the ranks on their own. The more ambitious memsahibs could find entryways into the lives of people with higher ranks through their own stratagems. After all, 'tuft-hunting'—that is, trying to ascend to the upper echelons of society by seeking high-status friends—was very common in the Raj because it allowed those of lower rank to rub shoulders with the rich and important. Whether it was army or civil service, some women hankered after the higher ranks quite desperately, hoping to find better means of more lively entertainment as well as other privileges that such acquaintances would provide. Such women were easy to spot and were considered quite odious in polite company. Florence Marryat found this to be quite vulgar.

It is perhaps admirable that even the heat did not deter women from socialising and attending parties. If they wanted to dress up and visit friends, they would do it irrespective of the temperature. They could even brave sunstroke and fever for society's sake. In fact, the exhilarating and high-powered social life of India was the only redemptive quality of long Indian summers. Christina S. Bremner wrote, "poor mem-saheb, in her tight dress and kid-encased extremities, sallies out with more of a smile on her face… I never heard of any lady being struck by heat apoplexy". Bremner, unlike most, was often happy to stay indoors in her dressing gown, and read her novel inside her darkened rooms, even as the distant strains of music wafted from the club for half the night.

Whether a memsahib chose to follow all the trends or become unconventional, the troubles of the Indian social life could hardly ever be sidestepped even by the most seasoned Raj ladies. In many ways, British women in India did not even have to step out to face perils in the Raj; they found them right within the confines of their homes, and more often than not experienced twice the adventures that sahibs did: some in the wilderness of India, and some in their very homes as 'memsahibs'.

3

"THERE IS NO SOLITUDE LIKE THE SOLITUDE OF A CIVILIAN'S LADY"

NOSTALGIA, BOREDOM, MARITAL STRIFE, AND 'GOING NATIVE'

As I watched him stride down the path, the dogs at his heels, I wanted to call out to him to stop, to take me with him or stay at home. A sudden realisation that I was going to be alone for the first time in my strange surroundings swept over me and I had to restrain the words that rushed to my lips… Suddenly as I sat there on the floor beside the trunk, my lap full of treasures, two large fat tears sprang unbidden to my eyes and rolled gently down my cheeks. Where and when was I ever going to wear this heavenly trousseau? Nellie Burney, who had helped Mother with my clothes, must have thought the jungle provided a social life that matched her gay whirl in Bombay and Simla and other civilised places where she had always lived. We had almost no neighbours… three miles down the river and then seven miles back by road lay a plantation where the Turners held an open-houses tennis afternoon every three weeks for the little group of white people who lived scattered around them at varying distances of two to thirty miles… I was *afraid and I was furious with myself for it. I seemed to fear so many things all at once. Most of all perhaps I feared myself.*

– Monica Lang, 1952

On ordinary days, memsahibs did not have much to do cooped up in their homes. According to Steel and Gardiner's *The Complete Indian Housekeeper and Cook*, the ordering of the household after breakfast could be done in half an hour, so ideally, in the morning, every good memsahib went into the storeroom, inspected the supplies, doled out the provisions for the day, ordered the meals, checked the cook's expenditures, inspected the kitchen, and chided the *ayah*, all in quick succession. If they had trained their servants well, the work was done even quicker, and they retired to their bedrooms well before noon. With nothing else to do, they passed time somehow until evening when they ventured out for a walk around the bungalows or played 'hot-weather badminton'.

On most days, the good memsahib had a sense of satisfaction at being able to dispense of her daily chores quickly and efficiently. However, too often for her liking, the sameness of the days, and the utter inertia of small-town life, began to feel oppressive. It is difficult to say who was impacted more by isolated postings—the sahibs who had enormous work pressure while posted in obscure corners of the country or their wives who were restricted to the oasis of their homes, without good company, and deprived of activities that were quotidian back home. Emily Eden wrote, "some are quite alone. No other European within reach. In a climate where for some months they can hardly get out of the house, and why they do not go melancholy mad I cannot conceive. Some do come back to Calcutta in a frightfully nervous state".

Because of the protracted periods of seclusion, memsahibs were often not able to suppress their nostalgia for 'home'. They would suddenly be seized with thoughts of their families and get depressed for the rest of the day. Mrs. Leopold Paget wrote at Christmas, "at this season the thoughts of home depressed me much—thus isolated from all I love, in a strange land". After all, as the initial whirlwind of settling in subsided, they realised that 'home' was actually very far away and nearly always impossible to go back to. A memsahib remarked (somewhat inaccurately) how "Home always means England; nobody calls India home—not even those who have been here thirty years or more, and are never likely to return to Europe; even they still always speak of England as home".

Most women missed their past lives sorely and could not ignore the pain of being separated from their friends and family. Emily Eden called it a "dreadful agony", like in *Oliver Twist*. Once, Lady Williamson told Monica Campbell Martin that she was so sick of the isolation that every time her husband came back from work up the line, he found her packing to leave.

Like any other exiles, memsahibs would be on tenterhooks waiting for letters to arrive from England, carrying news and gossip about the goings-on in the lives of the people they missed dearly. The magazines and newspapers would arrive once a month, giving them something to look forward to. They went over these religiously, in an almost vain attempt to keep up with everything that was happening at home. The day they would get the news of their monthly mail despatch, they would be thrown into a frenzy, speculating, calculating, hoping, and praying that the mail would arrive a few days or even a few hours before the usual time. And when mail did come in, news travelled like wildfire through the cantonment, and all other interests and concerns were forgotten for the day.

Mail, however, was lost or got delayed frequently: the August overland mail could be delayed to October, for instance, but even that was acceptable to those who would not hear from their families for several weeks or months. When Mrs. Paget's husband was posted in Mhow, which was a cantonment town in present-day Madhya Pradesh, she had a monotonous routine; the only excitement was the arrival of letters, and when they were delayed, it caused her "heartsickening anxiety" in her lonely life.

Memsahibs often lamented how not they not only had to suffer the agonies of not receiving letters for long stretches of time but also the dreadful uncertainty of whether they would get them at all. When mail got lost, they had to labour to retrieve it, but mostly it would be lost for good. The lack of word from home was excruciating, and during such times they would have to make do with newspapers to get information about England if they could procure them. They despaired because there would be several stories that were left hanging, several questions unanswered, and many conversations that were broken or fragmented. Several memsahibs became utterly frustrated because of the long wait between mails. Even as they kept writing home, they realised that it was mostly futile, as no one knew the fate of letters going out or coming in. When Emily Eden sent a short journal back home, she was aware that her relatives would probably never get it because of the dearth of Bombay steamers. The government had been trying a new experiment of sending a Chinese clipper, which was a little out of use, to Aden with mail and cargo. Eden still wrote long letters merely out of habit, almost mechanically. Victorians treated letter writing very seriously and observed proper etiquette while writing. Almost like a ritual, they chronicled their daily escapades, as well as struggles with boredom and loneliness in India.

Most of the memsahibs' letters that were sent back home were filled with longing as they made desperate enquiries about their siblings or friends. Their desperation to know every detail of the lives of those they had left behind in their beloved homeland was actually a way of recalling the lives they themselves had left behind. But while on the one hand it was a cathartic experience to record everything in letters, the lack of responses and the delays could still be disheartening. What they were most worried about was that if anything happened to their dear ones, it would be weeks or even months before they would find out. Eden had to ask her physician to prescribe her a little medicine to help her snap out of the dejection.

It is perhaps because of this that Lady Campbell Wilson wrote, "The contrast of past and present makes it all seem like a dream". Indeed, no matter how they tried to cling on, 'home' was far away and lost, often forever. They were also forced to accept that in India, their lives were irrevocably changed. It is thus likely that their frantic and obsessive letter writing and journalling stemmed from an anxiety of forgetting and being forgotten. Over time, many of them struggled and often failed to keep in touch with what they were beginning to forget, and ardently longed for, despite their determination to hold on. Their former lives became a distant memory, which they tried in vain to keep fresh, but their friends and relatives soon began to find them a tad annoying because of their constant insistence on keeping in touch. The memsahibs themselves were painfully conscious that their correspondents back home did not enjoy their long-winded 'journal letters', which could be dull and repetitive to them. After all, India was not as exciting and glamorous as it was made out to be, and there was not much to write about their monotonous existence as Raj wives, except about their gloom and nostalgic reminiscences of the past.

Distance and lack of communication were not the only cause for the despair that memsahibs felt in India. Various minor but significant factors contributed to their sustained periods of gloom. Indeed, to say that life in the Raj was always exciting would be painting a partial picture. While it is true that the vibrant society of British India, with its string of balls, luncheons, tea parties, picnics, theatres, and so on offered a gay and eventful lifestyle, there were periodic lulls in a memsahib's social life.

Sometimes, the hiatuses from partying were because of postings in barracks or remote areas where there would not be too many Europeans. In such cases, a memsahib would typically stay indoors, lonely except for the servants in the house, or the occasional caller whom she may not want to meet anyhow. On such occasions, she would instruct her servant to make an excuse for her and deny her company to the guest, preferring to play an old song on her much out-of-tune piano.

The image of the bored and lonely memsahib has long haunted the postcolonial imagination, often recalled with derision. Memsahibs have been widely disparaged, and their shifting moods and airs have been lambasted as symptoms of their lazy and spoilt tendencies. The idea stems from the countless literary depictions of luckless memsahibs suffering from severe melancholy and *ennui* in India, withering away in the heat, and pining for their husbands who would either be posted away, or travelling on official Raj-related work.

But memsahibs cannot be blamed for being melancholic and unable to shake themselves out of stupors. They had to spend days and weeks without company when their husbands were away, and even when their husbands were at home, they were often too busy to pay heed to their wives. The memsahibs indulged in various pastimes, but sometimes nothing worked, and they were often left with no desire to accomplish anything. Needlework seemed cumbersome, especially in the heat when the needle felt too dull in their hot hands. Even mundane activities that they had always taken for granted back home, like going down to tea shops or to boutiques, were impossible because there was simply nowhere to go. If they wanted to buy something, they had to call for the *boxwallahs* (street peddlers selling knick-knacks and small wares) carrying their merchandise, but more often than not, they had to wait for them to come around.

While women were seldom able to improve their state, they were perennially conscious of their signs and symptoms of depression. Due to lack of stimulus, they would frequently feel lethargic, which worried them as they had heard too many stories of melancholy taking over ladies in India. They recorded their feelings of restlessness in their writings, trying to diagnose their ailments and purge them. 'Hysteria' was a common phenomenon associated with women in the nineteenth century and was dreaded widely. It was said to have a crippling effect on the consciousness, and memsahibs were careful so as not to allow hopelessness to take over. In fact, mental health issues were a serious matter in India and had to be treated in time. A memsahib came to know of the term for what she was feeling: 'Burmese Ennui', which was said to be more likely to attack women than men specifically because of them having little to no occupation. It supposedly took the form of a settled melancholy, which, if not diverted by a change in scene, could cause mental and cognitive degeneration leading to 'idiocy'. A woman was sent back to England because of the 'Burmese Ennui', as she would neither drink nor eat, and sat all day long doing nothing, with tears streaking down her face constantly.

If memsahibs were not afflicted by signs of depression, they felt troubled because they were distanced from the work aspect of their husband's life. Barring some exceptions, men often did not discuss official matters with them; sahibs would only resort to consulting with their wives if they did not find any other sahib to consult with. Memsahibs, as a result, felt like they were mere appendages in the Raj, meant only to serve their husbands who were the lords and masters of the empire in addition to the home. There was a glaring meaninglessness to their existence, apart from being in charge of the domestic space, and although they were usually dutiful, aiding their husbands in their official duties, taking care of their needs, and ensuring that their houses were functioning well, they felt a deep void in their lives.

If it is diagnosable in this manner, it appears that women in the Raj suffered majorly because of an overpowering sense of purposelessness. This feeling was likely heightened by the awareness of their own limitations, since their actual role in the Raj remained peripheral because of their gender. To add to their discontentment, their lives were quite unpredictable. Their husbands would be called away to dispense some duty and would often have to leave at short notice, forcing the memsahibs to stop everything and help them prepare for their departure. Because of this, their painstakingly organised lives would be frequently disrupted. E. Augusta King's husband was once called away abruptly for a new duty in the evening when a note from a lady arrived unexpectedly. Helen D. Mackenzie's husband received news of an impending attack on the Nawab, the ruler of the princely state where they were located, and he immediately set out to give him assistance, even though he was strictly forbidden from interfering by the state. Then again, sahibs commonly went beyond the call of duty, and the memsahibs, in all cases, had to co-operate. Mrs. Leopold Paget and her husband were sitting quietly at home when a messenger from the Brigade Major arrived to say that there were orders for immediate turnout, and the force was to march in an hour. She immediately got the meal prepared, completed the packing, and then mounted her horse to go as far with him as was prudent.

Moreover, official leaves were given sometimes just a day before, causing much chaos in planning and organising everything. Sometimes, unforeseen jobs came up, adding to the pressure of everything. For example, the Kings were still in Meerut when Robert King received a letter with orders for him to get to Landour sooner, resulting in a great struggle to get their luggage packed quickly and sent off. When they reached Landour, E. Augusta King found that she had been made judge for a flower show, which she did not enjoy because there was always a lot of hatred and malice caused by the judge's award, leading to quarrels. Then suddenly, her husband was called back to his post in Meerut, and she called it a "black Monday" because she was separated from him yet again. She resorted to adopting a puppy to divert herself from the boredom, which hardly helped.

It was not uncommon for memsahibs to keep pets in their homes, and it did help fill up some of that void they felt within. Monica Campbell Martin had an impressive private little zoo in the backyard of her bungalow. Villagers who knew of her weakness for animals frequently brought her abandoned eggs and baby wild animals in need of shelter. Over time, her 'jungle babies' acquired great repute: she had an odd assortment of dogs, ducklings, peacocks, a myna bird, deer, cats, and a few stray tiger and leopard cubs that she raised on bottle feed and kept in her enclosure. Once, she kept a 15-foot python asleep in her bathroom and forgot about it. The villagers had brought it to her, and busy as she was, she decided to deal with it later. That day, a bishop came to visit them. After some time, he excused himself to use the bathroom and was terrified to see the snake coiled up lethargically on the floor. He shot out of the house screaming and yelling at her, thinking she had done it on purpose.

However, such rare moments of hilarity did not always help alleviate the memsahibs' worries. Mostly, they had no choice but to give in to the demands of empire work and were helpless even when there were dangers involved. They hardly ever received full information and would be tense if their husbands were away for too long. Often, they only managed to find out small details about the risky work that their husbands were doing far away. The telegrams carrying messages were usually unclear or abrupt as they could not contain many words and would only leave them curious to know more.

The suspense of not knowing, especially if their husbands had been engaged in battle or any life-threatening work, caused them great anxiety. Being widowed was perhaps the most common fear amongst the wives of British officers in India. E. Augusta King found that many married women in the regiment that left Meerut to go into active service were not only engaged to remarry in the event of their husband's demise but also engaged to several at the same time. This over-cautiousness was not unfounded, because women would go 'off pay' right after 6 months of widowhood and had no means of supporting themselves afterwards. To be left alone in India was a tough business. Orphaned daughters were married off as young as fourteen if their mother was widowed. Widowhood was in fact the worst fate that memsahibs could meet in India.

Furthermore, memsahibs were often faced with situations where they were required to accompany their husbands on long and hazardous work trips. If they chose not to uproot themselves, they were imprisoned in areas where often there were no means of recreation. When E. Augusta King went down to Dehra to be with her civil servant husband for a week where he was posted for work and was able to drive around in a carriage in the evening, it had been 6 long months since she had last taken a drive. She was so devoid of company that even though there was a massive landslide in the surrounding regions, she still ventured out. The trip was not all that rewarding, and she realised that the place was a "terrible jungle".

If memsahibs were able to move around with their husbands, the sojourns were rarely enjoyable. The sahibs' work took them to the dreariest corners of the country, and the memsahibs tagged along half-heartedly, trying to adjust to the strange places. Emily Eden wrote about her struggles with cantonment life: she found the social arrangements to be tiresome and felt no enjoyment in mingling with the regiments stationed there. In such places, all the days were the same, and if their partners were gone for work, there was nothing for memsahibs to do in a country where people did not even understand their language. The desolate landscapes, and lack of company, society life, and even normal conversation with someone they knew and could talk to, caused periods of depression. One memsahib was so listless that she confessed that her children were too much for her, her servants too much, life too much, and her means too little.

Sometimes, memsahibs found some relief in walking through the *bazaars*, going down to the churches, hunting for antiques, and so on as a form of recreation. Some memsahibs enjoyed catching butterflies and indulged in gardening. Some of them passed time by churning butter—an activity that was suitably time-consuming. Some of them sketched a lot, and sometimes, reading a book, gazing outside, or occasionally going for lonely rides were the only means of distracting oneself from pensive thoughts. However, even after such deliberate attempts to stay occupied, simple things like an unsuitable weather could trigger sadness: Mrs. Leopold Paget found the damp weather depressing.

Occasionally, they viewed monotony as peacefulness. Maria Murray Mitchell liked it when the whirl of social obligations ended as people moved to Shimla, and they finally relapsed into quietness. She and her husband started a Bible study group and found the meetings to be refreshing and lively.

Indeed, there were hardly any productive or remunerative activities to undertake. If the women could be engaged in some activity at a sustained level, such as philanthropic work, they might not have felt the lack of a proper social life so deeply. Isabel Savory wrote that if bungalows were homes to live in instead of lodgings to be left in a year or so when the owners should be ordered elsewhere, if gardening were a case of anything except sowing and planting for an unknown successor, if there were good concerts, good picture galleries, good theatres, good church services, good lectures to attend, and if the climate were less enervating, women would do more than fritter time away. Yet, there were none of these things. A lady moaned how the dearth of mental food, the second-rate companions, and the amateur art formed a sickly substitute for 'society'.

Inevitably, boredom led to loneliness. Lady Campbell Wilson spent time playing with dolls to quell boredom: "I have been amusing myself making a bassinet for her. It was like playing at a doll's house again, and it whiled away many an idle hour. It looked very sweet when it was all finished, and I put a tiny white shawl under the pillow for my little dolly". They were bored, and there was no cure for it.

Depression was not limited to pining or lonely wives. Emily Eden was accompanying her brother, George Eden, who was the Governor-General in residence, and she felt the same kind of despondence felt by officers' wives while tagging along wherever he went. There was no limitation to the facilities she had access to, and her life was quite eventful, with plenty of activities planned out along with tremendous amounts of travel and explorations as well as social interactions. Moreover, her brother even depended on her immensely and was very fond of her as she was his confidante. However, even though she was of great use to him, her heart was heavy, which she attributed to the "unfamiliar scenes". Moreover, she felt detached from the future because her past was much better. Another reason for her despondency could simply be the lack of freedom of movement or any kind of independence.

Lack of freedom was, in fact, felt by women of all ranks; however, it was the soldiers' wives, particularly, who had the most difficult lives. Veronica Bamfield has pointed out that most of these women were young and fresh from England, and although they were given money, they had no idea about simple things like what to eat or what to buy and suffered as a consequence. More often than not, they had no one to look after them, and were treated almost like animals, living day and night in barracks, in the same room with a crowd of rough and rude men. Domestic abuse was common in such cases, and they had no way of getting any legal relief. Moreover, the system was apathetic as they would also be sent here and there on postings, with hardly any consideration for a lady's comfort or convenience. Sometimes, the memsahibs were not even able to acclimatise themselves to the place they were posted to before they had to move away for yet another posting. Their stressful lives often caused illnesses, and deaths were extremely numerous. Bamfield mentioned how the bodies of women and children were often buried by riversides without any record or investigation. The administration did not pay heed to their plight.

Considering the abominable situation of some memsahibs, it is not surprising that their journals and diaries often contain long passages of self-pity. They remembered the old days when they were always lively and spirited, when they would have their 'coming out' parties at Oxford and make visits to Longleat with friends and family. They recalled their childhoods fondly, recording all the memories that they seemed to be forgetting too quickly in India.

Trouble in Paradise

The isolated life civilians so often lead, and the large amount of authority and responsibility committed to them at such an early age, probably accounts for the fact that you scarcely meet a young civilian whose manner has not far too much confidence and pretension to be that of a good society... But if the gentlemen in India are above the home average, the ladies are certainly below it. Young men constantly make inferior marriages; and girls, after having been deprived of a mother's care half their lives, are brought out and married far too young—before their education (if they have any) is finished, or their minds formed, and before they have enjoyed what, in the present deficient system, is often the best part of a girl's training—the advantage of intercourse with really good society. They have thus no standard of manners or taste by which to test the manners of those among whom they are thrown; they probably marry under eighteen, often under sixteen... I think the wives of military men are worse in this respect than those of civilians...

There is certainly a great amount of domestic happiness in India. Married people are in many cases so entirely thrown upon each other, not only for sympathy, but for conversation and amusement, that they become knit much more closely than when each has a thousand distractions, and separate ways of spending the day... The lady cannot spend her mornings in shopping or visiting, nor the gentleman at his Club. They generally drive or ride together every evening, and many married people, when separated, write to each other every day. Circumstances which tend to promote such a high degree of conjugal union and sympathy surely cannot be considered merely as hardships...

– Helen Douglas Mackenzie (1857)

Even as the memsahibs suffered, cloistered in their homes, the sahibs immersed themselves in official duties, hardly conscious of or sensitive to the wives' misery. The pressure of imperial work was great, and even the most attentive husbands were prone to neglect their wives. Moreover, difficult postings could cause severe strain on even the strongest of conjugal relationships. Flora Annie Steel noted that boredom and lack of activity was one of the reasons why marital discord occurred in the Raj. Sometimes, the challenges of ordinary life, coupled with the hardships of *mofussil* life, led to serious domestic disputes and caused the estrangement of spouses.

The toil of army life was something most women did not foresee when marrying officers. This is exactly what happened to Minnie Blane. At the time of her marriage with Captain Archie Wood, she was completely unsuspecting of the realities of life in the East India Company's army. Her idea of India was rosy and romantic, gleaned from her brief interactions with officers of the Company who were on leave and visiting home. Their vibrant personalities appealed to her, and she thought that India was full of chivalrous and brave gentlemen who were always smartly attired in their uniforms and charming towards ladies. At the time, she and her mother had only heard of Robert Clive's victories, and the growing popularity of India amongst young British men serving as officers. Neither of them had any actual understanding of the discomforts and dangers of army life, the harsh climatic conditions, or the vast distances in the East which she would have to constantly traverse with her husband. Archie had not stressed those facts either, so that all she knew of India before she left was that it was a mystical place with gorgeous views. It was only when Minnie first laid eyes on India, sailing up into the Ganges Delta, that she saw the truth: deadly swamps with palms and tangled mangroves rooted in the sticky mud. "It was a jungle shunned by man but teeming with wildlife: birds, monkeys, snakes, and crocodiles, all dominated by numerous tigers, those fierce kings of the jungle."

Minnie had grown up in a comfortable household in Slough, and her family had been a prosperous one. Mr. Blane, Minnie's father, was a respectable man who had served in the Civil Service and had occupied the position of Deputy Governor of the Australian Agricultural Company. He passed away just a few years before she married Archie in 1856. In the absence of a fatherly figure who would have made enquiries about his background, Archie had managed to conceal the reality of his financial condition from the family. Mrs. Blane had been easily impressed by his chivalry and his apparently strong affections for Minnie, whom he had flattered and wooed most determinedly.

The couple was engaged and married quickly, and when they landed in India, the truth came as a rude shock to Minnie. Their financial conditions were extremely dire even by military standards. She was already pregnant by then, and given Archie's paltry income, migrating and adjusting to an alien place proved to be extremely difficult, especially since small towns were surrounded by jungles and without normal society. She felt like a stranger amongst strangers and developed a crushing sense of melancholia.

It was not long before Minnie discovered that her husband was not only a man of poor means, but also in great debt. He even took to habitually asking Mrs. Blane to send them money without Minnie's knowledge. When this came out, it caused an irrevocable rift between the couple.

It was the tumultuous year of 1857. The great sepoy rebellion was simmering across the country while Minnie faced her battles at home. She was soon plunged into a severe bout of depression, intensified by the violence and bloodshed around her. Apart from the political turmoil, her hastened marriage and early pregnancy, combined with the severance of all ties with her homeland, had caused her severe mental stress. She wrote to her mother frantically, and most of her letters spelt out her dejection and near-suicidal tendencies. During the mutiny itself, because salaries were not being paid to officers, and their wives were hardly given any relief or support, Minnie was burdened with acute anxiety and physical and psychological strain, as well as dire financial troubles. However, her greatest source of tension was her own husband, who had turned out to be a fraud. Even at the time of their marriage he had withheld from her that he could hardly afford even ordinary expenses. Minnie barely had money for the essentials when her first child arrived during the revolt of 1857, and they had to ask her mother for assistance.

When her next child arrived, they had to beg for money from different sources without being able to repay the earlier debts. Most of their letters to her mother contain elaborate explanations about their pathetic financial state, their calculations of the money they had borrowed, and their plans of how they would repay their loans after receiving money due to them. Archie still wrote with elaborate details about their expenditures, apparently to justify his requests for loans from Mrs. Blane. This regularly caused Minnie embarrassment. It was indeed shameful that Archie was not able to support his wife and children within just 2 years of their marriage.

As is evident in Minnie's case, one of the biggest hurdles in the way of a successful marriage in India for low-and middle-ranking British couples was financial in nature. The husbands were the sole breadwinners, and running a full-fledged home in the outposts suitable for an English wife could often become unaffordable. Archie's salary was insufficient for supporting his wife, let alone his children, especially given his poor financial planning. He gave a full-fledged calculation of his expenses incurred from running his household to his mother-in-law on 8 January 1858, explaining that his pay per month was only 515 rupees, out of which deductions were made, meaning he was left with 384 rupees. However, their most basic expenditure amounted to a total of 490 rupees. In other words, the basic running of the household cost about 100 rupees more per month than Archie's take-home pay. Given the major deficits, Minnie eventually reconciled herself to the fact that without help they would be plunged into poverty. Her letters soon after the birth of her first child are particularly poignant for her repeated cries for help from her widowed mother. After her father's demise, her family was not wealthy any longer and could hardly afford for Minnie to return home. Neither could Archie afford to send her back, even during the mutiny when it was dangerous for a nursing mother to stay in deserted cantonments and flee from one place to another.

Minnie's letters began to get repetitive after a while as she constantly mentioned money matters, how poorly she was faring because of pregnancy-related ailments, and her never-ending fights with Archie. Very soon, they did not have enough money to pay rent for their house or keep servants. It fell upon Minnie to manage the house and her three little children. Some of her letters, which contained requests for small items like spools of thread, needles, and even cloth for stitching, indicate how deprived she was of basic necessities.

Indeed, she was unable to purchase anything and regularly had to beg her mother for shoes and bonnets for herself and her children. She wrote in May 1858 that she had no clothes to wear and could not buy anything from the local shops as she did not have any money to spare. Daily essentials had become luxury items for her and Archie. She wrote:

> Please, dear Mama, get me some shoes and socks for him, and two pairs of the former in black for me. Indeed, anything you can put into a box will be most acceptable out here. I cannot procure the boy's elastic belts, could you get me some as they look so nice... I have never known till now what it is to be in want of money. I do think it is *very* hard that all officers' pay is stopped for three months. It is most distressing, as one's servants are grumpy at not being paid regularly.

Some of her letters also reveal intense frustration and even anger directed towards her mother and sister who she felt did not send assistance frequently enough. She resented that while they were comfortably established in England and had easy access to daily necessities, she was languishing in India. She was particularly irritated that her sister could enjoy wearing lovely gowns while she spent her pregnancy in tattered clothes.

It is not surprising that Minnie's letters eventually began to describe intimate details of her problems with her husband—something which might have been extremely difficult for her because of the typical Victorian view that family honour should be preserved at all costs and domestic problems were not to be discussed with a third person. However, Minnie's situation was worsening with each passing day, and she grew more and more lonesome as her marriage began to show signs of fissures.

Minnie's intolerance was justified. Archie had proven to be unreliable and reckless. Eventually, because of his dishonesty, Minnie resorted to making enquiries to her mother about his requests for money and plans for repayment, but her utter helplessness in the face of his secrecy revealed how oppressive her marriage had become. It also tells us that the rose-tinted glasses had fallen from her eyes, and she had not only lost respect for Archie but also suspected his intentions at the time of marriage. It was around this time that she began to refer to Archie as Captain Wood and assume a sarcastic tone whenever she mentioned him. She also began considering her legal rights for financial assistance in case of divorce or separation:

> I regret to say that he is so insufferably lazy he never writes to anyone, attends to his affairs, nor does anything like other men. Consequently, everything with us and ours goes to the bad… I wish to know most particularly if you ever told my husband that I had 500 Pounds of my own. He is constantly at me about it… If I applied to the lawyer when I arrive would he allow me to have so much for me and children's use? We cannot live on Captain Wood's pay, viz. 191 Pounds per annum and Income tax besides.

It did indeed become apparent that Archie was unambitious and slovenly and was accumulating debts because of his own carelessness. His letters to Mrs. Blane evoke disgust in the reader as he goes into long-winded and verbose explanations about his own trials and tribulations as an army man. He became verbally abusive towards Minnie and even refused to give her money for herself or the children. He would hurl insults at her whenever his temper flared because of her questioning and soon declared that he had married her only because he thought she was an heiress.

Jane Vansittart, the editor of Minnie's compilation of letters, wrote that Minnie left for England abruptly when news of her brother's death came in. He was coming to India to visit her and had suddenly died after landing. Minnie's letters end there, most likely because her family probably burnt her final letters to avoid scandal. However, it is known that she left her three little children behind and departed for her home without warning (Vansittart, 183–4). It was unlike her to abandon her beloved children in the way she did, but she had suffered great trauma by then and news of her brother's death had somehow jolted her, compelling her to undertake such a desperate act.

When Minnie married Archie, she was full of hopes and dreams, anxious but excited, and yet very much conscious of the enormous responsibility of her status as the wife of an officer. As we have seen, there were many details that memsahibs had to learn to fully assimilate into India. Besides, the climate was alien, and Minnie particularly hated Calcutta—the smells and sights were disagreeable to her, and she longed to leave the 'City of Palaces' the same week she arrived.

Indeed, army wives suffered the most in India due to the difficult postings and lack of provisions. Barrack life was abominable and could frighten the most patient woman. Veronica Bamfield wrote that financial troubles were all too common, and some women took to peddling grog in their "Tin Baby"—a barrel with a wax face wrapped in a shawl—which they took around the canteen in the evening, selling the drink at a profit. Most of them slaved in the hospitals, caring for the sick and injured, even as they were subjected to harassment by the male officers. Once, a group of women were pranked badly when some men picked up the skull of a dead soldier who had been dismembered by jackals because of a shallow-dug grave and chased them around with it. During marches, women had to put up with dirt and body lice, which were humorously called 'infantry', while fleas were called 'light cavalry'. Sometimes women could be carried off during skirmishes and sold. The exact date remains unknown, but in the early 1840s the wife of a General, Laurentia Sale, heard of an attractive child, Tootsie Anderson, being carried off by Afghans who took her back to Kabul and tried to sell her.

Such mishaps and incidents of harassment were part of an army wife's daily existence, and for women like Minnie, it must have felt like the ordeal that began at sea when they first sailed out had never come to an end. Many made light of their situation in their letters and journals, having grown stoic in the face of such grave perils. Helen Wood, a well-respected lady who came to India with her husband, Colonel Henry Wood, and their children in 1878, endured many years of a deeply unfulfilling marriage, doing her duty as a wife and mother.

Indeed, unlike Minnie and Archie, an ill-matched couple who eventually divorced, many women could not consider leaving their husbands, even in the case of violence or infidelity. Most had no hopes of returning home because they had no fortunes of their own. Moreover, life as a 'grass widow'—a term used for women separated from their husbands or divorced—was not easy. Apart from fending for themselves in strange places and dealing with the locals who knew that they were often clueless and unable to converse, they faced the problem of extreme financial deprivation. Although women were generally able to secure a second husband, impoverished women who were unable to return home sometimes had to take to the flesh trade and joined brothels. Moreover, absconding from the marital home was a major disgrace. Women mostly chose to endure unfulfilling marriages, rather than risk social ridicule.

Sometimes, it was not just the country that took a toll on them, but the British society within it as well. Perhaps it was the heat, or the unforgiving lifestyle, but jealousy, sabotage, and hostility were all too common in life in India.

The Renshaws, who were stationed in Mhow in 1861, bore a great burden resulting from malicious behaviour. Captain and Mrs. Renshaw were a fine couple, until rumours about Mrs. Renshaw being the guilty party in a divorce case surfaced all of a sudden. Since divorce was not countenanced in the army, the couple was boycotted by the regiment, the 6th Inniskilling Dragoons. In general, army men and their wives were quite used to petty behaviour and viciousness. In a way, it was a known feature of Raj society, and over time many grew stoic in the face of it (Bamfield, 117).

The country wore out many army wives. Fanny Duberly grew increasingly despondent but rode to the end of her last campaign in 1857, in which her husband's regiment brought down the magnificent warrior queen Rani of Jhansi as she led her army. Although one of the tougher army wives, Fanny, like so many of her kind, suffered because of the hazards for army wives in India. Yet, there is no doubt that even in their suffering, many army wives displayed remarkable fortitude and resilience.

'Going *Jungli*'? Perils of *Mofussil* Life

> *My personal experience does not lead me to endorse... accusations of mutual boredom. I can never remember a time when the thought of India (the whole peninsula) did not immediately evoke emotion and stimulate interest. In fact, memories of India and my Indian friends have lightened hours of acute boredom since I left them all. I know I was blessed in coming of a family which (on my mother's side) served India for three generations. I also owed much to my father who insisted that I should learn at least one main language (Urdu) well enough to conduct a reasonable conversation, though I was too lazy to master the script and have regretted it ever since... How was it possible to be bored for a*

moment with so much to learn and do and see? So much colour and contrast, above all so much response to any advance made in friendship towards Indians.

– Iris Butler, 1969

Despite their industriousness in staying updated with what was happening back home, the British in India were something of a joke because of their strange lives. Women in the Raj were mocked for their 'hybrid' clothes, their Indianised taste in food, and their fashion taste, which was always outdated.

Moreover, memsahibs themselves realised that India was having its impact on them, as they had always been told it would. They scrambled to retain their 'Englishness', by preparing dishes that they grew up eating and religiously reading British novels from the local libraries, for example. But books and annuals arrived very late to India, and often got damaged in transit, and the local libraries would often not be stocked with any worthwhile titles. Sometimes there were no libraries around, and in all cases supply seldom met demand. Emma Roberts mentioned how the supply of books in out-stations was paltry, and one could only find proper books in places like Meerut or Cawnpore. Sometimes, consignments of books were brought into Calcutta, but they would come in through different mercantile houses and were sold by auction. Once, at the Cape of Good Hope, the beach was strewn with novels when a ship carrying books got wrecked. In Calcutta, hawkers sold substandard novels, which the memsahibs would not even have heard about back in England, but in India that was all they had.

Indeed, good British literature could be notoriously difficult to come by even under ordinary circumstances. People had to ask to use families' private collections. Memsahibs had to struggle to stay literate and updated. Emily Eden categorically mentioned in her letters back home that she and the others had read *The Pickwick Papers* and *Oliver Twist* as well as *Nicholas Nickleby*, adding that the latter was better, as if to prove that she was indeed up to date with current Victorian fiction. She went on to say that she was in such awe of Charles Dickens that she wanted to start a public subscription for him—a "tribute from India"—and everybody would subscribe to it. She said Dickens was the "agent for Europe fun, and they do not grow much in this country".

Indeed, memsahibs often had to assert that they had not in fact forgotten their culture and become barbarians after living in 'primitive' India. Very often, they had to remind themselves, more than the people they wrote to, that they were still very much British.

To some, the fear of becoming 'nativised'—or '*jungli*'—was more terrifying than the perilous journeys they undertook along isolated highways or the sinister forests that they traversed so frequently. Although this was mostly unfounded, they were even afraid that they would dilute their English accents if they learnt local words and phrases. Christina S. Bremner was shocked to find out that she had imbibed the local languages without realising it when she yelled out instructions to her *coolies* in Hindustani while she was travelling. Indeed, most women dreaded the idea that after spending months and years away from England, India would alter them.

Sometimes, it would happen that a certain memsahib living in some deserted station would turn up dressed in a mix of British and Indian ensembles, and it terrified other memsahibs to think that they would also become such a 'hybrid'. Many of them described it as a creeping malaise of some sort, growing undetected for years, until suddenly, they were transformed. But no matter how rigid memsahibs remained about their superiority to and separateness from India, the lure of the East was all too compelling. In the provincial areas of India, which were covered in forests, the postings were extraordinarily lonely, and it was not possible to remain completely unaffected by the exhilarating experience of the 'exotic'. Eventually, the 'strangeness and mystery' of India took over their minds. It was said that very few of the women who came to India could stay impervious to it.

Monica Campbell Martin, however, was not afraid of such 'nativisation'. Her husband was a forest officer in the northern limits of the Province of Bihar, the Bettiah Raj, where he was known as the "*jungli* sahib", and she was delighted by the epithet when she learnt about it. In fact, unlike many of her contemporaries and predecessors, she was most gleeful when she herself became *jungli*:

> For the two months before his retirement, we were to live with the outgoing forest officer, Mr. Cameron. From him Peter was to gain a thorough knowledge of what is termed in forestry the Working Plan in the area… From now on Peter was to be known as the *Jungli* Sahib. The word jungle in India is always taken to mean a wild forest and a *jungli* is someone or something of the wild forest. Villagers, and even your own servants, seldom use your name, because to them it is often unpronounceable. They speak of you by the work you do… I was now, in all brevity, the *Jungli* Mem-Sahib. But the word '*jungli*' has another meaning. Someone wild, or uncouth, is also described as *jungli*. Because of this entertaining secondary meaning, our friends always applied our titles with gusto. I became a *jungli* mem-sahib and loved it.

Monica's enthusiasm, however, was rare; Emily Eden, for example, wrote in 1840 that her "wanderings in the wilderness" had come to an end. As everything suddenly seemed to slow down, she was surprised to realise how her appearance had changed:

> … the right shoe of my only remaining pair has sprung a large hole, the brambles that infest the jungles where we encamp have torn my gown into fringes, so that I look like a shabby Pharisee, and my last bonnet is brown with dust… I suppose it will be very dreadful when we all meet. 'Oh! My coevals, remnants of yourselves,' I often think of that. What sort of a remnant are you? I am a remnant of faded yellow gingham.

It is to be considered that the title 'memsahib' was not a politically recognised title—it did not occur in official accounts as a recognisable designation, and instead was merely a social term for addressing someone important, a term of respect. It was not easily available to all white women in the Raj and indicated a certain type, class, or category of women. Therefore, it had a jealously guarded status, and memsahibs ensured that it was reserved only for those women who fit into the category. For a woman to be known as a proper memsahib, she had to have the social and economic status for it, and Raj society constantly reiterated the need for the performance of the 'politically correct Memsahib', with fixed characteristics, as an identity for English women in India.

In such a situation, any kind of deviant behaviour was said to jeopardise the status of the memsahib. Moreover, the idea of an

Englishwoman growing closer in custom or culture to Indian traditions was believed to compromise the very essence of Britishness. Memsahibs' ability to adhere to the strict rules, therefore, was seen as something that reflected their will and steadfastness in the face of constant temptation. Florence Marryat was scandalised to encounter ladies who were more Indian than English in their manners. In fact, of all the strange occurrences British women were prepared to face in India, an outward or inward 'Indianisation' was considered the most grotesque amongst some. 'Going *jungli*' was the single most shameful fate of memsahibs. It supposedly indicated a weakness of character and susceptibility to the Indian environment. In many ways, it translated as a 'fall'—a descent into a primordial state—which brought with it a sharp decline in social and cultural value.

Memsahibs preferred to establish camaraderie with other memsahibs, believing that it would help tackle the supposed threat to their Britishness and alleviate some of the anxiety regarding the dilution of their identity. They were acutely judgemental of those who did not seem to care and regularly dwelled on the fragility of their identity in the *jungli* space of India. Because of this paranoia, some memsahibs held on to the markers of their British identity and condemned those who failed to live up to the European standards, irrespective of the circumstances. They would get together in groups at parties and gossip about women who did not abide by conventions; there were many women to slander because 'aberrant' behaviour was all too frequent.

When a memsahib dared to waver even slightly from the path of a proper English lady, she invited tremendous social censure upon herself. Maud Diver, who was the author of several bestselling 'imperial romance' novels in her time, was perhaps the only memsahib who was non-judgemental of the various 'indiscretions' of English women in India. She had grown up in India and believed that it was the atmosphere of the Raj that created a pleasure-loving tendency in memsahibs and dissolved their 'natural' inclination for self-discipline. She argued that it was inevitable for memsahibs' hearts to be "strangely inflammable under the Indian skies... propinquity fans the faintest spark into a flame. Small wonder that lightly-dipped natures grow frivolous in such an atmosphere; that even the more seriously inclined succumb for a while to the irresistible charm".

Although memsahibs were not spared disrepute in cases of moral lapse, they were sometimes not blamed entirely, as Diver's opinions indicate. It was said that while a beautiful woman had one temptation to be thoughtless in England, in India she had many. This was seemingly because of the conventions of society that were prevalent in India, which regularly involved close mingling between the sexes: it was quite customary for men to call on women regularly, particularly in cantonments. Even married men made their first round of cantonment calls without their wives. This was because the sahibs had often kept Indian mistresses before memsahibs started coming out to India, and it was not possible to bring them into polite company. This custom of men visiting alone simply continued into the Raj era: bachelors and married men went to any house they wanted to go to. They sent in their cards as a way of introduction, and sometimes were willing to sit for hours with a lady they had never met before. Several memsahibs found this custom to be deplorable as the free mingling of the genders in this manner could cause trouble. Yet, they also enjoyed it because any kind of interaction felt good when they were suffering from the effects of *ennui*. The boredom could be so great that even the tedium of entertaining strange callers at odd hours was not unwelcome. The constant flow of unknown guests inevitably gave them a change of pace from their monotonous days, so that the *khitmatgars* were frequently told "*brandy-pani lao!*" (fetch the brandy and water!).

In this way, women sometimes even received and conversed with as many as a dozen men in one morning—men whom they had never met before, and whom they knew they would not even recognise if they met again in the future. The incessant tea dates and morning bridge alleviated some of the boredom and loneliness during prolonged separation from their husbands because even if the husbands were with them, they went to work every day for long hours while their wives remained homebound. The solitary living often drove them to despair and acute frustration. Florence Marryat wrote:

> Women in India are often quoted as being more careless and reckless… scarcely anything can be done or said in India without its being known; but granted that it is the case, there are greater excuses for it… She is compelled by the climate to lead a life of so much idleness that any excitement comes to her as a release; and that in many cases she is left alone and unprotected for months and even years, whilst her husband is away on Foreign Service, and she has not one of her own family, or his, to go to during his absence. Added to which, in England, a gentleman has to obtain permission before he can call upon a lady; in India he may call on whom he pleases.

However, more often than not the system of gentlemen calling upon ladies was due to the lack of any kind of occupation in dull stations and not necessarily because of licentiousness or romantic interest. The sahibs and memsahibs were thankful for anything constructive to do or meeting with any friendly face, as long as they could have a decent conversation and drink a cup of coffee with company. Besides, there were plenty of officers passing through cantonments, and there were plenty of idle women withering away in their homes as there was literally nothing to do before and after their afternoon siestas.

Sometimes, the loneliness was so great that women had to rely on unpleasant company just for the sake of having someone around. Emily Eden was alone at a pony race when she was suddenly very sleepy. She was compelled to ask a certain 'Colonel L' for his arm in a fit of desperation, even though he was a misanthrope and had always been very unpleasant. Still, having someone was better than having no one. Women, in fact, invested all their energy into cultivating etiquette and creating a system of proper social life in the Raj for lack of anything productive to do.

Sometimes, finding women alone, missionaries attempted to fulfil their agendas with utmost abandon and alacrity. Lonely women were defenceless, and the aggressive and determined missionaries had an easy time scaring them. A memsahib was shocked and frightened after being berated by a rude missionary in a very coarse strain, especially because she was all alone at home.

Such incidents gave rise to the idea that memsahibs, lonely as they were, would be prone to moral indiscretions. For this reason, memsahibs mingled with women who had the same concerns as them in India and eschewed Indians' company. Mingling with the natives beyond a certain point was a major *faux pas*. Such divides were more perceptible in the social interactions of women, as men generally did mingle and interact with Indians frequently because of their work and the social contacts that emerged from it. However, for women, striking up friendships with ordinary Indian neighbours was a thing to be avoided. The strict boundaries between the races had to be maintained in order to avoid the label of *jungli*.

Such restrictions were imposed upon British society mainly due to the segregation tactics employed by the British in India. Racial purity was an important determinant in the status of women, because not all white women had a 'pure' white lineage. This became complicated because as the Raj progressed, a 'mixed race' born from interracial couplings came into being. Since the memsahib was customarily a woman who belonged to the ruling race and was married to a white officer of the Raj, she was usually considered to be racially superior to a Eurasian woman.

By the beginning of the twentieth century, there were thousands of Eurasians in India. While they preferred to be recognised as Europeans and did not want to be associated with the Indian population, they were not able to gain superior status. Their keenness to shed their part-Indian identity contributed to their lack of acceptance as they deliberately distanced themselves from their Indian roots and adopted British ways but were consequently shunned for being inferior. It was said that their accents were pretentious—'*chee chee*' (dirty), signifying their mixed origins—and they were perennially yearning to go back 'home' like the British, even though they had never been to England and were born in India. Their supposed nostalgia for the British scenery appeared ridiculous and fake, and further worsened their overall social image. British clubs often did not admit Eurasians, as they did not admit Indians. In fact, Eurasians faced ridicule regularly for wanting to erase their then-stigmatised origins. Historians have commented on the subordinate position of the Anglo-Indians, as they were represented as "walking paradoxes" due to their identification with the British elite, even as they lived in poverty with other Indians (Blunt, *Domicile and Diaspora*, 34).

For the British community in India, however, Anglo-Indians were more than a statistical problem; they were an indication that the dilution of the white race was possible and, in fact, a reality that could not be ignored anymore. Most '*pukka*' British ladies were uncomfortable about socialising with Anglo-Indians and avoided their company whenever they could. They were afraid that being seen in public with the "half-caste children of the soil", as Emma Roberts wrote, would forfeit their claim to association with people of their own class and community. The new arrivals especially had to be wary of this, as mixing with Eurasians could prove to be fatal to their social status.

Perhaps the worst of it for the memsahibs was when young Eurasian women began to contend for the status of a 'memsahib'. These 'black-eyed beauties' had the behaviour and mannerisms of British ladies, but often looked more Indian than British. Most of them were recognisably 'mixed', and no matter how well they appeared, they were mocked, derided, and strictly excluded from British society as well as being labelled as '*chee chee*'.

Broadly speaking, the title of 'memsahib' was ostensibly for 'respectable' white women during the British colonial Raj in the subcontinent, so although the term adapted to newer power structures with time, socially the Eurasian memsahibs' position was highly contentious because of their tenuous status in colonial India. They had to constantly assert their racial affiliations and perform their Britishness. Very few Eurasian men and women managed to break free of their so-called 'tainted' background.

It took the British a long time to accept Eurasian women into the proper English circles in Calcutta. For a very long time, marriage was the only way in which such women could better their status and only if they married into a European family; otherwise, they remained the 'kali mem' (black memsahib). Yet, sometimes, even a higher social status on paper did not translate to equal respect in the eyes of those who had a similar income and employment and British birth. The stigma associated with ancestry was quite enduring, and the proper white lady remained at a higher position in society. Moreover, marrying into a European family was not very common as Eurasian women hardly ever had access to the white officer class. Mostly, the mixed girls and boys had no option but to marry within their own community due to their stigmatised social status. Those who did marry British men became the butt of jokes for being wily and ambitious. Emma Roberts noted that the charm of Eurasian women sometimes won them English husbands, but marriage with mixed classes was discouraged with banishment from society and sometimes even forfeiture of office. The white population held onto their Englishness, and the memsahibs held onto their sense of superiority as a marker of their identity and position in Raj society.

Given the rigid racial and gender hierarchies in colonial India, it is not surprising that interracial couplings were abhorred, particularly those between British women and native men. The bias against Eurasians is evident even in their depictions in literature. Eurasian women were frequently portrayed as markedly different from white memsahibs, whom they supposedly aspired to be like but whom they were almost always seen as morally inferior to. Moreover, Eurasian women were usually considered to be extremely attractive, but because of their 'shameful' heritage, they were typecast as temptresses and set up as polar opposites of the good Victorian woman with an all-white lineage.

The matter of white women's sexuality is crucial here. British society kept a close watch on the '*pukka*' memsahibs' sexuality and stigmatised liaisons or marriages with native men because of the threat of mixed children. Such associations were considered transgressive and threatened the carefully cultivated culture of British domesticity in India. It also threatened the sharp division between the 'coloniser' and the 'colonised'.

Thus, sexual management of British society in India was an important aspect of colonial rule, especially since white women were the bearers of Christian morality and order. Moreover, it was believed that they were under direct threat from Indian men due to racist stereotypes about the 'native' man's 'animalistic' sexuality. Such fears stemmed from various orientalist views about the 'sensual East' or India being a 'land of temptation'.

The term used for portraying the 'native' man's desire for white women was known as "Black Peril" (Cornwell, 441). This refers to the common notion prevalent in the history of the British Empire in Africa and Asia about the supposed likelihood of rape of white women by 'native' men, very often despite the absence of evidence. Such ideas were symptomatic of the fear of subversion amongst European women themselves, who might flout the colonial codes of sexual conduct and sidestep control. India, after all, was outside the controlled space of home, and British women had much more freedom and agency in the outposts. Sometimes, despite all efforts, there would not be any watchful eyes around, especially in the far-flung stations and *mofussils*. It was believed, anyhow, that women who had left for India were not respectable per se due to them having stepped out of the designated space of 'home', that is, England. The women who travelled to India exhibited a kind of independence which was understood to have great potential for sexual and moral indiscretions. That is primarily the reason why memsahibs' conduct was surveilled heavily. Such a rigid moral order also reaffirmed the strictly demarcated sexist gender roles in the empire and largely restricted women to domestic roles.

Nevertheless, interracial affairs were all too common, and mixed marriages even took place. Such relationships were mostly condemned and viewed as illicit and forbidden; however, that did not prevent British women from falling in love with their Indian paramours or indeed defying all norms and getting married to them. For some of them, their love interests, hailing from royal or aristocratic backgrounds, were all too desirable. These men were often educated in the West or were well travelled abroad and could easily mingle in British societies. It is perhaps well known that Indian princes and nawabs were exceedingly charming. To add to this, they were wealthy and powerful and compelling enough to entice the staunchest of British women. This was the case with the polished and glamorous Sikh Maharaja, Sir Duleep Singh, who was given the name Black Prince. His father, Maharaja Ranjit Singh, the first Maharaja of the Sikh Empire, was called the 'Lion of Punjab'.

Duleep Singh was married to Bamba Muller, a part German and part Ethiopian woman, and was later married to Ada Douglas

Wetherill, who was known as the 'French princess'. However, Singh became embroiled in a number of controversies and scandals and was arrested when he tried to return to India against the wishes of the British government in 1886. Both the marriages were exceedingly tumultuous, and neither lasted for too long. Both Bamba and Ada remain two of the more intriguing figures associated with Indian royalty during the British rule (Younger, 43–57).

The 'Spanish Rani' of the Maharaja of Kapurthala, Anita Delgado, yet another foreigner wife of an Indian nobleman, also did not find fulfilment in her marriage. She was a flamenco dancer by profession and was pursued by Jagatjit Singh until she agreed to marry him. After their Sikh wedding, she changed her name to Prem Kaur Sahiba; however, she found that while she had all of the material pleasures that Jagatjit's European mistresses enjoyed, she had none of the social recognition of a wife since he had Indian wives who were much more senior to her in rank (Younger, 74–88).

It is noteworthy that many European women who married into Indian nobility and royalty encountered similar problems of feeling stifled in their Indian households. Some of them managed to find hobbies and other pursuits to keep themselves occupied, but many of them had to face resentment and prejudice from different quarters. Some of them left India, never to return.

This is not to say that happy unions never took place between European women and Indian men; however, tragic love stories are often remembered more than happy ones.

4

"I NEVER FELT, OR INDEED WAS, SO DIRTY IN MY LIFE"

DACOITS, *DOOLIES*, AND *DAK*-BUNGALOWS

> *We travelled on till ten this morning, and during the whole seventeen hours, baby preserved the greatest serenity. The road was execrable, over large unbroken masses of rock, and we noticed several times in the night a strange rumbling noise about the carriage, and just as we drove up to the bungalow at Sindwa, where we intended to pass the day, with a crash our luxurious britska broke to pieces… and incapable of being mended, that we shall have to abandon it here, and proceed on in the country carts, thankful that the crash occurred at a Station, as in the jungle we should have been exposed to the fearful rays of the sun without shelter… The bungalow at Sindwa is the most filthy place I ever was in—mud floors, swarming with vermin, on which we had to spread our carpets and mattresses and lie down, for chairs were an unknown luxury. I never felt, or indeed was, so dirty in my life, and oh! The streaming heat!*
>
> – Mrs. Leopold Grimstone Paget, 1865

Travel was an inevitable part of life in the Raj, and the British officers and their wives were constantly on the move, as they undertook frequent journeys through the subcontinent, either because of official postings, or for recreational travels to different cities. Whatever the case, whether it was the season of intense heat and dust, lashing rains, or snow, the travel never ceased.

This highly peripatetic lifestyle added to the excitement of life in India, but at the same time, it could be daunting for the memsahibs as it lent a kind of impermanence and uncertainty to their personal and domestic lives. Travelling frequently and migrating ever so often could be physically exhausting, financially burdensome, and also emotionally draining. The Sisyphean nature of moving from one station to another on different postings or for official work, where they had to take up residence in new and unfamiliar surroundings, could be utterly frustrating. It was disheartening, especially because no matter how expert they were at arranging their homes, they had to repeatedly dismantle the carefully put together domestic setups and then reset everything in a completely alien location.

Indeed, news of transfers or official tours came abruptly, and memsahibs would immediately have to begin preparations for packing and moving. It was a great challenge to pack an entire household, along with an entire lifestyle, then transport it great distances and rebuild everything with the hope of being able to replicate what had been taken apart. To make matters worse, despite their laborious arrangements to secure and pack their belongings, something or other would inevitably be damaged or lost on the way.

What aggravated memsahibs' misery was that they usually had no idea what the next establishment or area would be like, and they always dreaded the lack of proper facilities. Several doubts plagued their minds even on the journey: were they going to get good servants? Would the bungalow be better than the last one or worse? Would the area be secluded yet again? Would they be able to make good friends? It may be said that while the husbands were busy building the great empire, the wives not only did the lion's share of the work but also paid the highest price for it.

When it came to travelling for the sake of travel, however, memsahibs often displayed an affinity for excursions into areas deep in the Indian heartland. Such adventures added excitement to their otherwise dull and lonely lives in the remote corners of the outposts. Emma Roberts, who was a travel writer and poet, wrote in her memoirs about her life in India during the 1830s: "in constant movements through wilds, however monotonous, the incidents of the march and the change of scene afford a salutary relief to ennui, which is not to be found in a fixed residence".

One of the most incredible things about travelling memsahibs is that some of them travelled with their children (even new borns) quite nonchalantly. They usually gave the *ayahs* separate *doolies* (litters) as they were best suited for children, and they were adept at various practical methods for road travel when children were involved. They knew that bottles for babies had to be kept filled to the cork so that their contents did not turn sour because of the shaking of the *gharries* (carriages) and that the children had to be well covered to keep them protected against fevers, since the carriages were very draughty. If they were passing through dangerous areas, they took their babies in their own carriage, but otherwise, the maids took care of them.

Indeed, since memsahibs regularly went on excursions, they quite uncomplainingly endured even the greatest of discomforts while navigating difficult passages. They planned their travels meticulously, and for this reason were mostly unfazed by any troubles on the road, such as low supplies or dangerous weather conditions. Emma Roberts wrote:

> An Indian night is superb; excepting at intervals during the rains, it is midways light enough to distinguish objects at a considerable distance; the heavens shine with stars, and the moonlight descends in flood. Beneath the midnight planetary beam, the most simple and unpretending building is decked with beauty; the mud hut of some poor native, with its coarse drapery of climbing gourds, shews like a fairy bower, and the barest sand-bank, topped with the wretched habitations of humble villagers, assumes a romantic appearance, outlined against the dark blue sky spangled with innumerable stars.

During their journeys, memsahibs usually made the most of their trips by witnessing as many wonders of India as they could. The usual trend was to visit multiple towns, monuments, or scenic sites by taking longer routes like Christina S. Bremner did when she came to India in 1891. She spent a month travelling in a *dandi*, a kind of palanquin, and touring Kasauli, Delhi, Bombay, Agra, Shimla, and other places in North India.

It may be said that the memsahibs had figured out the *dak* system and could manage it rather well, as every morning they would be ready to embark on the journey with a holler of "*Dak-wallah, dak-wallah, tiar hi?*" ("Coachman, coachman, are you ready?"). They were undaunted by the risks and difficulties of unknown terrains and climate, and several of their writings reveal that their passion for travel often outweighed their fear of dangers. In fact, when these hardy and itinerant memsahibs were not accompanying their husbands on official work or migrating to the hills in the summers, they were travelling the country by themselves, in their carriages and palanquins, with their *coolies* carrying their boxes and managing their entourage. They unhesitatingly travelled in the hottest of afternoons and the inkiest of nights, and in the process witnessed the most remarkable scenes, which they wrote about in their letters back home. Most of their writings about their travels record their encounters with the most wondrous scenes around different corners of India. And many of them focused particularly on chronicling the threats that they encountered while in transit, rather jubilantly detailing their adventures and exciting narrow escapes.

"Dusty Pores" and *Dak-Banglas*

The inhabitants of remote villages, also sympathise in the unconquerable alarm excited by the colour and costume of a European. Often has a benighted and wayworn traveller been denied assistance from villagers, who on such occasions uniformly rush into their huts on his first enquiry, and either preserve an obstinate silence behind their closed doors or answer the poor man's remonstrations with shrieks of terror. The language in which they are addressed is unknown to them, and superstition induces the belief that the white-faced stranger is surely some Rakush or demon, who will destroy them with the evil eye. Often have I heard of the torrents of invective showered in good hindostanee, on these trem-

bling people by luckless travellers among the roadless mazes of some jungle waste, who have vainly required guidance from the people of a retired hamlet; until, weary of remonstrance, the baffled wayfarer has been fain to stretch his tired limbs, beneath some friendly tree, to await the morning light.

– Marianne Postans, 1838

Before colonial rule began in India, various rest houses were built along the ancient commerce routes. *Serais* and *dharamshalas* (shelters and rest houses) have existed in India for centuries and were meant for pilgrims travelling through the dusty corners of the countryside. During the Mughal rule, inns called *caravanserais* provided shelter to traders, merchants, and buccaneers.

The Indian postal system was established by Robert Clive in 1776 in Calcutta, which ushered in the age of *dak* bungalows, also known as circuit houses. These buildings were much like the coaching inns of Europe and were built especially for British officers and civilians as they travelled through the hinterlands. Eventually, the bungalows came to be used by individual travellers for resting overnight while in transit. Since the British travelled regularly, such rest stops were a recurring feature of their highly mobile lives. Travellers could hire coaches, horses, palanquins, or even carts carrying mail and rest in the bungalows on the way where the mail coaches stopped. In contrast to the challenges of the open roads and dense jungles, these bungalows were a welcome shelter. They were built at distances of 15 and 20 miles along the principal roads, and on particularly long travels they were a sight for sore eyes for the exhausted men and women on horseback or in carriages.

Travelling memsahibs had a range of options available to them when they undertook long journeys. They usually had the opportunity to reside with their friends and relations on the way, enjoying the hospitality of their hosts' homes and relishing the *chota hazri*, the meal taken at dawn, and *barha hazri*, which was the main breakfast meal, all of which provided a welcome change from the difficulties of the road. If memsahibs were the wives of important dignitaries or military officers of higher ranks, they would be welcomed into the local rajas' palaces. But very often, they sojourned up-country where there was no one to host them. In such remote places, they lodged in abandoned old buildings and palaces being operated as *dak* bungalows.

Memsahibs, in this way, were privileged travellers as they had access to government resources and facilities. However, the experience of living in *dak* bungalows could seldom count as a 'privilege', and even the most nomadic memsahibs dreaded staying in such guesthouses. This is because the structures were usually dilapidated and lacked the most basic of provisions. Ordinarily, they contained no more than four suites of rooms, with each suite having three rooms, a bathroom, and sometimes, its own veranda. If they were lucky, the rooms had fireplaces because in the evenings, even in summer, it could become chilly in some areas, especially in mountainous regions or hill stations.

There was a good reason why *dak* bungalows, over time, acquired a poor reputation. Even if in some rare cases they were adequately furnished, they were hardly aesthetic or comfortable and were usually rather austere. The windows would often have no glass, the walls would be grimy and plastered, and the rooms would have floors of beaten earth instead of proper flooring. Occasionally, the floors were made of mud, and covered with coarse *dhurries* (rugs). Very often the memsahibs found the woodwork of the doors, windows, roofs, and furniture to be rudimentary, and sometimes even doors and windows were absent, and the servants would drape curtains to give the guests privacy. If there were doors, and the rooms were shut, there could be complete darkness inside because of poor interior design. Very rarely did the rooms of any *dak* bungalow have glass panes to permit light inside. The rough and crude construction would upset the memsahibs when, after a long journey, they would find that their rooms did not even have mirrors and basins. Even though *jharuwallahs*, who were sweepers, were usually attached to the bungalows and received small payments from travellers using their services, they did not always do a proper job, so the interiors often looked unkempt. Christina S. Bremner was lucky to get a porter to clean up the *dak* bungalow she was staying in.

E. Augusta King, wife to a civilian, who was travelling in India during the late 1870s and early 1880s, called the *dak* bungalow structures she lived in "thoroughly native". She wrote about the rest house in Banihal which was so poorly constructed that cold gales of mountain wind flowed inside from all directions due to the arched windows that had only latticework on them. Luckily for her, they had *kangris*, which were small earthen pots filled with hot wood ashes that could be placed under petticoats or under a rug spread over the knees in order to keep warm indoors. In Kashmir, *kangris* were even carried because they were so portable and could last all day. The basic *kangris* were cheap, priced at 3 pence, and the more ornamental ones, which were preferred by the memsahibs, were between 6 pence and 9 pence.

Memsahibs usually made it a habit to travel with some basic amenities knowing that the bungalows they would come across would be spartan and filthy. Most of the bungalows did not even have proper bedding, and they would have to make their own arrangements on this matter. Memsahibs set up their rooms with the help of their servants and the *khitmatgar* of the bungalow just after settling in. When Flora Annie Steel stayed in a *dak* bungalow in Kasur, she decorated her flat nicely because she was going to stay for a long period of time. She had packed rugs, quilts, hangings, stools, and good crockery. She allowed herself some sundry luxuries such as a soft pillow cut on English lines and a coffee grinder to make her delicious brew of mocha coffee that was locally purchased. She even had a great supply of fresh meat and bread. Her stay in several *dak* bungalows was pleasant; however, occasionally she came across a bungalow that was in poor condition. In one such bungalow, the living room was dusty and the mouldy smell was unbearable. In Saharanpur, the *dak* bungalow she stayed in was swarming with rats and mice. The bearers told her and her husband that nearly 500 had been killed already so they were reluctant to do more.

Despite all measures, the weary travellers normally did not find comfort in the poorly constructed structures of *dak* bungalows. This was probably because the establishments were government properties, and the tariffs were affordable and standardised. In

1864, the tariff for a bungalow with all furnishings, crockery, bed, and other necessities was 1 rupee per day—in some cases, 1 rupee a day for each room occupied, and in others, 1 rupee a day for each member of the party. These nominal rates were justified as everything was quite below standard. Still, the *dak* system in place supported and encouraged travel and did help women move independently and frequently.

Upon arrival, the lodgers would be greeted by the *khansama* (head chef) and the manager of the bungalow. At the reception, they would be given an oblong registration book where they had to sign before taking up lodging there. After the stay, when checking out, the lodgers had to inscribe their date of departure, pay the tariff, and provide feedback in the same oblong book. The registration books were collected by the Company for accessing the performance of the bungalows and their employees. If a particular *dak* bungalow received too many complaints, it was fined for not maintaining proper standards, although this method clearly did not work well as none of the bungalows maintained 'standards'. However, the Indian employees and servants were sometimes severely punished for not doing work properly. Since they could not read English, they could never understand if the feedback was good or not and could not manipulate it.

After making the registration, the travellers had to quickly secure their rooms, because other travellers could come in and reserve the better rooms since the system was first come, first served. This system was not completely meticulous, and travellers often had to accommodate additional occupants or relinquish their extra rooms. This was a great challenge for the lodgers and added to the inconvenience of long journeys, which already made everyone exhausted and ill-tempered.

Sometimes, the bungalows could be tiny and not large enough to accommodate more than one or two individuals. In cases of shortage of space, it was not uncommon for the previous lodgers to agree to accommodate the new arrivals by doubling up in single rooms. If the bungalows were full, then memsahibs were required to vacate the rooms should a Company officer come that way. It was worse if the bungalow was housing sick soldiers because travellers who arrived later could not make a stopover there. And if families or lone women travellers arrived, the memsahibs would also have to vacate their rooms and share another, particularly if these ladies were ill-tempered and quarrelsome (as they often could be). This frequently resulted in arguments and scuffles in *dak* houses.

The tired memsahib, "flying from the hot season of the plains", as Nora Gardner put it, usually asked to procure a bath as the first thing to do when arriving anywhere. Then they would send one of their servants off to purchase provisions as soon as they had settled in. Usually, they had their meals prepared by their own servants if they felt finicky about the hygiene of the bungalow. But it could be too costly to purchase provisions en route, and most *dak* bungalows, in places such as Chakrata for instance, were inconveniently located; therefore food supplies were sparse. It was usually better to get meals from the bungalows since the rates were cheap anyway.

Every bungalow had its own *khansama*, but the food was often not up to standard. It was a popular joke that the *khansama* would always appear before mealtimes to politely ask the boarder what they would like to eat. But no matter the request, the food prepared would be the same generic chicken with gravy that was rarely palatable. Sometimes even this would not be available. Once, E. Augusta King found that the *dak* bungalow she had come to did not even have bread and eggs, and she had to sleep without a meal (it was always the responsibility of the *peon* (low-ranking attendant) of the bungalow to make such an arrangement). In the morning, they managed to get one single loaf, which by then made them feel extremely grateful. Another time, at the *dak* bungalow in the snow-clad Nagthat in Uttarakhand, which was built for the use of the road engineer, she found that the facilities were wholly unlike what she had been told they would be. To her utter dismay, there was not even any cooking vessel of any sort, no water, and nothing to bring any in, and the nearest village was down in the valley. They had to send their servants out to find a water pot first thing upon arriving. The only washing apparatus they found was an old tin tub with a great crack in it, which she had to plaster with mud as a temporary fix. There were also no candles in the bungalow. Luckily, they had carried their own, but they could not be too extravagant with their supplies lest they ran out and the next bungalow turned out to be worse.

Mrs. Paget had to stop in a jungle bungalow once in Palasner, in present-day Maharashtra, which was extremely cold and dirty, and she feared that the insanitary condition of the place, as well as the season of fever, could be most unhealthy.

Nora Gardner, who came to India in 1892, wrote about her trials while travelling in *Rifle and Spear with the Rajpoots: Being the Narrative of a Winter's Travel and Sport in Northern India*, published in 1895:

> We tried to bribe the drivers to push on with promises of backsheesh, but "Bahut achha, Sahib," "All right, Sir," is all we can get from them… Whilst we were at luncheon a violent thunderstorm came on… At five o'clock we reach Dulai where we meant to stay the night, but find the bungalow has a leaky roof and is flooded with rain, so we push on to Domel…
>
> The river here roared hundreds of feet below us. It was a dark night, but occasional flashes of lightning gave us a glimpse of the water at the foot of a descent so sheer that the torrent seemed absolutely to rush under our feet… We were not sorry to reach Domel, where two Englishmen at dinner in the verandah of the bungalow looked cheery and home like.
>
> The road to the bungalow leads through the native village, and we had to pull up to a walk and frequently halt, to avoid driving over the numerous family groups, squatted eating or sleeping on the highway. No carriage except the post is supposed to travel after dark… the villagers bring out their beds, light their fires and thoroughly make themselves at home on the public road. Their houses on either side… Lighted up by numerous fires, it was a very picturesque scene…
>
> Thursday, October 13th—I think if I had not slept on that bedstead it would have gone for a walk by itself! It is explained to me that the rain drives "things" indoors. It certainly did. There is a tiny English shop here, and I am laying in tins of Keating's powder. The view from the bungalow is beautiful. Two rivers meet below, one quite blue, the other brown, and the mountains tower above us on every side…

The location of the bungalows, however, was not always picturesque, especially if they were located in the middle of the jungle, which memsahibs knew was inhabited by the deadliest of creatures. There was the risk of wild animals attacking them even around the premises of remote bungalows. At Mowana, near Haryana, wolves were common around the *dak* bungalow where E. Augusta King and her husband were staying, and they realised that they could not let their little child sleep in a cot outside because wolves snatched little children away even with others around. Cheetahs could be bold enough to come into camps and attack slight *coolies* or pet animals. As King noted, "a moonlight stroll loses its charm when a possible tiger is crouching in the bushes".

While staying at the only bungalow for European travellers in 'Campoorly' (it is likely this refers to Khopoli, also known as Campoolie, near Bhor Ghat in Maharashtra), Anna H. Leonowens found, much to her horror, that it was inhabited by a tribe of monkeys that created a great ruckus when they moved in. She hastened to find cover inside her room and counted sixteen of them, and they ran in and out of the half-deserted building, throwing fruits from the peepal tree outside. Some were peeping in at her through doors and windows, and some were swinging from the rafters, seemingly swearing at her in a human-like fashion. She had to have the servant drive them away as monkeys could be extremely vicious in the regions she was passing through and were even known to strangle passers-by.

In fact, the bungalows, rather than providing some respite, were extremely exhausting for memsahibs. They were built a day's march apart, and the constant packing and unpacking could be extremely wearisome. E. Augusta King fell ill just the day before they had to urgently depart to Murree, and it delayed much of the preparation they had to undertake, especially because the *ayah* also fell ill. She wrote that despite deeply exhausting illness, "one way and another, all was done that had to be done", and they began their journey as scheduled. Indeed, the chain of *dak* bungalows that travellers had to stop at during their journeys could be nerve-wracking as they never knew what their next one would be like. Moreover, it was not unusual if their own servants turned insubordinate or stole from them on long journeys. Since they could not quarrel too much with the locals due to language barriers, they were sometimes faced with risky situations.

Furthermore, there were times when memsahibs were forced to stop in completely remote and eerie-looking bungalows if they were not inclined to continue their journey at night. This could be extremely perilous because the other lodgers would mostly be men, making it more unsafe for the memsahibs. In fact, *dak* bungalows could be even more sinister if they were located in spooky sleepy hollows of distant towns, deep inside the jungles, or in the middle of arid areas. Once, a memsahib realised that the bungalow she was staying at had the reputation of being haunted by the ghosts of a resident and his two children who had been slaughtered in the room directly above, during the revolt of 1857.

The fear of ghosts was not wholly unfounded. British woman Ursula Graham Bower, anthropologist and guerrilla fighter, described how in the jungles of the Naga regions in the north-east of India, the supernatural was part of the local culture. There would frequently be mysterious lights in the hills which the locals called "spirit fires", and sometimes at night, there would be unearthly cries and eerie whistling within the bungalows where they lived. She did not believe in ghosts until a poltergeist actually appeared inside her house. It began in the village called Laisong, where there had been complaints of doors being shaken and flung down at night, and of disruptive pattering of footsteps that also somehow sounded like hooves. Bower was indifferent to the noises, but soon it sounded like someone blowing "raspberries".

Things escalated quickly, and there would be fearful crashes at night within the bungalow compounds, but when they went running to check, nothing had been disturbed. The manifestations were frequent and began occurring inside the bungalow where Ursula was staying. One evening, she was sitting on the veranda when she heard a pattering like the tread of a heavy dog nearby. She immediately thought of leopards and grabbed a flashlight to check. As she held the door open to see, the noise was directly opposite her, but there was nothing there. A few nights later, the same thing happened, and when she heard the noise, she did not even trouble to stir. However, the next appearance was quite sinister. She was having dinner with the hurricane lamp casting a circle of light around the table and through the doorway into the bedroom beyond. She had a book propped on a ketchup bottle and was halfway through her soup when there was an explosive raspberry just beyond the doorway, well within the ring of light. She immediately looked around but there was nothing. She went back to her food, as there was nothing to be done: "if a spirit wished to amuse itself by making rude noises in my bungalow, I could see no immediate way to prevent it".

Piqued by her indifference, however, the incubus resorted to more alarming methods. During the next incident, she was in the living room at eight in the evening, reading after dinner by the fire with a lamp on the table next to her and her back to two small windows. The shutters were closed and held together by a bar. Suddenly, a faint sound made her look around. There was the bar—which, being new and taut, took a sharp pull to dislodge—slipping out corner-wise through the window space as though someone standing behind her was handling it, and the next second, the completely freed shutter fell loose with a thundering clatter, which startled the living daylights out of her. She yelled for the men, who came running, and they searched everywhere for the intruder, but could find nothing of earthly proportions. It was clear then, beyond doubt, that it was the same troublesome poltergeist that blew raspberries.

Then again, one evening, she was taking a bath when suddenly the bathroom door, which adjoined the bedroom, began to rattle as though someone was trying to open it. Petrified, she threw a towel on and jerked the door open herself, but the bedroom door was locked and the room was empty. Besides, no one, not even a cat, could cross the room unnoticed because the floors were covered with bamboo matting which creaked under pressure.

The oddest incident occurred when she was left alone with one of her men, Namkia, as the rest of the servants had gone to the village. They sat up by the fire, and it was almost midnight when they heard a low murmur of voices in the cookhouse that was twenty feet away. Namkia got up thinking the men had returned and went to speak to the cook. Ursula sat by the fire listening to the continued murmurings, when suddenly, Namkia reappeared to say that the cookhouse was deserted and the men were not back. They quickly understood that it was the same incubus making appearances, though yet again they could not find traces of it.

It later came out that the entire area near that particular bungalow was haunted. Laisong was used as a burial ground in cases of suicides or "accursed" deaths, and people claimed that curious lights could be seen moving here and there in the small hours. A Zemi poltergeist, which Ursula came to know of, was also reputed to haunt a rest house at Hangrum. It was a ghost of long standing, and its presence added to the creepiness of the bungalow at night. It was also a much more malevolent spirit and had forced the caretaker and his family to leave the compound.

Sometimes the threat of staying in *dak* bungalows was of a real nature; E. Augusta King and her husband once found a dead body outside their grounds.

Given such untoward occurrences frequently taking place in and around *dak* bungalows, it is no wonder that they were thought to be quite dreadful and risky back in the day.

Dak-gharries, *Doolies*, and *Dacoits*: Travelling from Bungalow to Bungalow

> *By no means unpleasant. You could travel night and day if you chose, lying down or sitting up, reading a book or sleeping, just stopping at a dak bungalow for a bath and food and, if the time was your own, you could rest there during the heat of the day…*
>
> *Thugs abounded through the length and breadth of the country. Though I am not aware of any Europeans having lost their lives through these highwaymen, they really were a terror of native travellers…*
>
> *To return to these Thugs, there were two species of this genus Homo. One killed his victim for what he could get out of him, if only a few coppers, the other from religious motives. Thugs were all Hindus, and as such were full of superstitions. So the religious murderer considered, in taking the life of some lonely traveller, that he was pleasing his goddess Kali or Darree.*
>
> – Harriet Tytler, 1907

Memsahibs not only faced sudden shocks during their stays at creepy *dak* bungalows but also endured countless perils and crises on the road while shunting from one bungalow to another. Since they regularly made overnight journeys, the lonely and winding roads could seem ominous and forbidding. Sometimes, they fell asleep inside their carriages, exhausted as they were after traversing miles without a break, while their servants kept an eye out.

Keeping a lookout was highly necessary on the road. Mrs. Marryat, while travelling overnight in her open carriage, was terror-stricken when she saw the occasional gleam of a tiger's eye as the lanterns carried by her *musalchees* (torchbearers) threw light upon the surrounding foliage as they moved along. Wild elephants could suddenly cross the path, forcing them off course. An Englishman riding on his elephant was joined by a wild elephant that ran alongside him for a considerable distance until the man began to light matches to distract it, after which he finally got away. Once, a memsahib woke up in the middle of the night and looked outside her *doolie* to find the *coolies* stood encircling her with a ring of bonfires, beyond which she could discern, much to her horror, a troop of wild elephants who would have charged towards them but for the circle of fire.

Sometimes the memsahibs even encountered tigers on the way, and the *coolies* would promptly run away, leaving the wretched memsahibs cowering inside the *doolies*. Once Emma Roberts had left a house in Chowringhee to return home at night, when the bearers took a wrong turn, and set down her palanquin to confabulate amongst themselves. She could hear the calls of jackals as this went on for a very long time. But she was more terrified that the bearers would run away, leaving her stranded in the middle of an unknown road, than of being mauled to death by the creatures of the night.

Managing the *coolies* was another great task for these lonesome memsahib wanderers since the language difference was a great barrier in communication. They only knew some set phrases and instructions like '*Ootow*', which meant 'lift up', or '*jiddiejow*', which meant 'go quickly', but they often stood the chance of being tricked by the *coolies* and carried to the wrong destination either out of carelessness or if the *coolies* wanted to steal from them.

Christina S. Bremner's experience with *coolies* was not pleasant during her journey in the northern regions of the subcontinent, in 1891. In Ambala, she was first accosted by several native bearers who demanded *buckshish* (alms or payment) for folding her blankets in the train carriage, which looked no better than before. Then she was carried off to the wrong address by the *coolies* who barely understood her instructions and behaved 'insolently' towards her. There were several accounts of travellers who were stranded in the middle of the roads because their *coolies*, ran off, leaving the baggage strewn about, which was likely if the traveller was tyrannical towards them. But sometimes *coolies* would casually abandon memsahibs in the middle of nowhere and leave for a break or demand *buckshish* repeatedly. Once Constance Frederica Gordon Cumming's dog attacked a conglomeration of yogis, and they turned up at her *gharrie* to ask for alms as compensation. However, this time, she was so annoyed that she turned the tables and demanded *buckshish* from them for causing an affront to her dog, much to the amusement of the yogis, who let her go.

It was not only the servants accompanying a memsahib who were difficult to handle; the transport itself added to the trials of a long journey cross-country. *Dak-gharries*, which were horse-drawn or bullock-drawn carriages, were especially built for overnight transit by road, but they were hardly safe or speedy. Still, before the railways, it was an effective system for those wishing to travel long distances. *Daks* could be hired at the post office and ran from village to village for a measly sum with '*takuts*' (tickets), which were stamped papers given by the commissariat or police officers at the station they were leaving from. Prior arrangements had to be made because *daks* could be engaged for weeks beforehand. When proper *dak-gharries* were not available, *tongas* had to be used. These were two-wheeled carts drawn by two or three horses and carried six people including the driver. They could be acutely uncomfortable because of the seating arrangement, as the passengers had to sit sideways like in a wagonette. The car would tilt back because of the weight of the *syce*s who stood somewhere at the back and made the seating position a tiring one to maintain for over 6 hours of incessant jolting.

E. Augusta King described how the ponies trained for *tongas* were better trained than the ones for *dak-gharries* and moved much faster and more efficiently, though a slower pace was preferred so that the luggage carts and servants could keep up with the party. If horses were pulling the carriages, they needed to be changed at every station or every 5 or 6 miles. Additionally, every horse had his own *syce* who ran alongside the carriage and was supposed to be at hand if the carriage met with some accident or if the animal needed attention (which happened too frequently). These *syces* had amazing running skills and were famous for their speed and stamina.

In the case of bullock-drawn *gharries*, a light luggage cart could be attached separately, because the carriages did not have enough space for passengers as well as their numerous boxes. Usually, a board was put across the centre to make a plane surface, and cushions were laid on it so that the traveller could lie down. Some of the luggage went underneath. A net was put on above the head for light things, and there would be leather cases and pockets on the sides. The wheels needed to be greased periodically, and the spring was encased with strips of rawhide. If bullocks were purchased, then it was not possible to do more than 20 miles daily unless there were alternate animals. Mrs. Paget remarked that the bullocks' tails were twisted constantly to keep them going at a decent pace, which she did not like to see. On longer journeys, the animals were hardly strong enough to go at a decent pace. This could be acutely uncomfortable as the women jostled about in the *gharries* on uneven roads while slowly baking inside the carriages. E. Augusta King wrote how the roads were "terribly sandy and heavy" when she was travelling with her child and how "the jolting over the rough boulders beneath the sand was terrific, and made the framework crack and groan, Carlie [her baby] thought it capital fun".

Diligent arrangements and contingency plans had to be devised for *dak* journeys, especially overnight journeys. But during emergencies, *gharries* were very ineffective: Mrs. Paget remarked that in cases of military work, transporting troops was a great challenge because there was no organised mode of transportation in the country. The carts had to be placed under guard until they were wanted. Sometimes *hackeries* (bullock carts) were sent without the soldiers' baggage, if there was a shortage.

The carriages could not always withstand the rough terrain and often broke down in the most inconvenient locations when the wheels became loosened because of the bumpy tracks and the contraction of the wood in the heat. In such a situation, other carts had to be procured from the nearest station, and this whole process took several hours. E. Augusta King and her husband were travelling to Naushira when their cart began rattling and one of the wheels rolled off. They had to call for a blacksmith to fix the tyre, which delayed them considerably. When they started again, another wheel came off. Ultimately, they had to borrow a wagonette to the point where they could take a palanquin and a pony.

Wheels coming off was a rather common phenomenon. In order to avoid it from happening, they were taken off if the *gharrie* was being taken through a sludgy terrain or dragged through a river. Twenty odd *coolies* would be required to execute this feat, and they would strip down completely to avoid getting their clothing drenched. Together, they would tug and pull while shouting loudly to each other over the gushing currents. Helen D. Mackenzie and her husband travelled through a 3-mile tract of sandy plains and the dried waterbed of a river named 'Son'. They then had to cross several streams, and when they reached the last stream, their carriage was pushed onto a boat with a platform of bamboo. Their carriage had three pairs of bullocks. Such activity required a suitable *backshish* from the memsahibs later on.

On uneven terrain, there was always the risk of the carriage overturning or of more unlikely accidents that could prove fatal. E. Augusta King and her husband exchanged their *dak-gharrie* for a barouche on their way to Saharanpur, but the coachman was not alert and left the *syces* with the carriage. They had just taken their seats when the horses bolted, almost dragging the *syces* down. Robert King had to leap into the box and seize the bit off the horse just before they reached full gallop. During the same journey, the Kings almost met with another accident by way of collision with some bullock carts which were travelling on the wrong side of the road. It was known that the animals got nervous at the sight of army livery; they kept slipping their heads out of the yoke and would caracole all over the place until the drivers had to chase them around. Once, Mrs. Paget was travelling in a bullock *gharrie* when it fell into a ditch. Despite the chaos, the driver paid no attention. He merely sat around chatting, and after some time finally lifted the *gharry* out of the ditch. During another instance, they were driving by a river and suddenly the *gharrie* carrying her child swerved and one wheel went into a hole. The bullocks jostled precariously, and the entire carriage could have fallen into the water, but they managed to save it.

It was a great inconvenience that bullocks and horses were not always available. Much to her surprise, E. Augusta King found that in Saharanpur it was men instead of animals who drew the ordinary bullock carts. Elephants were useful in case memsahibs were riding with the royalty. Mrs. Paget's first time on an elephant was while the Pagets were in Mundergode. The Nawab of Savanoor had sent his elephants for them, with *howdas* (covered seats) on top. These were fastened on the elephant's back and had pillars all a round with mirrors in them. They also had curtains on all sides which could be kept open. Inside, there were pillows to recline against. However, the size was small for Europeans and the elbow room was limited for two people. The elephants were controlled by the *mahouts* who drove them with an iron spike. Helen D. Mackenzie was quite comfortable riding on an elephant and said it was a fine mode of journey, but she found the two-wheeled buggy extremely unsafe.

The poor condition of roads added to the troubles of the journey as the paths were seldom macadamised. E. Augusta King found that the road beyond Kohala, after crossing the Jhelum, was extremely uneven and gravelly, making the climb quite challenging. There was no shade because of the barren tracts, and the scenery was not at all pleasant. On her route to Chattar from Rhara, they went by river, and she wrote how the noise of the rushing water made conversation extremely tiring. The path was completely rough and uneven, and they had to make detours upwards or downwards as roads next to the river could have collapsed due to landslides.

Mrs. Paget's *gharrie* broke down in the middle of the road one night because of the uneven paths. Once, the road was so bumpy that she had to hold on with both hands and wedge her baby in between boxes so that he would not topple over because of the jolting, but even then "he was frequently tossed into the air", and she feared he might be thrown off the carriage altogether if she fell asleep.

Horse-riding journeys could be extremely dangerous because of the loose rocks, especially if the soil had been softened by rain. The paths were mostly extremely narrow with only 2 feet in width for riding on, and frequent landslides presented another risk in the hills. However, the memsahibs would mostly have no choice but to keep moving, even with their feet protruding over the edge of gaping cliffs of a few thousand feet. If the climb was steep, the animals slowed down on their own. It would be extremely tiring holding onto the animal on an upward slope, but the mettlesome memsahibs held onto the ponies' manes for dear life.

E. Augusta King once had a pony who refused to budge on the uphill road after going 2 miles. For this reason, horses and ponies had to be selected very carefully because the Europeans often did not know how to guide the animals, and they had to rely on their horse's training to transport them safely. King liked the Kashmiri ponies and said they were the best kind; she preferred them to the other kinds of pony even if others were more expensive and healthier. She said that even a poorly fed and shoeless Kashmiri pony was better than a sturdy pony from other regions when it came to moving through poorly constructed hilly areas. They were clever and took their time to navigate in treacherous terrains, stopping every now and then to choose the best track. Sometimes, these creatures went back and forth, almost with "human sagacity and caution". While travelling from Vernag to Banihal, they had to climb up extremely steep ridges and were forced to slow down significantly, with the added issue that the ponies had to halt every ten yards to rest before going further.

Horseback journeys in the hills could indeed be quite nerve-wracking. While riding along a particularly narrow road, E. Augusta King had to block the view of the rolling descent underneath her pony with her umbrella so as not to get dizzy and tumble into the valley. This was a good idea because as Constance F. G. Cumming wrote, a memsahib had fainted as her horse backed into the ravine, and while it struggled, she fell from her saddle, unconscious.

Despite all precautions, tricky routes could not always be avoided, and memsahibs' journeys took them into the wilderness, no matter how they tried to avoid dangerous passages. On the road to Chakrata, E. Augusta King had an accident. The bridge was narrow, and she stopped abruptly, but her husband rode over the rickety bridge, which promptly collapsed. He managed to escape, but the pony fell into the ravine. She wrote that if she had also ridden on, both of them would certainly have fallen into the stream below. Such accidents could be quite fatal and were unfortunately too common on the road.

On problematic roads, the animals could sometimes get extremely agitated. Savory was riding with camels, and ponies did not usually like to get close to them. One of the camels suddenly swung across the road menacingly, startling her pony. The ponies reacted immediately, and began backing the cart over the edge, but an accident was somehow averted. Still, her beloved pony fell into a ravine and would have taken her with it had she not thrown herself off the saddle.

E. Augusta King recounted the time when a particular pony pulling her *dak-gharrie* began jerking and pulling at the reins until the trace broke and she got her legs over the pole. She was behaving as if she was possessed and kicked until she got one leg behind the splinter bar.

Even if the animals co-operated, the roads could present bizarre difficulties. One of the scariest experiences while in transit was the challenge of crossing rivers and streams. The country had a great many streams and crossing them on bridges was much more dangerous because the infrastructure around most towns was not up to the mark, and constructions were often not maintained. Most bridges were fragile, raised at a great height, and made in a very rudimentary style. Sometimes, they were simply ropes slung across from rock to rock, from which hung a seat fastened to a triangle, which slipped along the main ropes as the traveller worked with his hands.

Once a memsahib encountered a broken bridge, and she dismounted her carriage to lighten the load and waited on the bank while the driver attempted to take the carriage across the river. But the carriage got caught on a stump and remained fixed on the bank, and because of the current, the splinter bar broke with a crack. Somehow, the horses were released, and the drivers dragged the carriage out on the opposite side.

If there were no bridges, there were sometimes pulley systems where those crossing the river had to sit on a coil of rope and were drawn over. These pulley mechanisms were so frail that there were several stories about the deaths they caused. The rains and heat could damage the ropes, and they were not reliable. Memsahibs often chose to wade through the river on horseback rather than use such a technique, but this was no less risky than bridges or pulleys. Mrs. Paget's horses sank suddenly in the middle of the stream, and the *coolies* had to rescue her.

Sometimes, memsahibs were carried through a *nullah* (stream) in a palanquin, as the *coolies* waded waist deep, with the torchbearers leading the way at night through the churning waters, even as the nervous memsahib seated inside sat petrified because of the swirling waters and constant tilting of the palanquin.

A rather remarkable method of crossing the rivers, recorded by the Abbott family in the early decades of the twentieth century, was that of inflating complete animal hides, preferably buffalo skins, placing cloth on top, and setting them out on the water. Jocelyn Abbott said it could not only float effortlessly, but also carry multiple people, as if on a raft. The *coolies* would hold onto the 'legs' of the animal hide-raft, as they protruded like poles. Another odd method was crossing in large copper pans. These seated four or five and were only used if there were no boats or bridges. To the great shock of first-time users, these pans spun wildly in a strong current, though they were not dangerous unless they hit a rock.

Sometimes, it became impossible to cross the swollen rivers altogether. Mrs. Paget once had to take a detour through a jungle and wade through bogs and ditches where the water was up to the horses' stomachs, just to avoid a swollen *nullah*. On her way to Hangul, however, she was unable to avoid accidents. They had to cross a stream so put everything on the seats of the carriage and, kneeling on top, made a *collie* go ahead to show them the safe route. But the current was too strong, and waves splashed through the carriage and freed the horses, so they went down too, struggling to gain footing and ultimately sliding down and taking with them everything that was in the carriages.

Journeys were, therefore, almost always slow and laborious. Apart from rivers and hills, there could be multiple hindrances on main routes because of traffic. Herds of cattle and mules blocking the way were a common phenomenon. Passing them could be difficult if the roads on the hillside were narrow. Once, Mrs. Paget crossed a conglomeration of Indian nomads, and they, along with their carts and animals, had completely blocked the road, causing her a needless delay. Moreover, if any of the animals got alarmed, it could cause complete commotion, with animals charging up and down the road precariously. If there were bullocks carrying items on their backs, a slight swerve could bring everything down onto the road. In fact, in Shimla, no wheeled vehicles were allowed towards the end of the nineteenth century for fear of accidents. Luggage was carried in bullock carts, and people had to ride or be carried by *coolies* in hand-drawn rickshaws or palanquins. It was in the late nineteenth century that the British discovered horse-drawn carriages could be used in hill stations, and the journey from Shimla to Kalka, which was earlier undertaken over 3 days, could be made in 1 day.

* * *

Apart from carriages, palanquin journeys were quite common, but slower and more cumbersome than *dak* journeys. *Doolies*, which Emily Eden described as a sort of bed with red curtains that sick soldiers were carried in, were very light but squalid looking and were slow and painful. If they were not balanced well, they could be tilted on one side, and if the bearers were not good, they changed positions constantly, causing too much jerking. If all the bearers walked with the same rhythm in their steps, the palanquin rocked too much, causing discomfort to the passenger.

Helen D. Mackenzie used *jhampans*, which were a sort of armchair for a single passenger, with a canopy and curtains, of which the canopy could be taken off. A short pole was slung by a leather strap between the side poles, both in front and behind, and carried by four men in a single file. But memsahibs would get nauseous and sick in the jolty palanquin rides and would yell *"niche rakh do!"* ("set me down!") to make them stop whenever they needed a break. Helen D. Mackenzie described a *palkee* as a long box or a portable berth, with cushions on one end and a shelf inside, carried by two bearers, in which one felt as if they were winnowing in a sieve.

Once, E. Augusta King had an unfortunate accident when her *palkee* (another word for palanquin) came crashing down with her in it. This happened sometimes, and so memsahibs had to dismount from their *dandies* due to rough terrains and walk while carrying their sandals in their hands. Constance F. G. Cumming preferred to walk rather than be carried by the *coolies* because one false step on the rocky narrow path and all of them would go catapulting into the ravine. Anna H. Leonowens described her hazardous journey to Poona from Bombay: "Now on foot and now in *palkees* we at length ascended these *ghats*, sweeping round and round, now ascending, now descending, passing by dreadful precipices, drawing breath under quaint natural bowers, following winding paths, and coming suddenly upon foaming cascades leaping from rock to rock."

The harsh climatic conditions were a constant source of trouble during overland travel. If they were in doolies or carriages, the sun beat down on the travellers mercilessly as they trudged through barren lands without the cover of trees. Whenever they could, memsahibs travelled with great blocks of ice to keep cool inside the suffocating carriages: they would place the block of ice in the middle of the carriage and cool their hands and legs before it, like warming hands before a bonfire. This option was not available in palanquin journeys or trains, which could be intensely uncomfortable.

Cold weather could just as easily make travellers feel miserable. Mist in higher altitudes posed problems because of low visibility. Emily Eden wrote angrily about the "regular thick Indian fog", which made her riding expedition an unpleasant experience. Constance F. G. Cumming said that she felt as if white spirits were floating around, impalpable and grave, and as if she could grasp the ghosts passing by.

If it had rained, it could cause little streams to cascade down upon them, making the ground soft and slippery. Constance wrote, "the path seemed gliding from beneath our feet, while streams rushed past, as though along their natural channel", but they had to keep moving even in the rains. It was worse if the journeys were being made on bullock carts because the muddy roads were difficult to tread on for the animals while pulling heavily laden *gharries*, significantly slowing the process. Hailstorms could even kill someone who was unfortunate enough to be struck by a bigger hailstone.

Landslides could occur, carrying away the travellers and their belongings. Isabel Savory and her party of trekkers were caught in an avalanche while going down a steep slope. They were going slowly and carefully, but then they suddenly heard a loud crack, and tonnes of snow came cascading down towards them. She slid down 30 feet, but luckily the velocity of their fall slowed down gradually, and the snow padded it. Because of such accidents, memsahibs lived in fear of crumbling roads and falling houses. E. Augusta King wrote about the destruction of her servants' house in their hometown.

During the dry summer months, dust storms could catch the traveller unawares, and envelop them in opaque waves of loose earth and debris. In the plains where the soil was alluvial, there was a tendency for dust storms to strike frequently before the onset of monsoons.

Constance F. G. Cumming found herself in total darkness moments after she saw a ballooning red cloud expanding on the horizon from her bungalow where she had a layover during her journey to Allahabad. They quickly shut all the windows but were still half-smothered. Dust storms could completely ravage houses, and in some cases, were so fierce that they could tear off entire roofs. One can only imagine what it must have been like to live through such a storm while in a precarious wagon or palanquin.

* * *

Getting lost was yet another common problem while travelling. Sometimes, the landscape looked the same for miles, and it was difficult to distinguish between routes. Anna H. Leonowens was completely confused while leaving Bidar because of the miles of wilderness around them which did not seem to look any different as they went along. The guide was not of much help and gave vague directions. They had to take refuge under a tree near a great stream that could not be crossed after dark.

Losing the way could be extremely dangerous not only because of bad weather conditions, but also because of crimes in secluded areas and empty highways. Indeed, *dakoos*, or *dacoits*, were a constant threat on highways and were notorious for robbing lonesome travellers. But getting their goods stolen was not the worst fate they could meet. *Dacoits* were fierce and swift, and in cases of an encounter, their lethal sabres ruthlessly slashed open the chests of *khitmatgars* who did not surrender their sahib and memsahib's belongings. The *Allen's Indian Mail* published that on 6 May 1878, at 4.30 pm, the policeman of a village sent word to the regiment that a band of *dacoits* had robbed a camel with a load of 5,000 rupees and killed several villagers on their route.

Dacoits usually moved in packs and committed organised crime. There were several known tribes of bandits, and stories about *dakoo* infestation on a particular road or in a particular area would float around, warning possible travellers and allowing them to change the course of their journey. Mrs. Paget found that the Sawunt Warree people were hiding in a forest on the way to Belgaum. They were firing at the travellers from the thickets as they ascended into the *ghats*, and two soldiers had already been wounded. There were multiple skirmishes between *dacoits* and the soldiers, to keep the former from attacking. Sometimes, it could take troops to disperse them, and jungles had to be burnt down to clear out robbers' encampments. Travellers often passed by such forest clearings, where the stubble was still smouldering, and knew that they were the former hideouts of gangs of *dakoos*.

Emily Eden was particularly agitated by the frequency of lootings that occurred on the important routes and generalised that India was a country of robberies where people lived by plunder. Thus, memsahibs believed it was important to ensure safety while in transit, especially since they were often travelling with valuables. In fact, memsahibs realised the need for war-like precautions and trained their servants and *coolies* with proper instructions so they would not be targeted by *dacoits*. Usually, if the luggage was too much, they sent one set to go with the provisions, such as wines and grains, along with a strong guard, and the precious items were always sent by daylight. At night, they sent another set of servants with the dinner things, furniture, tents, and so on so that everything could be transported by the next morning and in different batches. The rest of the things went with the main group in the morning when there were regiments present to ensure that they were safe. But if they strayed by mistake, *dacoits* were sure to rob them, especially in some regions where incidents of robberies and murders had been reported.

Once, a Colonel's horse was stolen from under the noses of five police officers whom he had deputed to guard it. The thief had cut the ropes, jumped on its back, and ridden off, and was never heard of thereafter. *Dacoits* stole white horses and painted them in different shades to disguise them. Some were painted in stripes, some in zigzag, and sometimes, they were given orange legs or red tails.

Lillian Ashby was a new born when she, along with her mother and father, were travelling on the Grand Trunk Road from Monghyr (Munger), in the Province of Bengal and Bihar, to Ranchi, in Orissa, where her father been transferred (Bihar was later separated from Bengal and joined to the Province of Orissa). They had already encountered a tigress with her two cubs, and had to erect a bivouac for the night, when suddenly, their bearer spotted two hooded bandits, armed with daggers and knives, beyond the fire. Lillian's father, a police officer, was not armed because most officers were able to carry out their work without weapons, but seeing the menacing bandits approaching them, he sprang up, fiercely yelling, "Fetch my rifle!", at which the bearer handed him a walking stick. The *dacoits* mistook it for a rifle in the dark and fled. Luckily for the family, there were only two interlopers; otherwise, they would easily have been killed.

Dacoits were especially prone to attacking lone memsahibs being carried in their *doolies* or wagons, knowing they would be defenceless. Mrs. Leopold Paget was travelling from Vengurla in Maharashtra in 1858, with her husband's battery, when they had to march through an area that was known to be populated with *dacoits*. Upon arrival, they were congratulated for reaching their destination unscathed because it had been reported in Belgaum that they had been murdered by *dacoits* in the jungle. Apparently, the chief of the *dacoits* had announced a reward for the head of every sahib that was brought to him.

The penalty for being a *dacoit* was severe in colonial India, and any person accused would receive harsh punishment. The sentences ranged from imprisonment in chains for up to several years, to banishment overseas for life. If villagers were found to give refuge to local *dacoits*, they were convicted just as severely. In October 1863, in Hooghly, five villagers were charged with hiding *dacoits* and having belonged to a gang. They were sentenced to transportation as a life sentence and 3 to 14 years' imprisonment. Transportation was one of the more serious forms of punishment authorised by the East India Company's government in India during the nineteenth century.

In the nineteenth century, a new sub-sect or cult of *dacoits* involving ritual strangulation emerged as a great threat for travellers on highways. 'Thugs' or 'deceivers', as they were called, were recognised as a separate brand of criminals. Their victims were lured away from the roads with the promise of food and water, taken to a secluded area, robbed, and then strangled. These thugs were often referred to as '*phansigar*' ('*phansi*' means to be hanged by the noose, while '*phansigar*' roughly translates as the one who kills by strangulation with a noose). They acquired the reputation of being fanatics, as they would kill as part of a sacrifice to the goddess Kali. The killing itself was a rather distinct form of strangulation which always involved strangling with a silk *roomal* (scarf) twist.

Highway robbery was not unique to thugs. Before this, Kazaks were known for highway robbery, as they were mounted bandits, while Budheks were branded as a 'criminal tribe'.

Indian travellers usually formed groups called *kafilas* and journeyed together rather than alone to avoid such bandits. However, at night, they took shelter in *serais*, making them easy targets for highway bandits. Soldiers who were on furlough would return home with large amounts of money, and they would be the prime targets of thugs looking for people to rob.

An enormous body of literature emerged on the issue of highway banditry that exoticised the thugs, depicting them as fierce barbarians. They were said to conduct killings for the sheer 'lust' for blood. However, it has been argued that *thuggee* (highway robberies and murders by thieves) emerged only due to the uncertainties and chaos caused by colonial rule in India.

Initially, the British administration did not respond to *thuggee*, treating it as an ordinary law-and-order issue. But in the 1830s, with the increasing number of killings, the suppression of *thuggee* became one of the priorities of the civil and military servants of the East India Company. Although most thugs were not known to attack Europeans, the sinister manner of their killings and the fear of coming face to face with groups of horse-mounted freebooters were always a concern for travelling memsahibs.

* * *

After the late 1850s, dangers of the road could be avoided through the faster and safer method of railway travel in some cases. Christina S. Bremner, who wrote about her travels in North India, lauded the efforts of the British as the railway circuit expanded over the years: "Before another season begins, the 'Dehlie-Umballa-Kalka' Railway line will be open and the thirty-eight miles dividing Umballa [Ambala] from Kalka will be travelled in a couple of hours in the comfortable carriages of the East Indian Railway." This ensured that they travelled in relative comfort.

Indeed, railway travel was the most feasible (and fastest) option in the nineteenth century, yet it was difficult in its own way. Constance F. G. Cumming was appalled when an Indian man got into the women's carriage because he would not leave his wife, who was observing *purdah*, alone. Moreover, the issue of racial segregation was quite unmanageable. As members of the colonising race, the British were expected to travel by first class and not mingle with the 'native' passengers. E. Augusta King and her husband managed to secure a first-class carriage on the Punjab Northern State Railway, but it was extremely slow. Their carriage had two back windows facing two windows of the cabins for natives. This made King feel extremely uncomfortable, as the Indian passengers stared at them openly and she described feeling as if she was an animal in a zoo. The excessive noise bothered her too since she was ill and was not comfortable while sitting or standing.

What's more, while rail travel spared memsahibs the exposure to the elements that they experienced in wagons and palanquins, it also left them in an enclosed space that was no more comfortable than the bungalows along the road. The sultry weather caused them intense misery on the trains due to the lack of proper facilities. Sometimes, the coaches were hideous and were extremely crammed. Memsahibs despised being cloistered in such closed compartments with rickety windows that did not open. The carriages had a mattress on an upper berth, allowing for one of the two travellers to lie down. These carriages had tanks of water attached to them because of the stifling heat of plains, and women had to frequently put wet cloths on their foreheads to avoid heat stroke. Constance F. G. Cumming wrote that people were frequently lifted from trains due to heat apoplexy, and the threat of death was a well-recognised danger of the heat of India, so much so that railway authorities kept coffins ready at every station to receive dead travellers who had met their end on their long journeys.

Christina S. Bremner grew frustrated because of the frequent delays during her railway journey and wrote: "why won't the train move on and create the much wished for drought, without which we swelter and gasp for air?" It was sweltering in the compartments, and she was acutely uncomfortable. Sometimes, she found aerated water at the stations, but more often than not she had to make do with lukewarm drinks, which made the heat feel worse. By the end of the journey, she was extremely distressed and regularly scolded the *coolies* and bearers.

Inland water travel was another option in India. The British used budgerows (long boats with long cabins, mostly used for travelling along the Ganges) to travel in waterways, and this could be faster than road journeys. The hustle and bustle of the riverbanks presented wondrous views, and memsahibs enjoyed gazing at the vignettes of the country scenes. Sometimes *dhobis* lined the *ghats*, washing linen and beating the clothes on large rocks while singing in chorus.

However, unfortunately for the worn-out and dust-covered memsahibs, these dreamy drifting little boats could often be as difficult as *dak* travel. The planks on the floor of the boat would mostly be rickety, and if anyone shifted even slightly, the whole boat could tilt precariously. The matting that covered the resting area would hang low so that it would not be possible to stand upright. If the currents were strong, it would rock the budgerows, and the constant bobbing loosened the luggage. A memsahib's parrot cage crashed into the water and almost went under, but she managed to catch hold of it before it was swept away. The parakeets, to whom she was quite attached, were safe although the water got into their throats, and they coughed and sneezed for a long time. In addition, boats were often not able to withstand violent storms that brewed up in the larger rivers. If it rained, the passengers would get completely drenched and sit inside shivering behind a flimsy partition.

When E. Augusta King travelled to Islamabad from Srinagar by boat in 1881, the journey took 3 days. The river winds were dreadful even though the scenery was breath-taking, and knowing how tumultuous it could get during storms, the travellers were constantly anxious. Apart from that, there was the fear of fire because of the portable stove and kerosene lamps on the boat. One night, they accidently set the mat roof on fire with the heat of the lamp. If they had not noticed in time, the whole boat would have been set ablaze, as the fire had already charred one of the poles.

Sometimes, the boats had to be anchored for several nights because of the tides. Emily Eden's boat was blown onto the banks once, and they had to anchor until the wind went down. She lost her trunks of clothes because the current was so violent that it upset the furniture stacked on-board. She later found out that her trunk was lying at the bottom of the sea. The waters near the coastlines could indeed be extremely choppy sometimes, and the boats beat about uncontrollably making landing extremely difficult.

The boats were usually also filthy and stank abominably. Memsahibs realised that even the smallest boats invariably had pests. Isabel Savory wrote that the *kishteys* (oblong boats usually used in Jammu and Kashmir) and *doonghas* (vernacular for a kind of houseboat also known as floating houses, which were used by some locals in Kashmir) that she travelled in overnight were filled with rats that kept scurrying across her bed clothing.

There were sometimes worse encroachers than rodents lurking on boats in the rivers. Robberies were common even on the waterways. River *dacoits* regularly attacked lone boats, especially if there were no men on-board. Harriet Tytler's aunt and another lady, Miss Menzies, were travelling in their boat one night when they heard music and "tomtomming", which seemed like a wedding party. This put them on their guard because they knew about *dacoits*, and Miss Menzies went out to check. They could see a boat with a wedding party on it, and just as they neared it, several robbers jumped in. Miss Menzies quickly donned her brother's hat, hoping that they would think that a man was on-board with them, but the robbers were not intimidated. Scared, she jumped overboard, and poor Harriet's aunt followed suit. She would have drowned if she had not been dragged out by her *ayah*. They spent the night in wet clothes on the banks, watching the boat drift down the river and disappear. When it was recovered later, it was found to be gutted of everything.

Ultimately, even the most nomadic memsahibs realised that undertaking journeys in India was not always rewarding. Sometimes the journeys were completely exhausting, and sometimes the destinations did not fulfil expectations. It was not unusual for them to express annoyance as their hopes were dashed because the views were not as majestic as they had imagined or heard, or the cities not as imperial. Nonetheless, they continued to travel, and wrote about their experiences with extreme alacrity, regularly making their own private discoveries in India.

5

"THIS COUNTREE VEREE JUNGLEY, MEES SAHIB!"

CAMPING, HUNTING, AND THE GREAT OUTDOORS

An enormous black bear cantered noiselessly out of the nullah… I en by the bushes. I had not even time to align the sights, and hardly expected to hit… When we had gone about a couple of hundred yards something stirred in front of us, and we suddenly saw the shaggy black head and shoulders of the bear standing behind a rock some thirty yards off. He had evidently heard or smelt us, and was moving his head to and fro and peering in our direction. A steady shot at the point of his shoulder rolled him over, to all appearances lifeless, and Rahman, in a state of excitement whipped out his knife, and rushed forward to take off the skin. He was a little premature, for, when we were within two or three yards, the bear suddenly struggled to his legs, and very clearly showed that he did not mean to part with his hide just yet. But a bullet through the side of his head finished him off, and he fell on his face, stone dead.

– Nora Gardner, 1895

By the nineteenth century, British women in India were travelling more than ever, both alone as well as in groups of friends and family. Apart from their annual retreats to hill stations and their extensive and often laborious travels through the mainland to join their husbands at postings, they also enjoyed spending time in nature and exploring different parts of the country. They would tie up their skirts with loops and strings to help them walk easily on uneven terrain, wear gauze veils to protect their delicate skin, and thoroughly enjoy their long treks and jungle adventures. They also looked forward to their periodic camping trips, where bonfires crackled, and hunting tales were told by deadly marksmen.

Some memsahibs got so accustomed to travel that they began to prefer it to all other activities. One lady felt that a "gipsy-life" offered the best kind of joy, as the scattered groups of merrymaking people enjoyed each other's company while sitting in circles around blazing fires, singing cheerful songs with the backdrop of majestic mountains and lush greens. The panoramas offered a great visual treat, and the experience of such camps made for beautiful memories that lasted a lifetime.

Emily Eden wrote about a friend who was completely addicted to outdoor adventures: "it is the only life she likes, never to be two days in the same place; just as if we ever were in '*a place*'". This lady's husband, however, was not as adventurous as her and suffered greatly because of her wanderlust. He wanted to make a whole pyramid of tent pins, put the flagstaff in the centre with tents neatly packed around, and then set fire to the whole thing because he thought it would be an act of humanity as nobody would have to undergo all the discomfort and boredom that he had undergone!

Indeed, some memsahibs had grown fond of the "wildlife symphony swelling and falling" in the jungles of India. They liked the familiar chorus of animal and bird calls, the orchestra of myriad insects, the silences of wilderness, and all the vagaries of forest life in India. The droning of the tree beetles, the ghostly jungles, the star-speckled skies, and the occasional calls of animals in the distance were all too irresistible to them.

However, they knew that deadly creatures crept in the darkness, that the soft bristly leaves of bushes were poisonous to touch, and that the rivers they joyfully drifted down were infested with watchful crocodiles. Still, they cheerfully embarked upon long-drawn journeys, one hand holding an umbrella to protect against the sun, and the other controlling the reins of their horse.

"THIS COUNTREE VEREE JUNGLEY, MEES SAHIB!"

The more daring women who lusted after action trailed and hunted wild beasts of prey, and for some of them, like Monica Campbell Martin, whose husband was a forest officer, chancing upon wild animals was so frequent while camping that it became a habit to carry a loaded shotgun at all times, slung over one shoulder or tucked under one arm and balanced on the nook of the elbow.

Aux Belles Étoiles: Camping in Style

We landed at five, and drove... through immense crowds and much dust to our camp. The first evening of tents, I must say, was more uncomfortable than I had ever fancied. Everybody kept saying, 'What a magnificent camp!' and I thought I never had seen such squalid, melancholy discomfort. G., F., and I have three private tents, and a fourth... leading from one tent to the other. Each tent is divided into bedroom, dressing-room, and sitting-room. They have covered us up in every direction, just as if we were native women... there is a wall of red cloth, eight feet high, drawn all round our enclosure, so that... we see nothing but a crimson wall. Inside each tent were our beds—one leaf of a dining-table and three cane chairs. Our pittarrahs and the camel-trunks were brought in; and in about half an hour, the Nazir came to say they must all, with our books, dressing-cases, &c., be carried off to be put under the care of a sentry, as nothing is safe in a tent from the dacoits... The canvas flops about, and it was very chilly in the night... it feels open-airish and unsafe. They say everybody begins by hating their tents and ends by loving them, but at present, I am much prepossessed in favour of a house.

– Emily Eden, 1866

Camping, whether exclusively for leisure or as part of military encampments, was one of the chief highlights of travel activities in India. Luxuriant as it could often be, it could also be extremely fast-paced and unpredictable. There could be sudden storms or even outbreaks of illnesses, although it was sometimes perfectly executed with no hurdles at all. During such times, the festivities of the night could stretch on until 2 am, just 2 hours before the servants would begin to pack up the camp equipment for the next day's travels.

When marching with a regiment, multiple tents were required. These tents could be expensive, and the finest kind were said to be made in Jabalpur, costing up to 400 rupees in the nineteenth century. The larger tents had to be carried by camels in most cases due to bulk and size. The smaller tents were about 6 feet square, and had light cots, bedding, carpets, a basin, and some tin boxes for storage called *pitarrahs or banghies*. If proper arrangements were made, a camp could have separate tents for sleeping and lounging. These would be airy and spacious, furnished with rugs, wall hangings, curtains for privacy, tables, chairs, and beds. The tents were usually covered in gaily hued chintz, the floors were well covered with rugs, and a convenient space in the rear was sectioned off for offices and bathrooms. There were movable stoves like the Spanish *brasseros*, and there was an Indian contraption called the *chillum chee*, which was a copper basin mounted on an iron tripod and filled with red wood, which diffused warmth throughout the tent. The single-pole tent was twice as convenient if it was first divided down the centre with a pole and curtains to screen off the beds. The interiors were made to resemble bungalows in order to mitigate the feel of the wilderness that lay directly outside.

Memsahibs were especially keen on maintaining the semblance of home while living in tents. Their seemingly natural propensity to plan everything in detail, combined with their inclination for extravagance in the Raj, meant that life in camps could be unexpectedly grand. The temporary tents and settlements had several facilities. The British were well acquainted with life under canvas and managed to make them resemble European marquees. In the evenings, the white canvas spread over a forest clearing amidst trees and mountains, with several fires flickering in the wind, made for a charming sight. At night, deep male voices sang folk songs as the firelight gleamed on the circle of sleepless faces. The organ-like notes of 'Shenandoah' flowed to the nearby river, in the shadow of the trees.

Since camping was frequent, the campers found ways to incorporate their normal daily existence into it and made it like the kind of *fête champêtre* that they were used to back home in England. For this reason, they carried various accoutrements from their domestic lives such as china, silverware, candlesticks, and even portable gramophones. Anything that could not be acquired within the range of 50 to 60 miles was brought into camp on the heads of an army of *coolies*. It came to be said, as mentioned by Isabel Savory, that the "track of the Britisher across the East is marked by soda-water bottles and kerosene oil-tins". Memsahibs were hardly ever in want of the conveniences of life during their sojourns in the densest of forests. The food was packed in leather cases and carried by about thirty *coolies*, each carrying their own share of the luggage. Bottles of brandy, sherry, whiskey, and wine were a staple. Compressed food such as preserved vegetables, pickles, cocoa, and syrups were essential.

If they were travelling with regiments, even the *bazaar* sometimes accompanied them, and fresh bread, meat, milk, and fruits were easily available. Special arrangements were made for filtered water because drinking water was not always available. Cold provisions of tea and Seltzer water were a particular favourite on trips, and hot grog at night was favoured in cold weather. Fresh fruits and vegetables were not always found on the way, so crates of canned food were carried to keep up the standard of cooking in camps. Tea and coffee were considered absolute essentials, and carried in canisters, along with items such as pepper, salt, sago, nuts, jams, pickles, and chutneys.

Memsahibs also carried tins of preserved provisions such as julienne and mock turtle soup, beef, peas, and carrots. If they were travelling during Christmas, they carried puddings and cakes, especially if they were travelling with their children. Plum puddings did not spoil too quickly if they were boiled in a round tin with a cover and kept that way. They could be sliced and fried before eating. But if milk and eggs were readily available, cakes could be baked quite easily on the roadside. For this, a small fire would be made in a pit, and when the ground got hot, the fire would be swept off. Then a few sticks would be placed in the hot pit, and a brass basin would be turned over the pudding and covered with hot embers.

The British were aware that the Indian servants' religious sentiments had to be kept in mind while staying in close proximity to them in camps to avoid unnecessary discord. Emily Eden wrote that they could not kill a cow in front of Sikhs, so they refrained from having beefsteak or veal cutlets and ate simpler meals. Nevertheless, to eliminate the frugalities that were associated with the long journeys, food was always sumptuous. In fact, mealtimes were surprisingly fancy affairs, and the sahibs and memsahibs preferred to dress up formally and dined under the evening skies wherever possible. They wanted to feel as much 'at home' as was possible while travelling through alien terrains.

A cooking machine, invented by Colonel Saly, became popular in the mid-nineteenth century, and this was extremely useful for preparing meals while travelling. It had two oval blocks containing the saucepans and kettles, which could be put in all at once with oil, spirit, or fire. It could be carried by a single *coolie* with the light burning so that cooking could be done anytime en route at short notice. Most of the time during camp, special dishes were prepared that were more feasible to cook outdoors or in case of scarcity of ingredients. The Burdwan stew was a staple in camp, and the 'Shikaree' was a regular camp sauce. A curry dish, 'Sudden Death' was a great camp speciality and was made with fowl (mostly poultry) that had been cooked within 20 minutes of being killed.

However, sometimes it was not possible to be as lavish while en route. There was the constraint of time, and it was not always possible to get a proper supply of fresh food from the locals. At times, meals could be as basic as biscuits and milk.

In fact, camp life could be easy or difficult, according to the campers' preparation. For instance, a basic rule was that a good supply of candles should be carried as well as lamp oil (which had to be carried carefully) because the forests could be extremely dark if the sky was overcast or if it was a moonless night. A Hitchcock lamp was useful because it required neither a globe nor a chimney, though a shade might be used. Kerosene oil was to be found in almost every village, but it was preferable to carry it in regular tin canisters.

Despite the scale of the arrangements, some of the expeditions could become unexpectedly difficult. The simplest of things such as soap, stationery, candles, quinine, chlorodyne, scissors, needles, thread, and powdered alum could become great luxuries while in transit; this was not always because of scarcity but sometimes because they would be packed away and difficult to locate in the enormous quantities of baggage. However, the sahibs and memsahibs did not want to compromise on the comfort of their stay in tents and made extra efforts to avoid problems of any kind if they could help it. Ironically, most writings by the memsahibs stress that living in tents was not always as comfortable and glamorous as was the popular perception.

Sometimes, the location of camps could be unsuitable. Once, a memsahib was horrified to realise that her campsite was located in the middle of a railway station on one side, a dirty pond on the second, a filthy prison on the third, and a graveyard on the fourth. When she protested, she was rebuffed by other campers who claimed that all the sahibs came there.

Moreover, sometimes there would be unwanted visitors in the night. The memsahibs often woke up to the sound of 'fairy feet', which were large mountain mice swarming all over the tents including over the top of them. Rains also posed a regular problem and could easily turn into deluges that could wash away the tents. Wet weather in hilly areas could be extremely uncomfortable, and the canvas of the tents could be soaked like a sponge. Even though the water might not leak inside, if someone accidentally touched the top of the tent with their head, streams of water trickled down. During such times, puddles formed around the tent and a ditch had to be dug to allow for drainage.

If the torrential rains did not abate, the campers would have to reach out to the *lambardar* (headman) of the nearest village to ask for shelter in a bungalow. They would then sit with their feet in hot water for fear of catching cold, which they were prone to do in the great outdoors, although avoiding illness was not always possible. The strenuous journeys, coupled with the lack of supplies and harsh climatic conditions, often weakened travellers. Emily Eden felt extremely exhausted during camping and wrote in her memoirs:

> We march early each morning; so after a racking night—and I really can't impress upon you the pain in my Indian bones—it was necessary at half past five—just when one might by good luck have fallen asleep—to get up by candle-light and put on bonnet and cloak and—one's things in short, to drive over no road.

She developed "Gugga fever" at the riverside, for which the doctor put leeches on her. Along with her, another travel companion also fell ill. They had to alter their routes so that they could get some rest on the way and recover from the illness that had weakened their bodies. In her letters, she wrote that all of India had fever in it: "you ought to see the hard-ships of a camp life. I wonder what the ships of a camp life are, which are not hard-ships?"

* * *

The men and women of the Raj were passionate about memorialising the magnificence of the 'empire on the move', which they did through photographs, paintings, and vivid accounts about their travels in the 'opulent East'. They travelled in large cavalcades, with complete pomp and pageantry of gilded palanquins, glittering silks, and vibrantly caparisoned camels and elephants. While embarking on expeditions, showcasing the splendour of the empire and its workers was considered necessary, for the visual appeal and for awing the 'natives' of the villages they passed through.

During most travels, the British moved with a substantial group of domestic helpers and *coolies* to manage the vast quantities of luggage they liked to carry on their journeys. The army of servants, dressed in white and swarming around the sahibs and memsahibs, not only made their journeys comfortable and lavish but also indicated the wealth and power of the British in India. Apart from the *coolies* who were meant to carry the load, multiple servants had their own separate roles. The head butler, washerman, watercarrier, bearer, and horsemen were extremely crucial for the smooth functioning of the camp life of the sahibs and memsahibs. The number of servants could range from anywhere between twenty to fifty, including the palanquin-bearers and carriage-drivers. E. Augusta King's entourage included six servants and twenty *coolies* carrying the baggage, not counting the palanquin-bearers and a lady's maid.

Sometimes, large retinues were deliberately organised to ensure safety and security in transit. Since life in the Raj was risky and unpredictable, larger groups could keep danger at bay as well as helping reduce the difficulties of the harsh climate and rough terrain. Emma Roberts' cortege was most elaborate: she took twelve camels, and her train consisted of a *khansama*, three *khitmatgars*, a *sirdar-bearer* (head bearer), a tailor, a washerman, a watercarrier, a cook and torchbearers, twelve bearers, *claishees* (men to pitch the tents), men to carry the suitcases, innumerable *coolies*, and a number of female attendants.

Servants were most crucial on such trips. No matter how long the journey or how early the departure, they were all too ready to conduct their duties. The bugles sounded early in the mornings, and the packing began. This involved meticulous pre-planning on the part of the women: if they were marching in the morning, everything had to be packed except for items like the teapot and cups, which could be packed quickly after breakfast. With children there, a large kettle and the medicine chest would be packed last. The tent pegs were loosened at the first bugle, so that there was a warning before they were removed. Even the pegs had to be counted in case they were stolen or lost.

To the great annoyance of the memsahibs, because of the hubbub early in the mornings, the luggage was always mixed up, and the boxes, which contained all the sundry items of camp life, would often present the most curious mix of domesticity. If the memsahibs were not careful, the servants would keep the plum cakes next to the sardine oil container so that the cakes would be saturated with oil by the time the next stopover arrived. The silver-topped bottles from the dressing bag would end up in kettles, which would be rolled up in skirts, and knives and spoons and cigars would wind up in the sponge bag. Once the servants left a memsahib's mackintosh coat outside while at camp, and several crows came and perched on top of it, pecking as they do upon sheep.

Keeping order amongst the army of servants was a source of great tedium for campers. It was customary for memsahibs to lord over their multiple *coolies* and servants, but managing them while on the way to ensure there were no slackers could be tricky. Still, they needed to keep strictly vigilant because there could sometimes be misbehaviour if the servants were not checked. Once, during the festival of Holi, E. Augusta King's servants and even the *syces* got extremely drunk, presenting a major inconvenience because of the delay it caused. The memsahibs even had to ensure that the luggage was evenly distributed amongst them, because some carried the bags on their heads, some had them on their backs, and some slung them over the shoulder. It was not always possible to make them alter their position, so it required a lot of thought and arrangement.

Memsahibs mostly liked to keep an eye on their luggage in case something got damaged or went missing. Advice manuals for memsahibs on packing luggage for camps made recommendations: "It is another camp axiom, that not a single box should be carried that has no use even when empty." For instance, if thin boxes, divided into two or three partitions, were packed inside the bags, the china would travel far more safely, and the boxes could be used as cupboards. E. Augusta King saw that the violent jolting on the road had loosened the bars of her birdcage, and the parrot had escaped. Once, Emily Eden's luggage was mounted on an elephant, and was sent to the port by mistake, leaving her without a change of clothes or any provisions for several hours. Thus, the luggage had to be sent several hours before the campers so that it could reach the next stop in time for the arrival of the sahibs and memsahibs, considering that there could be unexpected delays on the way.

For those who were travelling with officers, shortage of sentries could prove to be a problem. Emily Eden noted that a Colonel ordered off half of the regiment that had come to escort them to Allahabad, and 'Colonel B' sent word that he had only 300 men to do the work of 1,000 men. The sentries were withdrawn from all the private tents, and all the silver *howdahs* and wagons that were loaded with shawls, jewellery, arms, and so on from the *Tosha Khanna* ("the collection of native presents made to us") were brought into the middle of the street. She wrote, "I should have liked to have robbed it for fun".

Such disorganised behaviour could be quite risky because the campers could easily be looted. Nora Gardner's *ayah* was robbed while she was in a moving carriage. In the dead of the night, a hand appeared through the curtains, and grabbed the blanket right off her. She explained it to her memsahib the next morning in her broken English:

> Memsahib, I fast asleep feel my blanket pulled. I think it slipping; I pull, and see one man pulling too. Then I call to *ghari-wallah* (driver), and say, 'I robbed'. He say, 'You dream'. Then I see one hand put in carriage, and take my beautiful brass mug all made of copper. Then, Memsahib, I give *ghari-wallah* one push. He fell on road. I say, 'You go find my blanket; you not come back'. So he go, and says he sees man run away very fast. 'You not get your blanket again.'

While at camp, visits by travelling *jadoogars* (magicians) were common, but their tricks were not always received with pleasure. While rope tricks and ordinary disappearance acts were acceptable to most, the basket trick, which was particularly gory, ended up scaring some memsahibs. In this trick, a petite girl would be made to climb into a basket, and the magician would plunge a sword into it, making blood spurt through the wicker, even as the girl emitted loud screams of agony. In the end, the basket would be shown to be empty, and the girl would appear from elsewhere completely unscathed. No doubt, such violent tricks added to the thrill of camping in the jungles, but some ended up disapproving of them, speculating that the magicians used mass hypnosis to trick the audience (Nevile, 206–7).

These were not the only unwanted visitors in camps. The Pathans and the Pashto communities, called the Afridis, were known by the British for being the swiftest rifle thieves and often snuck into the tents of sleeping men and women to steal as many rifles as they could. They could easily draw them out from under the blankets of sleeping officers, who kept their rifles as close as possible, precisely to avoid them being stolen at night.

Then there were thieves, different from bandits but no less menacing, who followed marching regiments and travelling parties. These men were closely shaved and oiled their bodies in order to slip out of a grasp if caught. They would usually be armed with a dagger, which they did not hesitate to use. Such thieves crept into the tents naked, so as to be unnoticeable in the dark, and tickled the sleeper with a feather to make them turn onto the other side, upon which they literally drew the clothes off their backs.

A lady, Mrs. Beckett, woke up one night in her camp and found that she had no covering over her, not even her night clothes. Panicking, she called out to her *ayah* in the dark, and the poor *ayah* found that even she was stark naked. The *ayah* had to creep to the other memsahib's tent to ask her for clothes. Although this was an extremely grave incident, it made for a hilarious camp anecdote and was retold again and again by the mortified lady's fellow campers.

Another time, a memsahib woke up just before a thief was about to make off with all her possessions. He had tied everything up in a bundle, ready to be carried off at an opportune moment when the camp was quiet.

Thieves also came into camps to steal cattle. The thieves would sometimes put shoes that were facing backwards on the hooves of the horses or cows so that it would appear that the travellers had moved in the opposite direction to where they had actually gone. The ingeniousness of the thieves was remarkable.

Given the exhilarating and unique experiences that camp life offered, the ending of long camping journeys always gave rise to mixed feelings of relief and regret. The memsahibs, while perhaps glad that the gruelling journey had finally ended, were also disappointed at the dispersal of their fellow campers. Emily Eden looked wistfully at the breaking up of the camp after her adventures in 1840. The scene was of utter chaos: camp followers asking for rupees in every direction, boats being loaded and more wanted, all horses and furniture being sold off at the stables, and the crowd, which covered five acres, slowly dispersing. To celebrate the successful camping trip, there would be a ball at the end, and the campers would go to the steamer the next day. Boatloads of trunks would go in the morning, and many more would make their way to Calcutta in carriages or on horses, which would arrive a fortnight later.

Still, even for the travel-loving Eden, the end was a definite relief. She was glad to return home after spending days in those "wretched tents", as she returned to her "dear little villa at Kensington Gore".

Shikar in the 'Land of Promise'

When I first saw him, he was some distance below me, galloping round a slope, off towards his cave again. I waited for a space clear from undulating ground and rocks and took my shot. He spoke, but galloped on, untouched as I thought... The panther had done another twenty yards or so. I raised my rifle, but before I could fire again over he went, head over heels, rolling down the hill, stone dead.

I was never, I think, so pleased at anything before. And what a fluke! We measured and found that he was over 120 yards away, and I might have shot another forty times and never have hit him once... Several of them ran on ahead up to the panther, not staying to throw stones at him from a distance to make sure that he was really dead. I told them how well they had beaten—so they had—and what a good [setup] it was to have managed to beat an animal over that difficult lie of country anywhere near me. We measured him—7 ft. 2 in.—and they carried him back to the village to be skinned.

– Mrs. W.W. Baillie, 1921

The British discovered *shikar* (hunting) when the sport-loving princes of India introduced them to it. Various rajas and maharajas had built hunting lodges across India and established hunting as a standard leisurely pastime for royalty. When the British came, they decided that if it was fit for the kings, it was fit for them, and they ritualised it as their own favourite outdoor adventure-sport.

The *shikar* (hunt) was a thrilling exercise, involving long journeys into untamed wilderness, tracking sightings and carcasses, studying pugmarks, following trails, and sitting in wait for the animals to emerge from their lairs. The fecund forests of India were swarming with a remarkable variety of wildlife, making them a paradise for hunters. The heat, humidity, topography, insects, and unexpected predators in the jungles were a great source of wonderment and enchantment to sahibs and memsahibs alike. The great element of risk only added to the thrill of the sport.

Moreover, the British were aware of the value of their kill. They took great pride in collecting various mementos of the formidable beasts they had killed and passionately displayed their achievements. One has only to glance through photographs of such hunts to know how much they invested time and resources in *shikar*. In fact, they meticulously archived their hunts not just through photographs, written records, and official documentation but also by taking back game trophies in the form of claws, fangs, heads, or full skins. In June 1833, Lieutenant Clarke of the 26th Native Infantry, Bombay, travelled with his servants for field sports; he had wanted to hunt black bucks or hogs but encountered a pack of six lions. He shot a lioness, mortally wounding her, and when she returned to attack them, passed his rifle to a soldier who had been in his service for 10 years in an attempt to tease his servants. However, the man missed his mark, and the lioness attacked the Lieutenant. When the lioness was finally killed, he took her skull as a trophy of his victory.

It was perhaps unconventional in England, but in India, British women regularly accompanied men on the riskiest of expeditions, simply to witness the thrill of 'oriental' sports. Due to the mixed crowd in camping sites, the atmosphere would be extremely lively. The sahibs and memsahibs, in their khaki hunting outfits, mingled gaily over drinks with the maharajas and nawabs, who were resplendent in their colourful robes and turbans. The animals they rode would be dressed in brilliantly hued drapes and petticoats, looking stately against the backdrop of the thick jungles.

Constance F. G. Cumming marvelled at the impressive row of fourteen elephants, formed in a line to beat the tall grass, with the gentlemen mounted on their backs, ready to gallop in pursuit of wild boars and tigers. At night, there would be gay parties and dancing, even as wolves and jackals howled from the thickets, not daring to approach the riotous campers. The revelries were one of the prime attractions of such hunting expeditions. British travel writer and poet Emma Roberts declared that the

> truest enjoyment of field sports is offered to small parties of Europeans, who blend intellectual tastes with the love of the chase, who, while sojourning in the forest, delight to make themselves acquainted with the manners and habits of its indigenous people, and who not entirely bent upon butchery, vary their occupations by devoting themselves to botanical and geological pursuits.

It was said that in the jungles, males had it all their own way right down to the insects: "Happy the cicada's life, because he has a silent wife". But it was not so for British women, who went to hunt like the men did. Some memsahibs who were skilled at it, like Emily

Eden, often led hunting groups. Sometimes, they indulged in the more dangerous *shikars*, such as hunting wild hogs, tigers, leopards, and bears, often without British companions, much to the surprise of others in the camp as well as the Indian servants and locals. Some of them even wrote accounts of their *shikars* and everything else about India they witnessed on the way. Once, Emily Eden went on foot with 'Captain X' (she rarely named people in her accounts) and shot an antelope on one of her excursions.

'Howdah' shikar, with hunters mounted on elephants, was one of the more regal and traditional modes of hunting and was only meant for the aristocracy or high-ranking class of officers. Such expeditions were extravagant, and were relatively safe, so women were usually present. Memsahibs enjoyed riding on top of elephants, especially because the grandstand view was splendid. Bird-shooting activities on elephants were one of their most favoured sports. Some birds, like parrots, were considered destructive to crops, so killing them was also in tandem with the government's agenda. Emily Eden accompanied several such expeditions, with companions who shot quails and partridges.

One of the faster and more exciting sports that memsahibs enjoyed was 'pig-sticking'. Hogs were not just wily and fast, but also extremely aggressive once provoked. Hunting them involved chasing after them at breakneck gallop. Memsahibs had become quite practised in this and displayed great skill. Isabel Savory and her friend who loved pig-sticking were invited by Maharaja Jagatjit Singh Bahadur for hunting during peak season near Kapurthala, around 1900. During a hard chase, the friend fell off her horse into a ditch, and the enraged boar came charging towards her with its sharp tusks raised. With no time to do anything, she threw herself face down so that the tusks ripped her coat and left a gash on the small of her back. Still, the injury was not enough to scare her, and she mounted her horse again and went in steady pursuit of her prey. When everyone objected and said she needed to rest, she rode away saying, "I shall have all eternity to rest in".

Memsahibs also participated in the hunting of carnivores and wild cats, which was trickier, but immensely thrilling and action-packed. After spending time in the wild, they had learnt the signs that helped a hunter: the crow in a tree looking down at something and cawing meant a beast was at hand, and the grazing herd of deer that caught a scent on the wind meant that a bear was nearby. If a wild animal were around, the monkeys in the jungle would emit a cacophony of screeches, helping the sportsmen alter their course. Anna H. Leonowens described how during her tour of Mahabaleshwar Hills in the 1880s, the Indian hunters were always at hand to lead the adventures into the dens of tigers, panthers, bears, and wolves.

However, encounters with big cats and other predators, even when not intended, were quite likely in remote areas near forests. Mrs. Leopold Paget was due to go for a hyena hunt, but the animal was somehow captured beforehand. Later on, news came that it had escaped. One night, when she and her husband were getting ready for bed, a stranger rushed in through the door to inform them that while passing by, he had seen a wild beast on the roof of their bungalow. Her husband immediately ran out with a loaded revolver and searched the premises, still in his gown and slippers, but could not find it.

It was not unusual for creatures to prowl around residential areas after dark since hill stations or rocky hilly regions were infested with all kinds of wild cats, and black panthers were common on lonely winding roads through dense tropical forests. But hunting panthers was quite exclusive, and even the best tiger hunters rarely had a black panther or leopard skin to show. These creatures were particularly elusive, and if a party of hunters wished to hunt one, they usually arranged for it to be captured beforehand, and then released from the cage for them to pursue. Even then, the *shikaris* had to struggle to catch up on horseback. Sometimes, to add to the challenge, spears were used instead of rifles.

In 1893, Nora Gardner, who was a writer and photographer best known for her rather unembellished accounts of Indian camp life, went with her husband to accompany Maharaja Jey Singh on a hunt, for which a panther was released from a cage and then pursued. When they tried to pin it with a spear, the beast broke the lance clean in two with its sharp jaws. The Maharaja was unable to kill a second panther while hunting with a gun, and so he released dogs to go after it.

Leopards were cunning cats and equally tricky, so they were meant only for the best *shikaris*. Leopard-*shikar* had to be done at night, as they were nocturnal creatures. Sitting up for them required patience because the hunter usually had to first find the carcass of an animal they had maimed, to which the feline creatures were known to return later. Sometimes, they did not return for several nights in a row, by which time the carcass would become putrid and emit foul odours.

Florence Marryat and her husband, who was an officer of the British Army, were travelling with their close friend when a cheetah killed their friend's dog. The officer wanted to avenge his beloved pet, and they set out for a hunting expedition; however, Marryat was attacked by the beast, although she managed to shoot it square in the chest.

Amongst the animals hunted in the Raj, the most popular were tigers. If these hunts were to be undertaken in the company of nawabs and local rajas, the camps would be suitably lavish for the presence of royalty. There would be great red campfires, a multitude of servants to cook and clean, and large tents with all kinds of provisions. Challenging as it was, those who had killed tigers could earn the title of the 'tiger-slayer'. The sahibs and memsahibs were always looking to increase their tiger kill count. They looked forward to hearing about any tiger infestation around the areas they visited. A record was set by a lady, Mrs. Laurie Johnson, in the Jalpaiguri Duars, where she killed a tiger measuring up to 12 feet—the coat of which could be about 13 feet.

Hunting tigers often involved constructing platforms on treetops called *machans*, where the hunters took their positions after twilight. Hunters would use a bait (any kind of cattle or the remains of the tiger's previous kill—even if it was the remains of a human they had killed) to draw the tiger out of its den. However, such hunts could become life-threatening as tigers could leap up to the platforms where the *shikaris* sat waiting.

The most danger-loving hunters went on foot. They had to have immense discipline and skill and knew every sign and trick, such as the fact that when a tiger was around, there was usually a swarm of birds hovering over its previous kill, to which the tiger was sure to return later. A wake of vultures circling above the carcass was enough to tell the hunters to begin. When Isabel Savory went hunting, they had a narrow escape:

> The tiger moved on. I sat with my rifle at full cock, but he went up to Captain F.'s tree, looked up, saw him, gave a fierce growl, and then stood still about ten yards off. A loud detonation followed; but Captain F. must have made a poor shot—he hit him behind, much too far back, the bullet going down to his hock. The tiger looked magnificent still—he stood on a little knoll, lashing his tail and looking vindictively up into the tree. At one and the same moment Captain F. and myself fired; somehow or other we both missed him. This was rather too much. In one moment, like a flash, the tiger darted round, deliberately galloped at the tree, sprang about halfway up into its lowest branches, and, assisted by the natural oblique inclination of the trunk, swarmed up to the machan as quickly and easily as a cat. It was a terrible moment, one of those of which we pray that they may be few and far between; most of us can lay a finger on two or three such moments in our lives. Poor Capt. F., both barrels fired and helpless, had in desperation sprung to his feet, his hands on the side of the machan. Either the tiger's teeth or his claws tore his fingers all down the back of it to the bone… With my last barrel I fired. There was no time for a long and steady aim; but as the smoke cleared away—what relief—the tiger had dropped to the ground. With nine lives—cat-like—he was not dead; he walked off and disappeared.

If hunts were hosted by maharajas, they were conducted with the help of beaters known as *hunqahs*, who drove the tigers towards the hunters on elephant-back, to ease the process and ensure the kill. This too was rife with danger because an elephant could sometimes panic and begin rushing wildly at the sight of a tiger, endangering the lives of those mounted on its back. Tigers were also known to attack *shikaris* on elephants by pouncing halfway up to grab a limb and drag the hunter down. Sometimes, an elephant was thrown into a rage and would bend down over the tiger, attempting to pin it down with its tusk or crush it with its weight, thereby tipping the *howdah* over and threatening to throw the sportsmen off into the tiger's jaws. Monica Campbell Martin's fiercest of hunting elephants, Temi Bahadur (meaning Temi, the Great One), would dash at leopards and crush them within seconds. Funnily enough, neither Temi nor any other elephants could face a porcupine. Its rapine quills could hurt their delicate trunks, and once when a porcupine scuttled towards a line of elephants, they squealed and danced about like a pack of schoolchildren.

During the Raj period, the practice of hunting had become more than a standard sport or 'pastime' for the British and was co-opted into the work of colonial governance and administration. There was an abundance of wild animals in the country, and the vast and uncharted forests contained many mysteries for the imperialists to solve. But the British wanted to quickly control and 'civilise' the disorderly and mostly unexplored wilderness. This was also one of the principal arguments against bringing in regulations for hunting in India. They believed that hunting animals where there were so many would not harm the ecosystem and would in fact help them tame and conquer the subcontinent more effectively.

Frequently, organised government-sponsored hunting expeditions took on the proportions of extermination drives against animals that had claimed the lives of people or killed cattle. Before the Raj, hunting had never been conducted with the specific aim to eradicate species that were deemed dangerous. But with the British wanting to clear forests of dangerous animals, terms such as 'vermin' and 'pests' came up. Infestations of certain species became understood as an administrative problem due to a threat to life and property and were tackled methodically. Mrs. Paget was in Mhow in 1859 when she heard of a man-eating tiger who had devoured nine villagers. The hunters were attacked by a wild bear but managed to kill the tiger. People often had to light fires outside their homes at night to scare wild beasts away.

Sometimes, if there were attacks in a village that sahibs and memsahibs were passing through, they would take up the role of vigilantes and set about to kill the animal in question. Or if locals knew of sahibs and memsahibs camping near their village, they would gallop to the site to bring news of the sightings. Such hunts by the British were conducted at a personal level to 'protect' the helpless and vulnerable natives from the onslaught of the predators at large. During such times, the entire camp would be thrown into excitement as everybody, including the servants, would run back and forth to saddle the horses and strap the elephants with *howdahs*. A vengeful spirit would run high and could even turn the meekest memsahib into a heroic muzzle-loader who wanted retribution for the slain victims of the given beast. Isabel Savory went off in hot pursuit of the man-eater that had mauled one of the *coolies* in her entourage, much to the amazement of the villagers and her servants. The killing of man-eating tigers was always celebrated by the locals of the regions, with everybody congregating around the carcass to survey the slain beast as the sahib or memsahib *shikari* posed with their rifle over it. Indeed, hunting missions of this kind displayed the machismo of the British, who wanted to project themselves as the 'protectors' and 'saviours' of the weak natives, to awe them with their skill and bravery.

'Glamorous' as they were, *shikars* in hilly areas had their own set of unique complexities. There could be unexpected blizzards that could prevent setting up camp so that the sahibs and memsahibs would shiver in the winds, completely exposed to the elements while struggling with the tents. Moreover, pursuing animals in the hills was a sport in its own right because some creatures could be incredibly elusive. Very often, the sahibs and memsahibs had to hike a long distance on foot, in the forests, to find the right spot. This involved great discipline and skill because the terrain presented its own set of challenges, especially in mountainous regions. Hunting goat-like animals, like the Nilgiri tahr or the ghoral, was particularly difficult, and they had to be stalked for great distances in extremely perilous terrain. While pursuing the quick-footed antelopes, a loose rock could send the *shikari* or his assistants tumbling down the jagged ravines. The high altitude and unpredictable weather made things riskier as sudden gales could even push hunters off balance. Fogs in hilly areas could impede vision, and a single misstep or miscalculation could cost lives. In fact, whether in the hills or in the plains, if a hunter was slow to react or was taken off guard, it could quickly become fatal. One memsahib wrote that an officer was gouged by the tusks of a wild boar, slicing his body from head to toe and inflicting more than fifty wounds.

In hill stations, amongst the more challenging *shikars* was the hunting of mountain bears. Sahibs and memsahibs had to pitch camps along the way as news of a slew of bears came through word of mouth as they passed different areas. Nora Gardner and her husband were passionate about hunting and travelled for days in pursuit of the *bara shikar* (big game). Nora was extremely good at killing bears, and together they collected several bearskins in the mountains near Marbul Pass.

Brown bears were commonly known as *lal bhalu* and *harpat* in Kashmir and were mostly shy and harmless to humans, but the Himalayan black bears were violent and had a sharp sense of smell. While pursuing bears with a local Raja at Alwas, Isabel Savory had to go on a long trek, clambering 6 miles upwards for 5 hours and becoming one of the first European women to penetrate so far into Chamba.

Just as soon as they had walked around a little, taking in the scenery, their *coolie* ran up to tell them, "*This countree veree jungley*, Mees Sahib. *Bhalu*!" A bear they had already shot attacked them, and they managed to finally kill it with their 500-Express hunting rifle before it injured anybody.

Florence Marryat's husband had a rather unusual experience while bear hunting in Secunderabad. He chanced upon three bears sleeping, and when he shot one of them, it attacked the other two thinking they had injured it. Eventually, one escaped, and one of the two remaining bears was killed while fighting the other, even as the *coolies* kept shouting, "*Khabardar, sahib! Khabardar!*" (Beware! Watch out! That is a dangerous creature!). Florence's husband had to do nothing but bring back the skin and bear grease.

Crocodile hunting was also quite common in marshy areas or near riverbanks, but killing crocodiles was complicated because there were only two fatal points and only the .557 and .450 rifles could kill them. Memsahibs would go down the rivers, near their camps, to sit in wait with their rifles ready to shoot. In the dry region of Deoli, in Rajasthan, where the British built an artificial lake in the mid-1850s, spearing crocodiles was common. They could be harpooned from the bow of a flat-bottomed boat. However, in either case, it could be extremely risky as the motionless sahibs and memsahibs on the banks were perfect bait for these reptilian creatures, who could lurk just underneath the river's surface and leap up suddenly, grabbing their prey in their deathly jaws.

Elephant hunting emerged in the nineteenth century but was not too common. This was done mostly in cases where a wild elephant had caused destruction in a village or plantation area, damaging the property or killing people. These were also mostly those elephants who left their herd and became solitary wanderers. They were labelled as 'rogue' and were sometimes responsible for large-scale destruction around villages and settlements. However, elephants were extremely useful and intelligent creatures, and the government preferred to capture them alive. The ivory tusks of elephants, which could be up to 10 feet, were extremely valuable, and were a prized trophy for hunters. The Elephant Preservation Acts of 1873 and 1879 strictly controlled the *shikar* of elephants.

Capturing elephants was another sport. They were mostly kept in *khedder*, which were large enclosures where the great game was captured. Catching them in these *khedders* required great skill and precision, and special arrangements had to be made. First, hunters had to track the herds. Then they would put up tents in a clearing within a few miles of the place where the herd had been found. Several hundred locals would be called, and under the superintendence of experienced officers and hunters, the herd would be driven into a thick patch of jungle by the beating of drums. Then the natives would spread out in a circle surrounding the herd—a circle covering 5 or 6 miles of ground—and construct a makeshift fence of bamboo to prevent the game from escaping, even when suspicious elephants thundered out from inside the thickets. The sahibs and memsahibs would retire to their tents for tea and biscuits while the fence was being built, and once the work was completed, they would ride around it to survey the stockade. By evening, they would take some time for dinner—a scrumptious camp meal—to kick-start the adventure.

Isabel Savory seemed to be one of the memsahibs most passionate about hunting, and specifically called herself "a sportswoman", titling her memoirs *A Sportswoman in India: Personal Adventures and Experiences of Travel in Known and Unknown India*, which showed her commitment to the sport. She was both nervous and excited when she went on the expedition to capture elephants around the year 1900. Once it got dark, and they were ready to begin the process, bonfires were made around the stockade. By midnight, as watchers walked around with flaming torches, the excitement mounted with the piercing trumpeting of the beasts trapped inside. And then, the elephants appeared, one by one, charging straight towards the fence, and were immediately met with a shower of missiles, forcing them to retreat because of injuries. The hunters waited for the next one, snacking on cheroots, sleepless and anxious. By daybreak, nearly sixty elephants had been secured. And by the afternoon, the palisade was fortified, and after some days, the *khedder*—an enclosure of about 100 yards in diameter—was ready. When it was constructed, all the hunters gathered again, and hundreds and thousands of beaters began the beat to drive the herd into the *khedder*.

Isabel wrote that a mother elephant and her calf appeared, and the mother charged towards one of the sahibs, who had to kill her with an eight-bore Greener and ten drams, when she was almost at his feet. Killing elephants required a shot to the brain, and it was essential to get as close to the elephant as possible before aiming. The entire herd was eventually captured and made to mingle inside the pound with tamed elephants who had their own *mahout*. The tame elephants were used to gradually separate each wild elephant one by one from the rest of the herd, allowing the *noosers* (those who placed nooses) to pass ropes and chains around the hind legs of the captive elephants to constrain them until they were trained into submission.

Monica Campbell Martin loved elephants and had several of them. She wrote that they were gentle creatures who could be extremely faithful, sweet-tempered, and frolicsome once tamed. Isabel said she had been friends with elephants since her first experience of capturing them. She had a beloved elephant whom she named 'Jemima'.

Other large animals that were regularly hunted were the wild bison and rhinoceros. The bison was sought after because of its horns as well as for the meat, which was a delicacy.

Rhinos were known as a trophy animal because of the rarity of the kill, which required specialised skill and elaborate arrangements. Rhino horns were sold for large sums and were sent out from the borders of India to China as they were believed to have magical properties. It was said that Indian princes particularly coveted them and would keep one under their thrones as a symbol of fecundity. But by the early twentieth century, with growing concerns about wildlife conservancy and excessive poaching of endangered species, shooting rhinos became forbidden, and a fine of 1,000 rupees began to be levied on those who flouted this.

The sahib and memsahib *shikaris* enacted their conquests over nature and landscape through killing and capture. By the time the Raj period began, the figure of the *shikari* sahib was seen as the epitome of the white man in India. The risky hunting expeditions were supposed to demonstrate the manly vigour of Europeans who had overcome the fear of the unknown.

In fact, Indian Civil Service officers frequently took leave to practise hunting. In times of peace, it was supposed to keep up their spirit of conquering. Heroic narratives of sahibs and memsahibs killing predatory creatures circulated widely, projecting the *shikari* as the brave European. By the twentieth century, there was a wide array of works on *shikars* in the Raj, which dominated the imagination of the British even back home, and writers like Kenneth Anderson and Jim Corbett's works led to a certain thrill becoming associated with it.

6

"WOE IS ME THAT I SOJOURN IN THIS LAND OF PESTILENCE"

DIRT, DISEASE, AND DOCTORLY MEMSAHIBS

My poor ayah was taken ill with fever four days ago and died last night... It is the first fatal case among our servants... Her husband would not hear of her going to the hospital, but carried her off in a litter to his own home, where he sent for a 'magic doctor' to exorcise the devil with which the natives say she was possessed. Possibly the devil in going out of her killed her... The Commissioner has just returned from inspecting the Alighur district. He says that no death returns, frightful as they are, give any idea of the extent of the late mortality from fever. The village chowkidars, whose duty it is to report deaths, either died themselves or were too ill to know what went on, and in one village alone, where twenty-one deaths were reported, it was found from personal inquiry that in reality more than 200 persons had died... It is most appalling, and utterly mocks all efforts to save life; for even were it possible that quinine could be brought to the very door of each family, it would be useless without also sufficient warm clothing, nourishing food, and proper and continued medical treatment.

– E. Augusta King, 1884

In the documentary "The Lost World of the Raj", India-born Nancy Vernede recalled that one of the first things that happened to her when she came home as a bride after she got married to a young recruit of the Indian Civil Service in Lucknow was a severe episode of malaria after being bitten by mosquitoes on her honeymoon (Ep. 1, 6.40–7.10).

The British lived in perennial dread of various tropical diseases and infections in the Indian subcontinent. The spectre of death loomed above their *sola topee*-covered heads at all times, and memsahibs were morbidly aware of the likelihood of catching fatal illnesses even when they were in the prime of their health. Virulent fevers struck people around them with regularity, and they often heard of so-and-so's friend or acquaintance passing away.

Women, especially, were concerned about their susceptibility to illness as they were believed to be more prone to the harmful effects of the tropical space. Their writings reveal that they had a wide knowledge of the maladies caused by the insalubrious climate and confined *mofussils*. Since Western medical facilities were mostly scarce, they had to rely on their own faculties. Most were wary of the 'native' cures and remedies as they believed that it was likely that they would die of them rather than the disease or infection itself. Moreover, in India, superstition, religion, and science were inextricably entwined. Memsahibs noted that the 'natives' believed that unless the gods were placated with sufficient sacrifices and offerings, they could unleash famines and epidemics on them. Constance F. G. Cumming observed the curious custom of sheep and goats being circled around an ailing patient and then having their heads cut as a form of sacrifice to drive away the demons who were causing disease. If the man recovered, it was supposed that the demon was propitiated, and if he died it was deemed a work of fate or the doing of the gods.

To worsen matters, medical officers of the East India Company were infamous for being lax and were often ridiculed as quacks. *Real Life in India: Embracing a View of the Requirements of Individuals Appointed to Any Branch of the Indian Public Service* (1847), which was a book specifically written for those travelling to India or who were curious about the British in India, had a fascinating view on the doctors stationed there. The writer, who wrote the book under the name 'An Old Resident', stated sarcastically that "a man need only sleep upon a medicine chest for a single night to become perfectly qualified for office" (52).

In such a situation, self-treatment was preferred, and for the memsahibs medicine became just another survival skill, which they learnt almost as part of domestic management. Even before they came to India, they knew that in distant colonies they had to be aware of Western cures, especially for missionaries in remote areas where there would not be proper medical aid for them. *Remarks on the Uses of Some of the Bazaar Medicines and Common Medical Plants of India* (1874), by Edward John Waring, acknowledged this problem. The book gave information on multiple types of medicines including antacids, astringents, antispasmodics, diuretics, purgatives, narcotics, and even sedatives to help families administer drugs themselves whenever needed.

Thus, memsahibs were well aware of what medicines to bring to India and how to administer them on themselves and others around them. But no matter how well they prepared themselves and learnt all the remedies written in European medical manuals, sickness in India was almost an inevitability. They knew that being bitten by mosquitoes, for instance, was something no one could avoid. Nor indeed could anyone avoid getting cholera while living in the more pestilent areas or while camping. As a result, memsahibs sometimes had a kind of nonchalance about experiencing severe 'ague' or some other virulent fever, for which they knew there was no actual prevention or cure.

Flora Annie Steel wrote, quite jubilantly, "Certainly I am an animal: I have such recuperative power." This is not to say that memsahibs were unaffected by the suffering caused by physical and psychological ordeals during treatment and recuperation, but they had become comfortable in dealing with illness and had a proper scientific understanding of disease and infections.

Indeed, they could medicate children and domestic animals for a number of ailments. If someone in the neighbourhood fell sick, they were quite happy whipping up syrups and potions from their personal medicine chests which they carried everywhere. Castor oil, grey powder, rhubarb, and ipecacuanha were some of the staples in their personal medicine chests, and like physicians, they even memorised dosages. In cases of minor or medium maladies, they generously dispensed a number of pills that were supposed to address multiple ailments at the same time. For instance, Halloway's pills could cure headache, dimness of sight, disordered livers, and became quite popular in the Bombay Presidency.

When it comes to medical practices in colonial India, it is interesting to see the intersection of Western and Eastern medical practices in the experiences of memsahibs. Christina S. Bremner observed how Indians did seem to have faith in the white people's medicine if it was given to them by someone whom they knew. She never hesitated at "giving medicine for fever, or administering a dose of castor oil".

Indeed, to the locals, taking medicine and treatment from a sympathetic memsahib they knew was better than going to professionals who tackled them swiftly and clinically, often without consideration for their religious sentiments or reluctance. They avoided going to hospitals altogether because it was believed they were places people went as a last resort when they were likely to die.

However, despite the industriousness of these ad hoc 'doctor-memsahibs', Western medicine was not always received easily by Indians. Memsahibs wrote about the general aversion to Western medical practices in some regions. Emily Eden was dismayed to learn how Maharaja Ranjeet Singh, the 'Sher-e-Punjab' (Lion of Punjab) who reigned from 1792 to 1801, refused all medication when he was taken ill in 1838, shortly before he died. This kind of resistance in Indians was quite common and continued despite various educational and awareness campaigns. Anna H. Leonowens once gave some cholera morbus and quinine to her Sanskrit teacher, a *pundit*, but was met with severe reproach from an elder woman in his family who screamed, "You dare not come in here! You dare not! What reason have you for daring to give my son medicine? I want you hateful *Injrage* [English] to know that I would rather have him die, than be polluted by your vile drinks, made of devils' blood and pig's flesh."

This kind of scepticism amongst Indians towards Western medicine continued through the twentieth century. When Monica Campbell Martin's husband, Peter, the Assistant Mines Manager and Zamindar Manager of Domchanch, heard that twenty-one people in the village had been bitten by mad jackals, he immediately issued notes to the Sub-Divisional Officer requesting their speedy treatment. Five of them refused to go, and the other sixteen were treated for rabies, despite repeated warnings. Monica, however, always tried to do scientific things for the Indians around her. She ran a "rough and ready sick parade" in her veranda regularly to prevent malaria and lined up her servants and the local villagers to dispense basic drugs like Epsom salts. Sometimes, she gave first aid when it was required. She even encouraged the women to go to the hospital for childbirth. At other times, she helped with childbirth herself and was constantly chasing out the village *dhai* (midwife) who never maintained hygiene. She abhorred the way the villagers put the baby out in the blazing sun after smearing it with mustard to 'harden' it, and she protested against this in vain.

Sometimes Indians grew to accept their medicine despite their initial misgivings or religious restrictions. Helen D. Mackenzie, wife of an army officer who published various works about her life in India, offered some medicine to a Brahmin sepoy who fell ill with violent colic. To her surprise, he took it despite it being mixed with their water that was taken from a Muslim bearer and was kept in a bottle made of goatskin (which was supposed to cause caste 'pollution').

Constance F. G. Cumming mentioned how her servants, in the 1880s, were always asking for '*dawai*' (medicine) because they were prone to get a touch of fever. This shows that Western methods of medicine were in fact spreading through India in the nineteenth century, and memsahibs were part of that process at the micro level, even though, owing to the prevalence of various 'tropical diseases', disease would take its toll despite their administering proper drugs to locals.

Still, memsahibs were the stand-ins for doctors and physicians for their own families and their servants, and sometimes even distant villagers came to them to ask for medicines for minor complaints. E. Augusta King wrote about the time she became a dentist for some locals:

> Two villagers suffering from toothache came to ask us for medicine, and as, fortunately, I always carry a bottle of Bunter's

> Nervine with me, I was able to doctor them, with the help of some cotton wool and a long sharp splinter of wood. Their pain was relieved almost instantly, and, the fame of this medicine spreading, another poor fellow came presently with his face swollen.

Another aspect of the intersection between Western and Indian cures concerns those instances when memsahibs adopted certain native remedies. Memsahibs sometimes administered homeopathic medicine and used some common medical plants for themselves if European medicine was scarce, even if Western doctors discouraged this. E. Augusta King wrote about the time when her husband fell quite ill with lumbago and none of the Western medicines worked. Then one of their servants took him to a well-known *hakim* (native healer), who gave him some homeopathic pills, after which he was decidedly better.

Monica Campbell Martin, who was a staunch advocate of Western methods, also saw that some of the medicinal herbs were effective, such as correctives for dysentery called '*aishaph ghul*'. Neem leaves were useful for poulticing and fomentations, and she steeped them in hot water during summer to relieve prickly heat. Whenever there was a dearth of quinine, memsahibs resorted to *chiretta*, which was a kind of tonic and intensely bitter febrifuge that could be purchased in most villages (a *petit verre* was a good alternative although it was a forbidden luxury for many). Veronica Bamfield wrote about a lady who was cured with some blackish seeds that the family's servant procured from the *bazaar*, after several failed attempts at getting her internal infection diagnosed by physicians at the hospital. The seeds were administered with an apple, after which she got better.

Several, though not all, memsahibs believed that there was a great fuss created around the unhealthiness of India and that sickness could be prevented through some basic precautionary methods and timely detection of maladies. They felt that just as they took measures to guard against the damp and chill of England, they had to take measures to guard against the heat and wet climate in India. In fact, back home, they suffered quite a lot due to cold, cough, infection, bad ventilation, and poor sanitation. In India, all they had to do was develop their immunity in a similar fashion.

Most memsahibs also had confidence in their robust European constitutions and were more or less prepared for the tropical ailments they had read so much about. In fact, they conceded that life in India could be good if they did not weaken, treating illness almost as a psychosomatic phenomenon.

As we have seen, any number of health risks or illnesses did not deter them from experiencing adventures, and they went about their daily lives despite the frequent bouts of aches and fevers. The sheer frequency of deadly illnesses that they experienced themselves or witnessed around them made them blasé regarding death itself. A more or less easy acceptance of this deadly side of Raj life underlies their chronicles of sicknesses.

Muck and Miasmas in the *Kala Jugga*

> *With aching limbs, parched tongue, throbbing brow, and leaden eyes, I prayed that light might come. Phantoms pursued, and waves submerged me; half delirious, I rose to look for water. Alas! It was the house of strangers, and guests were not meant to be thirsty. There was none. I pushed into another room, and eagerly swallowed the remains of a glass left by someone the night before. The influenza fiend and fever had laid hold of me, and for three days, all I saw of Kasauli's beauties was the trunk of a gheel, which insufficiently darkened my window. I had almost forgotten I was in a great military station where our soldiers go to recruit their health... But fever potions worked out their cure... A few days of influenza are a light affliction that endure but for a moment, but the weeks, and even months of prostration that follow it, are bad to bear.*
>
> – Christina S. Bremner, 1891

Matters of individual health may not have been a great cause for concern among the hardy in British India, but with the rapid increase in the number of Europeans serving in the Raj from the mid-nineteenth century, the administration realised that public health matters were crucial to the sustenance of the empire in the subcontinent.

India's climate and topography were understood to be hazardous to the Europeans. But protecting only Europeans and isolating them from the native population was largely ineffective because during epidemics diseases spread like wildfire, impacting even those who remained cloistered in their enclaves. Thus, ensuring the proper health of Europeans required addressing the overall public health of the colony.

Before the beginning of the Raj period, since the beginning of the seventeenth century, the East India Company had been bringing in surgeons and physicians from England, and there were consistent efforts to ensure that Western medical practices became prominent in India. But 'public health' in India developed slowly. As the years rolled on, epidemics broke out throughout the nineteenth century in different parts of the country, sometimes lasting for several years and sometimes recurring, like in the case of cholera. These were recognised as a major impediment to imperial work, and speedy work needed to be done to tackle the varying tropical diseases.

This was significant because in the nineteenth century, as the knowledge relating to 'contagion' increased, awareness of communicable infections also developed. The Plague Commission, for instance, was formed in the 1890s, following decades of multiple discourses about the unsuitability of the tropical climate for Europeans, especially women. Special research was conducted on tropical diseases and ailments, and institutionalised tropical medicine focused on vector theories, which linked the environment to the infections. Colonial therapeutics and medicine focused on dealing with illnesses that were specific to or were heightened by the wet and warm climate of India, such as dysentery, and a specialised regime of health and hygiene was promoted for the Europeans' sustenance in the subcontinent.

It was in the latter half of the nineteenth century that the matter of sanitariness emerged in public discourse. After the 1857 rebellion, concerns regarding the health of men in the ranks mounted due to the shockingly high rates of sickness and disease-related mortality. For instance, due to a lack of cleanliness and proper facilities, dysentery was common, and jaundice occurred frequently because of contaminated water, so much so that even quinine had no effect. Mrs. Leopold Paget was concerned about the decomposing dead bodies left out under the sun after the mass killings. Many of her people fell ill because of the stench and unhealthiness of the air since everything festered very quickly in the tropical sun. Indeed, the wet air worsened matters.

India was haunted by the memories of such deadly epidemics, and people knew that disaster could easily strike again. Sometimes, even exposure to heat and sandstorms could cause illnesses. This was most frequent amongst regiments because of poor medical facilities causing numerous cases of ophthalmia. Because medical facilities for the army were so poor, the sick had no shelter except for their tents, and those could become very crammed. This was a concern even before the 1857 conflict. Helen D. Mackenzie noted that Lord Hardinge, who served as Governor-General of India between 1844 and 1848, wanted his 800 rank and file to be lodged in five tents, each of which was supposed to hold only eighty.

As a result, the issue of hygiene and cleanliness became hotly debated, and there was a huge uproar about the death rates amongst officers in India as they could have been prevented. Consequently, sanitary commissions were set up, mostly to investigate the state of military cantonments (Harrison 8), and the matter of hygiene became formally regulated by the 1860s.

The administration also knew that diseases were linked to insanitariness, not just overcrowding. There was a severe threat of cholera almost throughout the nineteenth century, and the government acted quickly to develop massive campaigns and public health measures to curb the contagion. Around the same time that cholera spread from lower Bengal to other parts, the dangers of the tropical Indian environment became clear to the British administrators yet again. The risks of 'miasmas', simply meaning filthy, disease-carrying air, which were linked to the tropical conditions of India, became known. There was a need to curb the spread of infections and diseases in overcrowded sites because most diseases were highly transmissible. *Practical Observations on the Hygiene of the Army in India* (1861) by Stewart Clark, Inspector General of Prisons, stated that congregating in ill-ventilated workshops and barracks also caused sickness. Disease was everywhere.

A stringent spatial segregation between the Europeans and non-Europeans was believed to lessen the impact of diseases on the

British families living within the cantonments, plantations, hill stations, 'civil lines', and so on. In the cities, the native parts of the towns, outside the European enclaves, were called '*kala jugga*' or 'Black Towns'; it was there that the problem of unsanitary public spaces was most acute. The affluent native population lived in spacious bungalows with verandas, and the lower classes lived in small huts made of clay and roofed with dried leaves, but the Black Town mostly consisted of houses made with bamboo, wood, and mud, and unpaved roads meant for the natives. The entire area would be densely populated and have several pockets of commerce. The *bazaars* would be overflowing at all times, creating further filth and disorder. When Maria Graham visited the *kala jugga*, she remarked at the overcrowding in the small area.

Eventually, therefore, the focus expanded to the sanitariness of rural spaces as well. When Mackenzie reached Karnaul she noted that it was a very unhealthy station with occasional epidemics. In general diseases spread in places where there was a high density of people. At pilgrim sites, for instance, where huge masses of people conglomerated, diseases spread rapidly. In 1884, Constance F. G. Cumming was worried about the squalid condition of the places where pilgrims camped while on the way to the Jaganath festival held at Puri, where fifty to three hundred thousand devotees assembled. Due to sanitary regulation and quarantining measures, the vast pilgrim site was located outside the city to prevent the outbreak of disease caused by filth and overcrowding (94).

However, the diseases claimed the lives of those who lived in the purer and cooler mountainous regions as well as those in hot 'miasmatic' and overcrowded areas. Cumming was in the Himalayas when there was a sudden outbreak of cholera. She felt a strange hush as the entire valley was decimated by the disease, which she called "a mysterious and terrible scourge". Many of the villagers had fled the area and nothing seemed to stir.

In 1896, bubonic plagues broke out in Bombay and came to be reported in several other port cities. When Monica Campbell Martin was in Bettiah, she was alarmed when the plague broke out in the *bazaars*. The virus was carried by rats, and when a dead rat fell from the rafters of the roof, it meant that the plague had come to town. There was no time to lose, and the administration took stock of the situation quickly and began inoculation. The serum could affect people badly, and many of them fainted right after, but the efforts helped curtail the spread.

In 1858, while travelling with her husband's battery near Belgaum, Mrs. Leopold Paget was worried that the smallpox was raging amongst the natives in the *bazaar* nearby, and she wanted to have their baby vaccinated.

Indeed, during the nineteenth and early twentieth centuries, various medical theories emerged, and enormous amounts of research went into understanding pathogenicity, treatments, and cures. 'Sanitarianism' as an idea also became widely popular during the nineteenth century, and it was believed that cleansing, cleaning, and clearing public spaces could prevent the spread of certain infectious diseases. Certain elite circles in Bengal, particularly those of the middle class who were privy to public discussions on health and health practices, grew concerned about the transmission of diseases. Rabindranath Tagore established the Sriniketan Rural Reconstruction Project (1922), which aimed to address the health problems faced by the poor villagers, along with a more ambitious project of village development.

However, prevention, containment, and eradication proved immensely challenging due to the variegated climatic and topographical conditions. Moreover, there were various hurdles in the way of sanitation drives and public health policies. In Calcutta, the issues ranged from religious to cultural, while in Bombay they were related to finances. After the epidemic, Bombay was recognised as a hot seat for cholera, but reforms and measures were still lacking in the municipality. Madras was as badly afflicted, again due to financial constraints. The sanitary establishment was not up to the mark, and the foul state of the streets, the nauseating stench, and the filthy corners posed a grave threat. The *Madras Manual of Hygiene* (1880), compiled by Surgeon-Major Henry King, listed the various substances and objects that could be poisoned or contaminated leading to illness. In the manual, the issue of cleanliness and ventilation was paramount.

Moreover, it was believed that the perennially wet or humid seasons in coastal areas increased the chances of vector-borne diseases. In the 1830s, F. P. Strong, a Calcutta surgeon, wrote that malaria was produced most abundantly in those parts of Bengal where the jungle was not cleared, although the connection between mosquitoes and malaria was not established until decades later, a gap in knowledge which severely curtailed preventative methods.

Danger lurked everywhere. In fact, like Nancy Vernede who caught malaria as a newlywed bride, memsahibs discovered immediately upon arriving that one of their biggest enemies in the strange land of India was nothing larger than a grain of rice: the mosquito. They braved the jungles, lived in the vilest of conditions, faced wild animals, pirates, *dacoits*, and even mutineers, but to their surprise, they could be undone by this fiend on wings that buzzed in their ears all night long.

Indeed, aside from the risk of fevers, mosquitoes were a particular nuisance to the memsahibs, who were not used to them. Sometimes, a memsahib's face would be speckled with tiny bumps due to being bitten all night despite the mosquito curtains. They were usually unsuccessful in swatting them in the dark, and several women recorded long nights of misery as they battled with the buzzing pests, unable to catch any sleep. With that, they declared war on mosquitoes; they wore their anti-mosquito sleeping drawers and were careful to wear their canvas boots while going outdoors. Their beds were always draped with fine netting to keep the mosquitoes away, although they knew they would be bitten one way or another. They employed several extreme strategies and sometimes they worked: their beds were soaked in paraffin, but the odours wafted around them, making them giddy throughout the night. The mosquitoes were in such abundance that Christina S. Bremner referred to them as a 'curtain' that constantly hung over her as she slept fitfully at night. She wrote:

> They bit me in the winter when everybody said there were none. My face and person were bedecked with bumps raised by mosquito poison when all declared they could not bite… I grew wonderfully expert at killing the enemy. Whilst the more heavy-moving masculine animal was slowly gathering himself together preparatory to an onslaught, I had laid a row of corpses on the table, victims of my agility… Nothing but ether and chloroform will prevent me thinking of them.

It was near the end of the nineteenth century that the Nobel Prize-winning doctor Sir Robert Ross discovered that the parasitic fever called malaria, which had such a staggeringly high mortality rate, was linked to mosquitoes. The illness could hit people suddenly with force, and memsahibs wrote how they would be bed-ridden and delirious for days. The fever would be accompanied by chills as well as breaking out in a sweat in the middle of the night. It could also strike a person multiple times in the span of a few months and leave them weakened. Rosamund Lawrence struggled with her fever for days, and lay quaking, surrounded with hot water bottles under layers of rugs and carpets, just to get the fever to break. She experienced typhoid and malaria together and was completely diminished at the end of it (Macmillan, 85).

However, for some, malaria was so common around them that it became banal and not even a significant subject for discussion. If a memsahib came down with it, she simply scribbled to her friends that she was down with malaria, and there would be no questions asked, no offence taken, and no alarm caused. Monica Campbell Martin caught malaria multiple times while living in a malarial district, Terai, in Nepal. There was a special type of malaria in the area called 'aoul'. She had no choice but to suffer through it, since the nearest doctor was located 42 miles away.

The administration, no doubt, took rigorous measures to rage their battle against the vicious insects. There was steady research on the cause and treatment of malaria, focusing on eradication and cure. The Malaria Committee of the Royal Society, who had been to Africa, came to India in 1902, and they toured Calcutta, the Duars, Jeypore Hills, Punjab, and other places, trying to make their assessments in relation to atmospheric and topographical factors. Centres of industrial work, plantations, mills, and so on were recognised as cesspits of malarial fevers. Jungles, forests, and hilly districts were also recognised to be the spaces that were the breeding grounds of mosquitoes. In Calcutta, since flooding was common, filthy pools and marshy ponds caused malaria epidemics. Factors like the construction of the railways, irrigation networks, inadequate drainage systems, and improper sanitation drives exacerbated the problem of stagnant water, which in turn allowed for the breeding of mosquitoes.

Anna H. Leonowens was travelling in Calcutta in the early 1880s when she wrote about how the city was at one point one of the unhealthiest parts of India. The entire landscape was flat with several muddy lakes, which were breeding spots for malarial mosquitoes. In places like Calcutta, there were a number of dense forests on the outskirts, but the streets had been carefully drained, and many of the stagnant pools of muddy water had been converted into gardens. However, the air remained impregnated "with impure exaltations arising from the low jungles in the vicinity of this city, called the Sundarbans". In fact, memsahibs constantly exhibited concerns about the habitability of the colonised space in their writings and frequently expressed their disgust at the insanitary conditions of cantonments.

The war against malaria was mainly waged with a few tablets of quinine. It was taken plain or mixed with tonic water, and sometimes even gin. In fact, the British had such enthusiasm for it that pills of quinine were passed around at dinner tables. It was the only sworn treatment for malaria, and the only hope against it.

Problematic Pregnancies and Women's Health

Delhi, December 11th, 1838.

... When Henry's troop was ordered to march, he volunteered to join; nor could I object to his doing what was obviously his duty... and I kept up, by God's help... On that day we set out, and the whole journey seemed to me like a funeral procession; and that the place of parting was to be the grave of my happiness. It would be long to tell you the pains and troubles of that week; baby very ill, myself apparently sinking fast, yet obliged to push on, that we might get a nurse for the baby and advice for me... At Meerut we had ten days on the full stretch—days that I cannot yet look back on without agony... My Henry is among those that remain [stationed in Ferozepur]; *and I am setting off to join him. The journey is long and formidable. There will be an abundance of discomforts, living in a tent fourteen feet square, on a sandy plain...*

– Honoria Lawrence, 1936

In tandem with the expansionist aims of the empire, memsahibs became central to the colonial project of settlement for their ability to bear children for the Raj. Indeed, children were the future of the empire in India and a clear sign that the British race was propagating itself. Motherhood thus became understood as the 'white woman's burden'.

However, in the far outposts, this role was often riskier than any sahib's imperial duties. As mentioned in the previous section, surgeons and physicians were hard to come by, and the absence of medical care at crucial moments could be dangerous and often fatal. Sometimes, women would be in transit when they realised that they were in the middle of labour and would have nothing but assistance from their servants or the locals. Puerperal infections were thus common and could worsen quickly. Healthy women could suddenly develop uterine or ovarian ailments and suffer through immensely difficult pregnancies and childbirths.

While motherhood was an important role for memsahibs in India, repeated pregnancies because of lack of contraception were a great bane for the women. Veronica Bamfield, who wrote *On the Strength* (1975), about the life of British army wives ranging from the seventeenth to nineteenth centuries, wrote that for army wives, unwanted pregnancies, which occurred very frequently, were a major setback; they often went to considerable lengths to terminate them. Hot doses of gin and quinine made the ears buzz and eyesight become faulty, but it was the only method known to the women out in India to abort foetuses. More extreme measures included crawling upstairs backwards, jumping off chairs, riding hard to hounds, and even worse. However, knowledge about prevention of pregnancy was limited, and often there were no means for it. If memsahibs had had sufficient knowledge about their biological processes and had been given better institutional support, then one lady, whose extreme case Bamfield mentions, would not have had to go to the Indian *bazaars* for abortions six times, jeopardising her health severely. Often, memsahibs had no idea about birth control at all and got pregnant multiple times in quick succession. Bamfield wrote that when one lady discovered birth control, she was immensely relieved that after four children she need not have more.

It must be stated that pregnancy, even in general, was a great gamble in the Raj. Apart from issues relating to fertility and conception, there was a fear of complications during and after birth, which could sound the death-knell for the healthiest of women. Frequent pregnancies, repeated abortions, and miscarriages could also be harmful, debilitating their gynaecological health.

One of the principal risks in relation to maternal health was miscarriages, as well as mother and infant mortality. Many times, physicians were ill trained in dealing with women's issues, and could be insensitive and rough with women. It was also common for pregnant women to not get access to trained physicians or surgeons at all. Sometimes, hospitals were ill equipped to help women in such matters. And very frequently, the good hospitals were inaccessible due to the great distances in the outposts. To make matters worse, army surgeons did not take women's illnesses seriously and were liable to dismiss major health emergencies as 'hysteria' or exaggeration. During Captain Sherwood's term of service in India in the 1840s, women were admitted to men's wards only if beds were available.

Gynaecological and obstetrical complications were extremely common, and memsahibs were warned that they would not have access to adequate provisions in India, especially in provincial towns. The extreme cases of such disorders and maladies could be fatal in the long term. Sometimes, lack of awareness and knowledge about the details of their bodily functions worsened small problems, and often their own neglect and carelessness exacerbated infections leading to major complications later on in life. For instance, although dietary issues were always prevalent amongst the British in India, in the case of women, they sometimes led to severe uterine complications.

Moreover, physicians repeatedly stressed how menstrual troubles and uterine ailments were all too common amongst European women in India, supposedly due to the 'chronic inflammation' of their wombs, caused by excessive exposure to heat and frequent travels in rough conditions. India's climate and topography were considered most injurious to women's organs. In fact, the nineteenth-century gynaecologists and obstetricians believed that memsahibs' wombs were 'permanently damaged', and their uteruses ulcerated and congested. This was taken as an unavoidable corollary of living in a tropical country, especially in cases where the woman had been too exposed to the tropical climate.

As a result, there was a great profusion of medical literature for women, particularly in the form of self-help and guidebooks, specifically for European women in India, to help them understand and avoid gynaecological and obstetrical problems. Edward John Tilt says in *A Handbook of Uterine Therapeutics, and of Diseases of Women* (1869):

> Debility is not only caused by the physical effects of habitually intense heat, but sometimes by malaria, and always by the comparative inactivity and complete change of habits, which soon imparts a certain amount of Oriental indolence to the once hardy Englishwoman. It is well known that this confirmed debility renders the more important viscera very liable to subacute inflammation; and there is no reason why the womb should escape this influence, or why it should not be then more forcibly acted on by its usual exciting causes of inflammation. No wonder, then, if Dr Boggs should consider anaemia an important cause of the extraordinary frequency of uterine inflammation among European females in tropical regions (369).

Most books like Tilt's medical manuals were steeped in Victorian science and tropical therapeutics and constantly highlighted the adverse impact of excessive movement and travel on ovarian and uterine health. According to Tilt's treatises, menstruating women, in particular, were to avoid vigorous activities such as long walks, shopping, riding, dancing, parties, and theatres. Even though the memsahibs liked travelling, medical discourses often discouraged it because of the impact on the reproductive functions. They were instructed to not exert themselves or be excitable at any time.

In a situation where women had little understanding of complex biological matters, the available medical treatises on feminine health and hygiene were often their only viable options. They were particularly favoured in remote locations where medical facilities were not up to the mark, or missing altogether, so that women could be well-equipped to self-diagnose and cure their ailments without being dependent on anyone else.

What becomes apparent is that in addition to multiple restrictions imposed upon women because of the gendered space of the empire, the practical restrictions imposed on them by such medical texts, which contained a moralising and cautionary tone apart from scientific discourse, were rigid and often incontestable. This is because these texts contained assertive scientific jargon and were strict in their dictates. They also made memsahibs believe that not following the elaborate instructions could cost them their or their child's life.

However, even if they wanted to, following certain medical rules was simply unfeasible. As we have seen, travel, mobility, and even constant activity were synonymous with life in the Raj, and memsahibs had to regularly accompany their husbands on official tours and travels. Thus, the medical advice given to expectant mothers, warning them against excessive movement or going out in the sun, was simply rendered redundant. Most aspects of imperial work required their constant participation and striking a balance between their maternal roles and conjugal roles as memsahibs was nearly impossible for most women in the Raj. Very often, they had no choice but to ignore the medical advice altogether.

Consequently, their health was compromised. The sustained exposure to various climatic conditions as they kept moving from one place to another caused severe health complications for both mother and child at times, especially if the child was in its infancy. Minnie Blane was 7 months pregnant when her husband was posted to a new station in Jhelum, and she had to pack everything and move at short notice. She wrote about her difficulties in managing her pregnancy during the arduous process of moving to a new house after travelling a great distance. The climate was intolerable and worsened her health problems. To make matters worse, the doctor whom they had employed was a brash military surgeon who was hardly gentle with her and made the entire process of delivery extremely traumatic. This happened in the year 1857, and amidst the chaos, she had to journey to safety in such a delicate state. The intense heat and fear and the ordeal of travelling for so long worsened her wounds, which became infected, and delayed healing. The birth of her next child worsened her health even more.

Honoria Lawrence also had an extremely stressful time directly after giving birth because of a long journey. After the ceremony, she had to undertake an extremely difficult palanquin ride because of her husband's official duties, during which she had to change from the palanquin to a buggy and was jolted around on rough terrain for a whole week. The child was sick and colicky, even as her husband rode on ahead, quite oblivious to their suffering. Both mother and child arrived at their destination seriously ill and took a whole week to recover. She wrote:

> Oh the anguish of that hour… as I carried my babe about till I almost fainted. At last I laid him on my cloak by the roadside; but he cried so fearfully that I at once took him up again. I thought he would die there and then; and I was so worn and weak that I had no self-control to sustain me. Just as I got back into the doolie, Henry rode up. The bearer had never gone near him. He had only turned back from surprise at my not appearing. When we reached the dak bungalow he got some goat's milk and water for the baby and a cup of tea for me. Then I went on in the doolie, and my Henry took Alick with him in the buggy.

No matter how careful they were, even when they were not on the move, mishaps could occur frequently. Life in India was hectic, and there were always too many chores to supervise and too many guests to entertain. When Maria Nugent went into labour, she concealed her pains as she went about her daily work, writing letters and conducting her household duties, until it became unbearable, and she had to send for a doctor and nurse. Afterwards, she fell ill again: "My baby continued most prosperous, but I suffered sadly myself, from violent pains in my head, from want of sleep, and my eyes became very weak in consequence. The doctor says, it is all nervous, and so perhaps it is, and no wonder".

There is no doubt that memsahibs found childbearing, deliveries, and women's health burdensome in the Raj. Not only did they have to deal with unreliable medical provisions and ill-trained doctors, but they were also often alone and had to fend for themselves in the absence of friends and family. First-time mothers were particularly wracked with fear.

Indeed, most memsahibs in India had little to no experience and meagre knowledge gleaned only from some theoretical books, or worse, vague and often contradictory instructions passed on in the form of old wives' tales. Back home, they would have had a circuit of experienced mother figures and sisters to care for them and guide them in such intimate matters. However, in India, they were alone, and often without proper information.

On top of their fears for their own health and performance as mothers, memsahibs were terrified of losing their babies. Children could be stillborn if the delivery was not carried out in a safe and proper manner, and even if the child was alive, anything could happen to it in its infancy. Sickly babies were particularly vulnerable and could die of infections. Harriet Tytler's baby, who was born during the Indian rebellion of 1857, was born with dysentery, which was extremely perilous at such a young age, and she did not expect him to live beyond a week.

Accidents could also endanger unborn or newborn children since speedy medical attention was seldom possible. Lillian Ashby was told of a young memsahib who had died in a most unfortunate incident when there was a fire in the armoury near her residence. The lady was hastily dragged from the burning building and the trauma and stress induced premature labour. At that time, there was no midwife or doctor, and three days later, she succumbed because of the lack of proper care.

Ashby recalled how in a small town, Mohespur, there were no medical facilities for women, and treatments were mostly of herbs administered by *ayahs* or *hakims* "whose practices were the antithesis of antisepsis". There was no chance of getting a midwife. Of her own birth in 1876, she wrote, "With the thermometer registering one hundred and twenty degrees, in a room with a door and windows tightly closed to shut out the daytime glare, beneath fanning *punkahs*, I was born".

What made matters more challenging was that none of the matters relating to women's intimate health, hygiene, and gynaecological and obstetrical concerns were spoken of freely, and they were even downplayed in women's own writings. Postpartum wellbeing was also given little attention in the nineteenth century, and memsahibs were simply warned against 'exertion'. Confinements were considered particularly beneficial in India because of the added concerns of the harsh climate. There were clear instructions given to the lying-in mother about her recuperation during this period of confinement with regard to diet and domestic arrangements, such as keeping the room cool and free from draughts at all times. Confinement diets had to be followed properly, which was advantageous for young mothers because the recovery was quicker and less painful, although there was always difficulty in regaining strength afterwards.

One striking phenomenon particular to British India was the tendency to starve women after childbirth to avoid "chills". This could be highly detrimental to them unless the woman actually had a fever, and just points to the lack of scientific understanding on most women's health-related matters.

Moreover, there were hardly any mechanisms to help them deal with their problems. For instance, no matter what precautions were taken post-delivery, memsahibs usually had pains. But chloroform, which sometimes helped, was not feasible because it evaporated because of the heat. More often than not, memsahibs could only take recourse to teas to alleviate some of the pain.

Apart from physical postpartum ailments, psychological problems such as depression, ennui, and stress were common. Memsahibs were prone to have maudlin thoughts of their children dying, or that they themselves might die during or after childbirth, which they witnessed happening around them ever so frequently. Honoria Lawrence received news of a lady called Mrs. Ottley who had a successful delivery of a "*very* small daughter" when she was pregnant herself and she was curious to know how the new mother was faring. She was surprised to learn that the lady, "fresh from the perilous birth", was apathetic towards the infant. This disturbed her considerably. Postpartum depression was possibly quite common. Minnie Blane was so acutely depressed that she even became suicidal after the birth of her children.

The constant dwelling on matters of death sometimes brought on philosophical moods in memsahibs. Life and death were certainly unpredictable in the Raj. A person would be healthy one moment and dead the next. Ursula Graham Bower, the anthropologist who lived among the indigenous tribal communities in the

1930s and 1940s, felt the perilous conditions in India actually helped her to appreciate life better. She wrote:

> Death was never very far from anyone in that malarial, doctorless country, and thinking back, I believe it was chiefly that which held one so firmly in the present and prevented too great a building of hopes for the future. Certainly, to enjoy every simple pleasure as though it were for the last time sharpened the senses and gave life an extraordinarily rich texture.

7

"THE 'SIMLA WOMAN' IS FRIVOLOUS"

HILLS, SUNSETS, AND SCANDALS

Jack's own Jill goes up the hill,
To Murree or Chakrata
Jack remains, and dies in the plains,
And Jill re-marries soon after.

[This] *clever little verse presents one side of the picture only... Jill is not always wafted hill-ward by the first whiff of hot air from the dread furnace to come. She does, on occasion, stand by her husband, through bitter and sweet, through fire and frost...*

Mr Kipling's Jill is the type of Anglo-Indian wife best known to English readers; and yet how much less than little do they know of the subtle temptations which beset her at every turn! So serious are the charges made against the... morals of [India's] *wives in particular—that it is impossible to present any adequate picture of Anglo-Indian married life... the random assertion that the tone of social morality is lower in India than in England, is unjust and untrue... India tests a woman's character to the uttermost...*

[Yet] *in a Hill station—more especially in Simla—it is irresistibly infectious... for a woman who is young, comely, and gifted with a taste for acting, Simla is assuredly not the most innocuous place on God's earth. Here frivolity reaches its highest height.*

– Maud Diver, 1909

Some of the most tantalising stories of Raj India that made their way back to Britain were of memsahibs' holiday escapades in various hill stations of the country. Every holiday season, which usually began at the end of April and could be up to 8 months, various high-altitude destinations welcomed an exodus of a mixed group of women, children, convalescing men, members of the Secretariat, and officers on furlough. These sojourners were keen to avoid the physical and psychological effects of the dreaded 'Indian summer', when, according to some possibly exaggerated accounts, temperatures rose to 65 degrees Celsius out in the sun (Hicks, 175). Long retreats in cooler climes were the only escape from the sweltering heat, and come the end of spring, many left for the hills with their troops of servants and *coolies* carrying their enormous quantities of luggage. Many of them had temporary residences in the hill towns of the Himalayas in northern India or the Nilgiris in the south, or rented bungalows or inns for the season in any of the popular hill stations.

Memsahibs' summer sojourns are one of the main reasons why they have been ridiculed so widely in popular culture. Their willingness to stay away from their husbands for long stretches of time was taken as a sure sign of selfishness, as they were regularly accused of prioritising their own needs and comforts over their conjugal duties and guiltlessly enjoying their holidays. The vibrant social life that hill stations were famous for did not help their case. However, such accusations are misleading because they were merely partaking of a well-organised system of imperial culture in India.

Indeed, during the second half of the nineteenth century, the Raj had a keen interest in the development of hill towns as summer-stations for the seasonal inhabitation of the British in India. Apart from their popularisation as recreational centres, these towns were suitable sites for administrative work. In fact, Shimla in the Himalayas became one of the most crucial seats of imperial power and hosted multiple significant political meetings and conclaves. While the administration initially had misgivings about the development of hilly areas as destinations for large populations, given the topographical conditions and rough terrains, Shimla, Darjeeling, Nainital and Ootacamund (Ooty) were eventually made into government headquarters. It was common for officers of the government to pick up all of their work and simply accompany their wives into the hills. In the 1910s, the husband of Lady Anne Campbell Wilson (a notable author and wife of a British civil servant best known for the letters she wrote back home from India) did the same, but much to Lady Campbell Wilson's chagrin, he remained occupied throughout the day:

> In spite of the romantic surroundings Jim sits at an office-table disposing of 'files'. That is the insignificant name bestowed on gigantic folios, sometimes printed, sometimes containing in manuscript the opinions written by different officials on some subject, which a new development has again brought under discussion, and which demands widespread advice.

In 1827, the Governor-General of Bengal, William Amherst, visited Shimla and stayed in the Kennedy House, and a few years later, Shimla hosted the first political meeting between the Governor-General of India, Lord William Bentick, and the emissaries of Maharaja Ranjit Singh. By the latter half of the nineteenth century, the Viceroyalty began migrating to Shimla during the summer season. Sir John Lawrence, Viceroy between 1864 and 1869, moved his entire officialdom to Shimla from Calcutta for the summer.

The significance of various prime hill stations grew over the next few years, and between 1876 and 1880, Viceroy Robert Lytton undertook further planning of Shimla when he occupied the seat. Lord Dufferin assumed the role in 1884, and upon the completion of the Viceregal Lodge, was able to occupy it in the summer of 1888 with his wife. By this time, many branches of officialdom had transferred to the hills and operated from them each summer.

The arguments in favour of the costly and cumbersome annual migrations to hill stations were precisely that the heat of the burning, dusty plains in summer had enervating effects on the officers, which hampered imperial work. In contrast to the plains, the pristine sprawling greens combined with a climate like 'paradise', temperate enough to have healing qualities, were believed to increase the officers' productivity and facilitate better administration. Indeed, these spaces were known to be restorative, and became a haven for the ailing. As a result, a system termed "medical leisure" (Bhattacharya, 84) came about as sanatoriums were developed in places like Darjeeling in West Bengal, where the elite of India could convalesce in comparatively private and peaceable conditions, away from the debilitating effects of the fiery summer. Over time, hill stations became the lodestones of the Raj and a paradise for those who were nostalgic for the English air. The actual magnetism of hill stations thus lay in their being—in Cumming's words—an "atmospheric elixir". In fact, memsahibs were medically advised to move to cooler regions, since women were considered particularly vulnerable to heat.

Moreover, children were sent to the hills as well, either because of the boarding schools that had been established there or because they too were susceptible to heat-induced sickness. Naturally, their mothers were required to go with them. Rumer and Jon Godden, who co-authored *Two Under the Indian Sun* (1966), which was based on their childhood memories of India from 1914, wrote that even though they were not affluent, their parents took the whole family to different hill stations during summer where they rented a cottage for the season. Over the years, they went to Shillong, Assam, and Darjeeling in Bengal and as far away as Kashmir in the North or Coonoor in South India where the eucalyptus and mimosa trees grew. They would reserve compartments in trains and cram into them with their own bedding and tiffin baskets, and their entire luggage in holdalls. They carried many bottles of soda, lemonade, and regular water. Sometimes, the bread went dry and the butter melted, but they loved these road meals. It could take them 4 days to arrive at their chosen hill stations, but those journeys were truly memorable. To reach Mussoorie from the northern city of Dehradun, they were carried in *dandies* or in carrying chairs, which native *coolies* carried on their backs. They wrote delightedly about how "every hill station had a different flavour, and the beauty, the climate, and the people of each were quite different".

And yet, the stereotype of the 'hedonistic memsahib' enjoying the hills still persists. In many stories of the Raj, one comes across the pitiable sahib-husband toiling for long months in the plains, stuck behind his desk, while his carefree and inconsiderate wife enjoys sumptuous repasts and pleasant company in the cool weather of hill stations.

Apparently, even George Curzon—Viceroy of India from 1899 to 1905—was not able to escape the supposed fate of the unfortunate lonely husband slaving in the heat while his Vicereine sojourned in Shimla like all other memsahibs. He was miserable in Calcutta and wrote to her, "I am dogged tired… all my days are the same, work, work, work" (Nicholson, 125).

The 'busy idlers' and their 'party fever'

Yesterday I went down to lunch and dinner, and to-night I hope to go to Roberts' fancy ball… Thursday there were races, and a big dinner and dance here, both of which I was able to follow from my bed immediately above. First, a clatter of swords near my door, by which I know that His Excellency has been fetched, and that having descended the stairs, he is being taken round the guests… I hear 'God save the Queen,' and I know they are marching in to dinner, the Viceroy and Lady Roberts, Blanche and Sir Frederick, and a long line following; Blanche in a state of extreme nervousness at the very idea of sitting in my place and assuring Sir Frederick that 'nothing would ever induce her to do such a thing again'.

– Lady Helen Blackwood Dufferin, Vicereine, 1889

Shimla, one of the most popular and glamorous hill stations in the Raj, offered plenty of options for recreation and entertainment to the holidaymakers. In 1891, thirty years after Lawrence made Shimla the "Summer Capital" of the Raj, a narrow-gauge railway was opened linking it with the foothill town of Kalka, significantly increasing the numbers that flocked up the slope every year during peak season.

Shimla was to the British in India what Brighton was to England, symbolising fun, adventure, and flirtations. The deep ravines and gushing waterfalls were incredibly scenic, and the azure skies were a great change from the murkiness of the plains. The scent of hill stations was also very distinct—woody and musky from the pine trees and fresh foliage. As the British men and women ascended the hills, the scent of the lovely flower appropriately named 'traveller's joy' wafted in the air and bright red rhododendrons, which Yvonne Fitzroy (private secretary to the Vicereine, Lady Alice Reading) described as an "amazing sight" (Butler, 28), could be seen blossoming all around. The vegetation was also familiar, and the sight of petunias, sweet peas, verbena, and lilacs transported them back to their homeland.

The Himalayas captivated the British completely. During the day, the memsahibs went out to see the breath-taking views, which appeared and disappeared through the clouds swirling just beyond the ridges. In Shimla, especially, the public buildings along the roads were handsome, and the municipal structures, which included a concert hall, a gaiety theatre, a dancing room, a supper room, a library, and so on, added to the charm of the town. The Shimla theatre held performances several days a week, including 5 pm matinees and late-hour shows after 9 pm. On the Mall, there would be striking military visions on horseback as dapper colonels and lieutenants made their way to the United Service Club, where the excellent eating and drinking went on throughout the day.

One of the many favourite exercises for the young and the carefree at Shimla was to ride down to Annandale for horse races. During mild afternoons, memsahibs would be invited to games and picnics in the pretty glens where men would be present. Late evening walks along the winding roads under the star-speckled skies were incredibly romantic, and *jhampan* rides through the serene spaces were things they frequently wrote about in their letters. Some of these spaces were thought to be haunted by *churails*—female demons—lending a spooky air to the misty hill roads. In the evenings, the sombre deodar trees rustled in the twilight as the memsahibs were carried in *jhampans* down to the *bazaars* lined along the cliffs. Shivering slightly as they rode through the Mall Road, they enjoyed the cold winds, giggling as they held onto their bonnets lest they flew off. The marketplaces were full of exuberance, and the serpentine roads were ideal for evening perambulations. If clouds began to gather, indicating it would rain, they hurried off to their favourite tea shops and clubs to chit chat with their friends all evening.

The memsahibs particularly delighted in the Englishness of the scenes as hill towns like Shimla were built exclusively as British spaces. The cultivation around such stations was also deliberately designed to be European, and the caretakers industriously grew fruits and vegetables that were grown in Britain, to be able to cook authentic Pigeon pies and Irish stews. There would be scores of excellent European shops and boutiques, and recent arrivals from everywhere could be seen at the popular clubs and cafes. The architecture was also more European than anywhere else in India, with its gothic and Tudorbethan structures dotting the landscape and pretty villas so unlike the typical colonial bungalows of the plains. These villas had proper slanted roofs and bow windows, giving them the look of English cottages or even of quaint Swiss chalets. Every house had its own gardens, shaded by sweeping willows and majestic apricot trees laden with fruit. Lovely glens looked down on the houses. Sometimes, the houses would be perched right at the precipice of a ravine and would have the most enchanting view of the valleys down below.

When E. Augusta King reached her dwelling in Landour, in 1880, she saw to her amazement that it was at the extreme end of the narrow rocky ridge on which Landour itself was located. It looked "southward down, down, down to the scorching plains, and northward over all the intervening ranges to the great snow range". There was a lovely garden in front of the house, beyond the veranda, with a railing around the edge, from which the hills fell into a precipice of 1,000 feet.

The interiors of the houses in the hill stations were also built in European styles. The roof was always plastered so the ugly beams would be concealed and the woodwork was mostly varnished. There would be fireplaces in all the right places, which the memsahibs used every evening. Usually, they brought in their books, pictures, and piano, and set up their temporary houses to be cosy and homely. Emily Eden ecstatically wrote, "I shall be chilly! This dear Simla! It snowed yesterday, and has been hailing to-day, and is now thundering, in a cracking, sharp way".

Memsahibs who moved to hill stations for the whole of the summer to stay in their privately owned summerhouses travelled with a sizeable group of servants; Emily Eden had more than sixty servants to lodge in outhouses near her bungalow in Shimla. After housing the servants, they would set about modelling and remodelling their lodgings with the carpets, chandeliers, and shades they brought with them. If something needed repair, they brought in carpenters and blacksmiths; after all, the houses had been empty for months and required thorough fixing up. They also called gardeners to tend to the potted plants of violets they brought with them, remove the overgrowth, and liven up the backyards. They then set about mending the draperies, sofas, and rugs. Later, they went to examine their kitchen gardens, which could run down to almost half a mile. After settling in, the memsahibs would begin their neighbourly interactions.

The social climate in such hill stations was tailored to resemble the practices back home, evoking nostalgia for their old way of life. But a mode of interaction peculiar to the Raj was the system of 'chits', which were basically scraps of paper with messages on them exchanged between neighbours in quick succession. This system was enforced quite strictly in the more cloistered neighbourhoods of hill stations, due to the close proximity of neighbours.

Contrary to what one might imagine, the ordinarily company-deprived memsahibs often suffered under the burdens of such speedy message delivery systems. If a neighbour sent a chit, they had to respond immediately, or be considered rude. Lady Campbell Wilson was quite annoyed with such chits while she was sojourning in Sakesar, the highest mountain range in northern Punjab (now in Pakistan) in 1889, as they asked sundry domestic queries such as "would it be convenient to kill a sheep tomorrow?", or "who could mend the roof of a house, and whitewash walls?", or even "might Mrs. X. see today's papers, and could I oblige her by sending some tape, thread, and buttons?". They could be quite tiresome to someone who wanted to maintain some seclusion in their home, particularly because they were holidaying in the hills, away from their regular memsahib responsibilities.

However, hill stations were small, and everybody recognised everybody, so it was usually difficult to maintain privacy. Sometimes, the relationship between neighbours became extremely strained because people were suddenly thrust together. Lady Campbell Wilson mentions the story of two couples in Sakesar who ended up "cutting each other" when they met one evening for their walks on the narrow circular road in one of the hill stations because of some dispute over the daily supply of milk.

It turned out that there was no escaping the role of the memsahib for dignitaries like Lady Alice Isaacs, Marchioness of Reading and wife of the Viceroy Lord Reading, who served from 1921 to 1926, no matter what corner of the country they were in. Indeed, the social relations in hill station were just as tight as in other circumstances, despite the marked casualness of the atmosphere; rank and ceremony never ceased to matter even in the more relaxed society of the hills. Lady Reading always wished to slip into the crowds in marketplaces in incognito mode in order to enjoy the ordinary pleasures of hill-towns.

It may be said that the social customs and practices were more nuanced here than in the other places. Moreover, since government authorities began migrating to hill stations with their work, the importance of ceremony within these holiday zones also increased. Christina S. Bremner wrote in 1891:

> The relations of the ladies at a station is a delicate topic which should be touched on with fear and trembling… "You need to know the ropes out here", said one who did; but even she occasionally found she had pulled the wrong ones, though she devoted a naturally fine intelligence to their study. "It would not do to invite Mrs. D.; her husband is a ranker."

Lady Campbell Wilson was anxious about the social etiquette observed in hill stations amongst the British circles. Before her first dinner party, she was worried about the "Indian bible of precedence" and did not know about anyone's official position and title, far less about grades and steps, whereas every other person knew about such matters. She did not even know her own family's place in the official hierarchy and hoped to learn quickly because frank allusions were made to such things on all occasions. She took comfort in the fact that another person amongst her acquaintances was as ignorant as her about the laws of precedence. Lady Reading, however, was unconventional in this respect, as she did not shy away from inviting Indians to her special parties at the Viceregal Lodge, which were not only for official memsahibs and sahibs.

But not all vicereines relished the social expectations on high society in the hill stations. When she was at Shimla, Lady Mary Curzon lived in a large colonnaded bungalow with long verandas and a riverside garden. There was a Gothic-styled church nearby and a golf course. The Viceregal lodge, which had been built by the Dufferins in a beautiful Jacobethan style, was luxurious with its multiple suites of apartments and large halls. However, it failed to impress Mary Curzon who called it absurd and cheap. She also did not enjoy the social life in the hill station. The hectic schedules were so overwhelming that it was said that Shimla had worsened Lord Curzon's insomnia; however, social duties were not a matter of choice for individuals occupying high office in the Raj, and there were no exceptions for the Viceroyalty. On top of their regular hosting duties, the viceregal couple were duty-bound to entertain large groups of people on a regular basis, and to attend picnics, camps, polo matches, concerts, and theatre performances, especially during their stay in Shimla. They even had to mark their presence at some weddings and prize giveaways at competitions (Nicholson, 124).

Some of the memsahibs' writings reveal a kind of frenzy that seemed to come over them in places like Shimla, where they were simply unable to avoid or resist attending parties again and again. India was supposed to be the 'land of dinners', as England was the 'land of 5 o'clock teas', and the memsahibs, especially those who had been posted in isolated towns, dived into the custom almost desperately. It seemed that as soon as someone set foot in hill stations, they were gripped by the 'party fever', obsessively keeping up with the flurry of dinners and dances. The nervous *debutantes* of every season were particularly eager to see and be seen. Emily Eden mentioned a Miss T., who had ridden for 42 miles on the steep hills without stopping, just to make it to a dinner in Shimla. The sun was scorching and the skin on her shoulder had burnt through her habit, but that had not deterred her.

British women also attended *purdah* parties, where even women practicing '*purdah*' would attend, and it allowed them the rather rare opportunity to mingle with upper-class Indian women who would usually be sequestered in their domestic spaces. At such parties, the Indian women remained in a separate segregated space where only ladies were present. '*Purdah*' literally means 'curtain' and was a religious custom practised widely in the nineteenth century amongst Hindus and Muslims in India, in which women would keep their face concealed behind a veil, especially in male company or in public, and mostly remained secluded in specified female-only quarters of their homes. Lady Alice Reading wrote about such parties around the year 1921; she enjoyed them for the eclectic mix of people present. In Iris Butler's edition of her collected letters, an excerpt is provided highlighting how both she and Yvonne Fitzroy enjoyed them fully:

> July 5th: A very full week starting with the Purdah Party which I really think was a huge success. Miss F., the girls (Mary Mond and Doris Robson who had arrived to stay) and helpers were splendid. The Aides were much chagrined when I told them how little they were missed! We had the Hindoo ladies behind a screen in the ballroom with their fruit, sweets, and about 50 of them, the other 50 at small tables, but the Hindoos were so afraid of missing they continually appeared from behind the screen, had to be shoo'd back.

In 1887, Lady Dufferin attended twelve big dinners, twenty-nine small dinners, one state ball, one fancy ball, one children's fancy ball, six dances, three garden parties and two evening parties during her sojourn in Shimla. The total number of events was fifty-four, and the number of guests she dined with overall was over 600. It is no surprise that the endless parties and gatherings caused illness and exhaustion, particularly for women who would be in charge of overseeing the arrangements if they were hostesses. Lady Dufferin found herself ill on the day they were supposed to host a big dinner. She was too sick to leave the bed but too anxious to relax and followed everything from her bed by listening to the sounds below. This was not the only time that she was unable to resist the urge to participate in gatherings, willing to risk severe complications for the sake of a party. Even after days of feeling unwell and weak, when it came to a ball they were invited to, she was determined to go and wrote, "I must consider myself convalescent, though feeble".

Hill stations weren't always synonymous with party-filled holidays, however. Some towns developed their status due to the commercial value of such areas. In the 1830s, the British government had begun looking for new methods of tea production in India after the East India Company lost its monopoly rights in tea trade with China. Darjeeling became one of the first hill stations to be made into a summer residence. Lady Dufferin was travelling there with some women in the year 1887 and recorded her travels in her photographs and journals. During her upward journey to Darjeeling, she visited convalescent homes, women's schools, and even photography shops. She marvelled at the indigenous communities such as the Lepchas and Gorkhas and was fascinated by their unique cultures and ethnic attire. She was particularly charmed by the colourful praying flags hanging all around, rippling in the winds. In Shimla, she carried along her magnificent boudoir and writing tools to add to her repository of personal accounts of her sojourns in hill stations, which she penned from the Viceregal Lodge.

Mussoorie, the 'Queen of the hills', was yet another popular hill station back in the day. It was closest to Delhi, and although it was smaller than Shimla, it was just as vibrant and picturesque and much less expensive. It was called the 'the Happy valley', with its 'gymkhanas' (gentlemen's clubs or places for sporting events), breakfast clubs, and hotels like the Savoy, which were frequented by the British and Indian elite. Fanny Eden, sister of Emily Eden, who came to India to visit their brother the Governor-General Lord Auckland, mentioned in her journal written in 1838 how the hotels were built so impressively by bringing in all the furnishings, liquor, and so on from the plains.

Moreover, Mussoorie was quite accessible from the nearby plains where officers and their wives were stationed, so people came in from all around. Every morning, the officers would go to the public room for breakfast and spend hours in the company of women. At noon, the memsahibs would mount their horses and ride around, before going to the clubs for lunch. The clatter of knives and forks during mealtimes at the clubs was incredibly exciting. To add to the charm, there were majestic views from any window they looked out from. From the back of the clubs and houses, Dehradun was visible, just about a mile off, and in the distance, the eternal snow-capped mountains and the lush forests could be seen.

The Mall Road in Mussoorie was a fashionable promenade, which was frequented by the British, and some hills like 'Jakko' and 'Camel's Back' were tourist hotspots. If a sahib saw a lady making her way to the *bazaar* to buy a bonnet, he would ask to accompany her, then join another party to dine. In the evenings, the crowds listened to performances of 'Pop Goes the Weasel' and other English songs with Indian tunes, performed by Indian conjurers and performers (Lang, *Wanderings*, 7–8). Stargazing was a popular social pastime. Lady Dufferin was amused at the conjuring trick of making "two eggs fight". She enjoyed visiting tea plantations and gazed at the scenes through her telescope.

Memsahibs were completely drawn into a life of fun and frolic in the hills and were pleasantly surprised when they found themselves to be the centre of attention because there were many parties to attend, and the gentlemen were always asking to escort them for the evening. They would not even have enough dresses and accessories to keep up with the volley of dances. Some of them spent their days sewing new dresses to wear to such and such a party from materials they purchased from local shops. It did not matter what the quality of such cloth was. In places like Shimla or Mussoorie, it was simply important to have a variety of dresses and look beautiful at all times.

Emily Eden wrote in her journal in 1839 about Lola Montez (then known as Mrs. James), whose arrival in Shimla that year caused a significant stir. Montez was bewitchingly exquisite, and eventually became notorious in the English circles for being a cunning seductress and adulterer. After her separation from her husband, she had become a dancer and then a mistress of King Ludwig of Bavaria. She later became a lecturer in New York and authored books. In Shimla that year, she was the beauty of the season because of her striking features and made every lady jealous of her. She was engaged to be married to a Lieutenant who was 15 years older to her, which caused some gossip at the time.

Fetes were popular in Shimla, and sometimes they were arranged exclusively for the members of the Viceroy's office. During such events, there would be tall arches and impressive *shamianas* (tents) all around with hanging decorations and decorated tables. Sometimes, the organisers would even hire Indians for *tamasha* (a form of street performance, sometimes involving dancing and singing), in which hundreds of *tamasha-wallahs* (performers) gathered in a racecourse while the British sat above, watching them. Bands would be hired to play music in an illuminated space, and there would be a handsome carpeted area, which led up to the theatre. The cannons would go off at intervals, and there would be men in uniforms appreciatively gazing at every woman who passed by. They would sometimes go down to nearby areas like Mashobra for temporary sojourns where they would have handsome picnics.

Hill stations were mostly meant to provide the seasonal migrants with a temporary escape from the dreary *mofussil* life of India. They also offered the British a kind of simulated 'home' as an alternative to going back.

Yet, these spaces were exactly the opposite of 'home' in some senses. These were places where people shed their ordinary social and moral codes, and in that they were impermanent anti-homes, removed from everyday life.

"The *Chota Peg* of Sinful Delight": Love, Romance, and Scandals

the Neilgherry Hills are very much 'like 'board ship: few enjoy them who have not the amusement of making love to fall back upon… It is a grand place for courtship… and many a young man who goes up there for six months or a year on sick leave, comes down with perhaps a worse burthen in the shape of a wife, for which the only consolation is, what can't be cured must be—the other thing.

There are always plenty of females on the hills, consequently the hills are dangerous to the idle man. There are the wives who can't live with their husbands in the plains; the "grass widows" (or widows put out to grass), as they are vulgarly termed; and as won't might very often be read for can't, perhaps they are (without any reference to the amount of their charms) the most dangerous that the idle young man could encounter. Then there are the young ladies whose parents are not able, or not willing, to send to England just yet, but who are too old to live with safety in the heat of Madras.

– Florence Marryat, 1868

Hill stations in colonial India were described as like a long voyage on a ship because there would often be little news about the world outside except what would arrive in mail. Perhaps it was because of this that these cloistered spaces, where constant mingling and interactions between the sexes took place, were seen as fertile ground for flirtations.

Moreover, the cultural scene of hill stations was quite rich, and conducive for all matters of love and lust. As various theatres sprang up, they were identified as major dens of sin and vice as they offered a pleasurable deviation from daily monotony, and exposed people to undue temptations. In these towns, gossip was common, which was to be expected in spaces that had conglomerations of British people attempting to have a sense of home outside home.

It is, therefore, not surprising that hill stations became synonymous with 'release' of various kinds, for providing an escape from the propriety of British society. Eventually, they acquired a reputation for being hotbeds of extra-marital romances. In fact, scandals were one of the prime features of hill stations in colonial India. Maud Diver's novel, *Candles in the Wind* (1909), mentions a woman in Shimla who became involved with a young man despite being married, and how she became completely obsessed with her lover, reached "the end of her tether", and wanted to elope with him. When a mother of young girls bemoaned that her daughters would never find husbands, they said: "Who cares, Mother? We're having lots of fun."

It is likely that extra-marital liaisons occurred because hill stations were populated mostly with memsahibs who were sojourning solo in the hills while their husbands worked in their posts in the plains. The young officers who regularly went up to hill stations to recuperate from illnesses or fatigue were only too willing to provide them company. Lady Reading said of Shimla in her letters: "Every Jack has someone else's Jill!"

Several racy real-life incidents in hill stations even inspired writers like J. G. Farrell and Rudyard Kipling, the latter of whom dramatised the events of hill stations in the memorable *Plain Tales from the Hills* (1888). The so-called 'frivolity' of British women in hill stations was quite infamous. The Shimla women were so notorious that it was said that their presence even distracted the Raj officials who were stationed there for government work.

Purportedly, the hill station also influenced the last Viceregal couple of India, the Mountbattens. In May 1947, just weeks before he announced the granting of dominion status to India and the partition of the country, Louis Mountbatten took his family to Shimla to spend a few relaxing days in the cool weather, away from the heat of Delhi. During that trip, Jawaharlal Nehru, soon-to-be Prime Minister of a newly independent India, and V. K. Krishna Menon, High Commissioner of India to the United Kingdom, joined them at the Viceregal Lodge.

Amidst salacious rumours of a passionate affair between Nehru and the Vicereine, Lady Edwina Mountbatten, the pair went on rides together in public, making frequent appearances on Shimla roads. It was clear by that time that they were not afraid of being seen together, and in fact Shimla became a special milestone in their unnamed relationship. When Edwina's letters were retrieved years later, one of them carried her admission: "I have fond memories of Simla—riding and your touch" (Lownie, 470).

In many ways, the entanglement between Nehru and Edwina is one of the most compelling romances of the empire. It was tender yet wildly romantic, forbidden, and hidden in plain sight. Exchanges between Louis Mountbatten (aka 'Dickie') and Edwina revealed that he, at least, was aware of the relationship; however, despite being cruelly mocked for being 'cuckolded' by a 'native', he had accepted the ambiguity of his wife's feelings for Nehru. The extent of his complaisance was seen when they were at Mashobra near Shimla, in 1948, and they went on a walk outside one evening, and as usual, Edwina and Nehru became engrossed in each other. Mountbatten then mindfully fell behind with his daughter, seemingly to let them converse freely. In fact, whenever the two were engaged in deep conversation, Mountbatten would tactfully leave to give them privacy. Edwina's daughter, Pamela Hicks, in her autobiography *Daughter of the Empire: Life as a Mountbatten* (2012), acknowledged the consolidation of Edwina and Nehru's already deepening relationship during the trip to Mashobra. She recalled how at that time she could not sense that her mother's regard for Nehru was stronger than deep friendship, but the trip did seem to bring them closer.

It was known that Mountbatten cherished his friendship with Nehru and did not want to intrude on Nehru's friendship with Edwina. He once confessed that although he was hurt by their relationship, he did not feel jealous. It was understood that he had immense trust in them both, even though the people around considered it odd that he gave Edwina so much liberty. However, it is likely that he gave his wife so much space because he was aware of his limitations as a husband. Edwina was constantly isolated and intellectually deprived, and Nehru fulfilled the role that he could not because of his administrative duties. He had often been confronted by Edwina for being constantly buried in work and for neglecting her, and it was only after her association with Nehru progressed that her outbursts towards him abated. He was glad to have her occupied (Lownie, 431).

There is uncertainty about the exact nature of the bond between Edwina and Nehru. Lady Pamela Hicks herself was unable to decipher whether their relationship was sexual or wholly platonic, despite her closeness to both (Hicks, 228). Pamela wrote that she could be sure that they never had the opportunity to be engaged in a physical relationship as they were always accompanied by others, surrounded by staff, police, and other official personnel. Edwina's biographer also indicated the same. Nonetheless, there seemed to have been an "element of the physical alongside the spiritual" (Lownie, 480). Nehru and Edwina had once been seen embracing each other alone in a room. In the 1950s, after India's independence, Nehru went to meet her in London, and it was speculated that they might have lain together (Tunzelmann, 650). Moreover, in one of Edwina's letters to Nehru, later recovered, she wrote,

"Dickie will be out tonight—come after 10.00 o'clock", and "You forgot your handkerchief, and before Dickie could spot it I covered it up" (Tunzelmann, 386), suggesting their clandestine meetings were perhaps illicit in nature.

In any case, Edwina, before anything else, shared a deep platonic relationship with Nehru, finding in him an intellectual partner who filled the void of an equal and compatible companion in her life. They were both lonely, and their friendship provided them both with emotional support (Lownie, 479–80). Nehru had been a widower since 1936, and his daughter, Indira Gandhi, was married and involved in her own family and her career as a member of the Congress Party. Pamela Hicks wrote in her memoirs of an intimate token given to Nehru by her mother:

> As we took our places, I saw her fumbling with something around her neck, an urgency to her movements that betrayed her calm exterior. She whispered something to her PA and passed her something in a closed fist, motioning for her to leave the plane. It was only later that I discovered the PA had been sent out with my mother's precious St. Christopher to find a safe pair of hands to get it to Panditji [Nehru] (231).

Edwina and Nehru's rumoured dalliances in the mountains are a rather sensational yet fitting illustration of the typical perception that hill stations were morally 'risky' spaces because of the easy opportunities for liaisons. Memsahibs were available in plenty, and the chivalrous officers lavished their attention on them knowing their husbands were not around.

This was particularly true for hotels. Several of them flourished in the days of the Raj in hill stations for British men and women wanting temporary boarding. Affluent sahibs and memsahibs who did not have their own residences in the hills stayed in these hotels, which then became centres for social events and parties. Moreover, such hotels gave men and women relative privacy and were regularly used by couples having secret affairs. Since a lady could not call her lover to her own house, and a man could not expect her to visit him at his, couples came to an arrangement where for the duration of the liaison of 2 weeks or so, they would move to a hotel. In such cases, the memsahib and her lover would not take the same room to avoid suspicion but would instead take rooms on the same floor. After lights went out at night, the man would discreetly move into the lady's room and leave after some hours. The establishments were mostly aware of such goings-on and turned a blind eye, but one of the hotels was particularly sensitive: they employed a half-blind man who walked around the corridors with a bell to warn the sahibs to go back to their own rooms in case they had nodded off so that they would not have any awkward incidents in the morning when the servants turned up to clean the rooms ("The Lost World of the Raj", Ep. 2, 51.00–54.00).

In the 1930s, Lillian Skinner stayed at the Hackman's Hotel in Mussoorie, which was located prominently on the Mall Road. It was a popular spot for dining and drinking and had a proper sprung floor so people also came for dancing. Mrs. Hackman, who ran the place, had decorated it tastefully and was very particular about what everyone wore and how they behaved. Guests had to observe proper etiquette at all times, but despite the watchful eyes of the hotelier, flirtations were common. Lillian Skinner once caught the eye of a Maharaja, but unfortunately, he came up just to her nose, so it was a great challenge to dance with him ("The Lost World of the Raj", Ep. 2, 45.00–47.00). It was well known that hill stations were like 'playgrounds' for rajas and maharajas who enjoyed European women's company. Shimla had many restrictions and protocols that discouraged this because of the presence of the government, but Mussoorie was much more liberal, and it was said that "those who came to whoop it up, came to Mussoorie" ("The Lost World of the Raj", Ep. 2, 39.00–41.00).

However, the presence of Indians destabilised the normal proceedings of hill-society, and mixed dances could cause controversy because of the close encounters between the British and Indians, especially the mingling between Indian men and single or unmarried British women. Lillian Skinner recalled how one of the maharajas once made a 'pass' at the then Viceroy's daughter and was subsequently banned from Shimla. Indeed, prejudices towards Indians were prevalent even in the liberal and 'saturnalian' spaces of hills, and most British men and women remained disinclined and sceptical about freely mingling with Indian men, due to stereotypes about their morality.

Emily Eden was similarly hesitant. In 1839, when she was in Shimla and there was to be a ball, the ladies had decided that they would not dance because a Sikh deputation was present, and they had no idea how to dance before 'natives'. This was because the general perception was that Indian men had only seen women dancing as *nautch girls* (professional dancers who performed for the entertainment of an assembled audience). Although the viewers were not always males, such forms of entertainment were tied closely with erotic performative arts meant for the pleasure of men. It made British women feel awkward, and scrupulous women avoided dancing completely. Eden wrote that this was inconvenient because it was too late to change the plans as the envoys had already been asked. A memsahib finally stepped forward and declared that she would dance every quadrille to show the other women how idiotic their decision was. As it turned out, eventually almost every other woman came onto the floor, dressed elegantly and dancing with complete abandon before Indians. In fact, they were delighted to see that Indian men were exceedingly chivalrous. Each lady was engaged for seven or eight quadrilles, and there was no room on the floor. Emily Eden wrote later, "Two of them had seen English dancing before, and were aware that the ladies were ladies, and not nautch-girls… I own, when some of the dancers asked for a waltz… I was afraid the Sikhs might have been a little astonished; and I think Govind Jus gave Golaub Singh a slight nudge as General K—whisked past with his daughter; but I dare say they thought it pretty".

There is no doubt that the British were wary of such socialising. In Kasauli, where Christina S. Bremner was staying in 1891, a noted Indian prince came to visit, accompanied by his entourage. During a dance where he was present, everybody waited with bated breath to see if the Indian Raja would dare to ask an Englishwoman for a dance and put his arm around her waist. This would have been a major '*faux-pas*' because there were rumours about the Raja's character. And even though this was merely speculation, a military officer's wife declared that she would consider it an insult to even be asked by him.

The forbidden nature of such mixed-race couplings gave hill stations a kind of cultural dubiousness owing to the apparent precariousness of British standards of moral conduct. Indian men were believed to be liable to negatively influence British women, vulnerable as they were due to being alone in the hills. However, there was no evidence to actually point to the presence of 'native' men 'corrupting' the British in the hill stations—they were often quite willingly getting 'corrupted', or simply busy corrupting one another! One officer found his wife in bed with his best friend and caused a great furore, after which the couple and the lady's paramour had to leave the station (de Courcy, 187).

As Viceroy between 1872 and 1876, Lord Northbrook became infamous for the problems in his personal life, which suddenly became very public. He had been doubly bereaved after the demise of his son and wife and, in 1875, found comfort in a "notorious white woman", Mrs. Searle, in a hill station called Ranikhet—an affair that invited controversy at the time (Hyam, 28). His son, Frank, had also become embroiled in an "unfortunate attachment" with a married woman in Shimla, causing a lot of gossip and intrigue (de Courcy, 186).

In the hill stations, anonymity could be maintained if the couples were careful, but a single oversight could expose affairs. Despite hotels, there was no actual privacy, and in cases of longer liaisons, the truth came out eventually. In fact, licentiousness seemed to be the norm, and if people saw a man and a lady leave together, they knew the reason. Everybody knew everybody else's activities, and if a lady and a gentleman were spotted together frequently, it was automatically assumed they were having a fling. Even extra-marital affairs were all too common in places like Mussoorie.

Mixed-race extra-marital affairs took place with remarkable casualness among the lower echelons of British society. A salesgirl in Mussoorie became involved with an old Maharaja and appeared some days later in a liveried rickshaw. When everyone asked her where she had been and what the Maharaja had done to her, imagining all sorts of orgies and sexual feats, she simply said that all she did for the Maharaja was bathe a number of times a day in his beautiful suite of rooms with a lovely shell bath, while he did nothing but sit and watch ("The Lost World of the Raj", Ep. 2, 49.00–51.00).

Although uncorroborated, there is a famous romantic legend about a love affair in Shimla that is still recounted zealously by local guides to fascinate tourists: it is the legend of the 'Scandal Point' in Shimla. The story goes back to the 1870s when the Maharaja of Patiala was said to have abducted the daughter of a Viceroy, an enchanting lady whom he fell passionately in love with. Another version of the tale suggests that the lady was not abducted and that the couple fell in love and decided to elope to avoid social censure. Although there is no historical proof, this urban myth just serves to demonstrate how gossip spread quickly through hill stations and often took the place of reality in people's imagination.

It must be said that for all the fun and parties, the official British line was extremely critical of memsahibs engaging in philanderous behaviour. Emily Eden, horrified by the corrupt mood of hill stations, wrote that it was dangerous for women to be left alone by their husbands in a country like India. There was no doubt that hill stations were romantic places (they continue to be popular honeymoon destinations even today), but the moral climate was always too liberal for some colonials. The Vicereine Mary Curzon wrote with contempt about the social environment of the hill station; she found the frivolity of the place tiresome. Lord Curzon also said that Shimla's remarkable feature was its "sinister novelty, always having to begin again and again with each year a new set of idlers, gossips and liars" (Nicholson, 124). John Lang, an Australian writer, journalist, and lawyer who worked as a barrister in India in the nineteenth century, wrote:

> The mall is crowded. Ladies and gentlemen on horseback, and ladies in *janpans*—the *janpanees* dressed in every variety of livery. Men in the French grey coats, trimmed with white serge, are carrying Mrs. Hastings. Men in the brown clothes, trimmed with yellow serge, are carrying Mrs. Merrydale. Jack Apsley's wife is mounted on her husband's second charger. 'Come along Captain Wall', she calls out to me, and goes off at a canter, which soon becomes a hard gallop. I follow her of course. Jack remains behind, to have a quiet chat with Mrs. Flower, of his regiment, who thinks—and Jack agrees with her—that hard riding on the mall is a nuisance, and ought to be put

> a stop to. But as we come back, we meet the hypocrite galloping with Miss Pinkerton, a new importation, with whom—much to the amusement of his wife—he affects to be desperately in love. The mall, by the way, is a great place for flirtations... What can a man do when a pretty woman like Mrs Apsley says, 'Come along; let us have a gallop' (Lang, *Wanderings*, 10).

On the other hand, Maud Diver, a British-Indian writer, argued that Shimla had already acquired a bad reputation over the years, and the space itself impacted women, no matter how virtuous they were, turning them into coquettes. She wrote in 1909, "the Simla woman... is frivolous and free and easy in both mind and manners". Her attempt at redeeming British women in hill stations was mostly to demonstrate that they could not be 'blamed' for immorality. She attributed the flirtation and 'debaucheries' to the multitude of widows who were genuinely alone and lonely, and for whom the attentions of handsome officers were understandably welcome. She was extremely critical of the continuous gossip around women in Shimla and was extremely generous to the so-called 'roving' memsahib, arguing that the husbands ought to have sufficiently warned and protected the women against the dangers of hill stations like Shimla. She argued that instead of just condemning the foolishness of the wives, part of the blame should be put on the indifference or lack of wisdom of the husbands. According to her, the British colonial wife was merely a victim of her circumstances. Amidst the slander piled on the "Simla woman", her attempt at understanding the cause for the supposed "frivolity" seems somewhat kinder.

Undoubtedly, the hill stations that produced a heady and liberating 'holiday effect' on the psyche of the sahibs and memsahibs were both liked and despised. Moreover, despite the apparent sleaziness of the hill stations, they remained the preferred summer destinations for memsahibs across the ranks, throughout the British period in India. In fact, it is quite possible that it was precisely the deplorable reputation of the hill stations that drew large crowds every summer.

8

MISSIE BABAS AND *BABA LOGS*

THE JUNIOR IMPERIALISTS, THEIR MOTHERS, AND THEIR *AYAHS*

> *India is fast losing its old appellation of 'exile' and becoming the real home, or at least the second home, of hundreds of men and women… A sad time, however, awaits the wife in India, and that is when the children have reached the age of five or six, and the dreadful question of sending them home arises. Now comes the real wrench, and she has to choose between staying with her husband or following her children. "Shall I go, or shall I stay?"… The husband generally wins the day, and the cries of joy and woe of the little ones are no longer heard on the verandah, and night after night the mother goes to sleep with an aching, yearning heart, wondering if her children are crying for her. No page in life is sadder than this one in the story of Anglo-Indian experience. Yet, perhaps, there is one thing sadder still; and that is, when we walk through an Indian cemetery, to see the number of tiny graves. The average mortality of English people in India is about three in 200 men, three in 200 women, and nine in 200 children.*
>
> – Adeline Georgina Kingscote, 1893

The arrival of a child in a British-Indian household was not just a matter of familial joy—it was a matter that concerned the future of the whole community. These children of 'British origins' were unlike their parents in that they belonged to the land more organically, signifying that the colonial settlement project was progressing. They were deemed to be the future sahibs and memsahibs, and their mothers fashioned them as such, knowing that the fate of the empire in the subcontinent was in their hands.

This formed the basis of motherhood within the British colonial project. Needless to say, parenting was the sole responsibility of the mothers, and as soon as a memsahib got pregnant, she knew that her real work as an 'agent' of the Raj had begun. They believed that making preparations for the arrival of their babies was a good way of utilising time as they spent many idle hours indoors. They also found that the extensive needlework, feeding, training, and so on could be soothing to the nerves. Decorating the nursery was also customary, as it was back home in England, and many memsahibs delighted in importing items from London. If they were not able to do that, they had ample options such as Whiteaway, Laidlaw & Co., Calcutta.

However, the task of child-rearing was a great challenge as tending to babies in India was not the same as it was back home in England. The general practices of British mothers that memsahibs were familiar with did not apply to India, and neither did the advice that poured in from their families in letters. For instance, while it was common practice to let the babies wet their cradles without changing their napkins constantly, especially if they did not wake up, in the hot climate of India it was considered prudent to keep the diapers under the body without pinning them up to let the air pass around. Memsahibs purchased the waterproof sheathing at Ranganatham and Co., Madras, and placed them in the beds of slightly older babies who wore short clothes. The napkins were also of a specific shape and meant especially for the 'Anglo-Indian' baby (Anglo-Indian was a term applied to persons of British origins and not just people of mixed descent).

The very overwhelmed new mother struggled, especially if there were financial constraints. But if money was no object, she had useful facilities at her disposal. Still, little things in childcare could become a great challenge to memsahibs who found themselves alone and confused in secluded postings, yet under pressure to follow strict measures for tending to their children. In the absence of their own relatives, these rather bewildered new mothers sometimes asked other memsahibs who might be in the same place as them to come in and check on them regularly.

To deal with their difficulties, memsahibs read manuals meant for new mothers in India, such as *The English Baby in India and How to Rear It* (1893) by Adeline Kingscote, an English author who wrote several novels under the pseudonyms 'Lucas Cleeve' and 'Mrs. Howard Kingscote'. This manual was culled from her own experiences in India where she lived for several years and was meant for the use of "Anglo-Indian mothers and specially ... the wives of the British soldiers". The book contained several directions and warnings, as well as anecdotes from her own life to tell the readers the lessons she herself had learnt while her children were growing up. For instance, she wrote that the Anglo-Indian baby's delicate skin was prone to insect bites and allergies and serious mishaps could occur even within the home if the mothers were not diligent. She mentioned a memsahib who kept her baby in a bamboo basket, which was dangerous because such baskets were the favourite breeding places of insects and pests.

Furthermore, health concerns of the babies were a major priority for the new mothers. They were painfully aware that the first month was extremely critical for their babies due to various aggressive 'tropical diseases' that they could succumb to. Some diseases could cause speedy death or permanent disfigurement, and they inoculated their infants religiously.

It was commonly understood that India weakened the physical constitution of the Anglo-Indian baby, as the changes in temperature made them vulnerable to colds and heat strokes. Edmund C. P. Hull and R. S. Mair, in *The European in India or, Anglo-Indian's Vade-Mecum* (1878), wrote that the European child required the most care in the first year, as India could easily prove to be fatal to children. Others asserted that later childhood years were more dangerous. In *The Management and Medical Treatment of Children in India* (1895), Edward A. Birch wrote:

> There is a pretty general medical opinion that the Indian climate does not in any way injure the health of the European infant during

> the first year of its life; further than this, the conviction is prevalent that with proper precautions up to the age of 5 or 6 years the child may be reared nearly as satisfactorily in the plains of India as in Europe; but beyond these ages all are agreed that physical and moral degeneration occur. The child then "exhibits the necessity for change of climate by emaciating and outgrowing its strength". So profoundly does the climate, after the period of immediate childhood, influence the constitution that the effect of a more prolonged residence is rendered permanent throughout life (14).

There was no end to the recommendations memsahibs found in the books and manuals, and they tried to incorporate as much as they could in their own baby's care. However, this was not always easy because they usually employed a nurse—'*ayah*'—directly after giving birth, and sometimes old nurses were not open to instructions. The young mothers had to keep an eye on them despite their own frail health. For instance, they had to ensure that the babies' nipples were not broken, as was the habit with some of the old-fashioned nurses.

Negotiating with their *ayahs* was not always easy as even the good *ayahs* had their own preconceived notions about childcare, which kept undercutting the memsahibs' wishes. In any case, conveying to their *ayahs* the entirety of the Western manner of rearing children was an altogether impossible enterprise. Since communicating with them across the language and culture barriers could often be a challenge, it was also difficult to give specific instructions, and expect them to follow through properly. Thus, British mothers often felt that there wasn't enough coordination between them and their help.

As mentioned in Chapter 2, there was also a tendency amongst memsahibs to have an attitude of mistrust towards domestic help at times, and when it came to babies, new mothers were particularly protective and felt they had to constantly police the nursery, even if their *ayahs* were experienced and efficient. Besides, there were enough stories about 'lax' Indian nurses to make them wary. They had to repeatedly insist that the child was washed twice daily with Pears or Castile soap, unless they were of delicate health. The temperature of the bath had to be checked because washing a baby with cold water could be fatal. Mothers were advised to mind the way the nurses bound their infants because tying them up too tightly made them flatulent. They were also told to watch what was being fed to their children because giving them sugar or butter, as nurses sometimes did, could be detrimental to their health.

Memsahibs controlled their children in the ways that they could, but not all of the tight control they attempted to exercise was down to social and cultural prejudice. Sometimes there were legitimate practical reasons to keep a close eye on children in India, such as the risk of infectious diseases. It was a common practice to employ Indian wet nurses for feeding babies, but memsahibs believed this could be dangerous because it meant that the child would be constantly exposed to the germs carried by them in case of any infections. They were particularly concerned because the nurses would be less likely to have been inoculated or to have access to medicine, and certainly less likely to subscribe to emerging Victorian ideas of sanitation. Once a lady discovered that her *ayah's* child was suffering from smallpox, and that she went to suckle it twice every day, in between feeding her mistress' baby.

It was widely believed that leaving little children with *ayahs* for protracted periods could sometimes be alarmingly perilous. Kingscote warned that as far as she had seen, *ayahs* sometimes took to drugging children. Some did it because it made it easier for them to manage work, and some did it out of a mistaken sense of pity for the crying babies. They apparently believed that enforcing sleep on a baby if it happened to be suffering due to even small ailments like stomach ache would be beneficial for it. However, they gave the children *arrack* (alcoholic spirits made of fermented sap, mostly distilled locally), which could prove to be fatal as it could cause a temporary paralysis of the stomach.

Kingscote mentioned that this had happened to a couple when they employed a local to be their newborn child's maid. This child unfortunately died soon after birth from a mysterious illness, which even doctors could not understand. 2 years later, a new baby was born, and it was healthy although rather restless. The monthly nurse left it after 4 weeks, after which the same *ayah* began to take care of it. It was 6 weeks old when its health suddenly deteriorated as it refused a proper diet, despite having had no trouble following this earlier on. After some time, the baby refused food altogether and lay sleeping, looking flushed at all times. The symptoms were the same as the previous baby, and the parents realised this child too would die. Finally, a doctor was able to see that the baby was being drugged. It was then that it came out that there was a common practice of dipping the tips of one or two fingers in a solution of drugs and letting it dry. Then whenever the *ayah* wanted to administer a dose, they made the child suckle the fingers. Sometimes, they even used a form of cannabis, called Indian hemp, which usually induced cheerfulness and then slumber. Although this practice was not very common, memsahibs tried to stay alert to any signs of drugging in their infants.

Many panicking new mothers were advised not to worry too much and not to investigate too closely what was going on around them because trying to control everything their *ayahs* did could simply be futile.

This need to turn a blind eye to things, for the sake of one's own sanity, became evident once when a Major and his wife moved to a house next door to Kingscote. The Major's wife had a baby within a month, but a fortnight after her confinement she came down with measles, which she was likely to have caught on-board the troop ship. Her English nurse and baby also caught the infection, and her eldest was sent to Kingscote until they recovered. Kingscote, fearing infection for her own children if her clothes were washed with the clothes of the Major's family (since *dhobis* (washermen) took all the clothes from the neighbourhood and washed them together near the river or a common tank), took the precaution of giving the washerman separate washing tubs and soaps. She also doubled his wages on the condition that he was to wash their clothes in her compound. The *dhobi* agreed to it, and she was happy with her ingenious method; however, some days later, she spotted an enormous pile of dirty clothes being brought across the road from the Major's house into her compound to be washed. Instead of taking the ailing woman's clothes to the tank and washing hers in her compound, he saved himself the trouble and simply washed both of the families' clothes in her compound.

Little *Babas* and their *Ayahs*

> *As a young child, I rarely saw my mother. During the day, Nanny Vera looked after me in the first-floor tower room nursery. She was the centre of my world and occupied me for hours: playing with me, taking me for walks, knitting clothes for my dolls, and generally being my champion. I was kept away from my sister, Patricia, for most of the day so that she could concentrate on her lessons in the schoolroom with her governess, Miss Vick—Vicky. At least, that was one reason. The other reason was that Nanny and Vicky did not get on at all, were constantly at war about this or that, and therefore it was only at teatime that my sister and I were allowed to play together downstairs. We were always pleased to see each other and had a number of imaginative games on the go, a rich make-believe world of our own.*
>
> – Lady Pamela Hicks, 2012

One of the strongest yet most strained relationships that memsahibs developed with Indians was the one they had with their *ayahs*, including wet nurses. They could not deny that these matronly and experienced Indian women were usually the primary caregivers for their babies. And their presence was a great comfort for the often physically weakened, socially isolated, and emotionally overwhelmed new mothers.

Indeed, not only childbirth, but motherhood on the whole could be immensely burdensome in India even with an ample number of servants at home. Moreover, there was always a scarcity of European nurses, and as a result *ayahs* were indispensable. References to them are quite common in memsahibs' accounts of motherhood in India. These oft-nameless women, simply referred to in memsahibs' diaries and letters as "my *ayah*", were constantly by their side, accompanying them on the long tours and trips, and clutching the white babies to their bosoms along with their own, as their employers were busy with other work.

However, memsahibs were wary of the closeness between their children and their *ayahs*. This was because the bond between an *ayah* and a British-Indian child could grow strong over the years, along with their influence over the mind of the child. The constant proximity and attachment on both sides was to the British mind 'excessive', given the Indian style of parenting that was more touch-oriented and emotion-driven. Monica Campbell Martin noted that a "spontaneous affection" existed between Indian servants and white children, which, to her racialised colonial mind, was probably because Indians were "innocent" and "simple" as little children were, and therefore they got along well together. She was amused to see that while her children would be reluctant to mingle with grown-ups of their own race, they would have no hesitation with a new *ayah* or bearer.

Moreover, memsahibs thought that Indian women had no sense of discipline and were concerned that their children would become slovenly and ill-mannered because of the indulgent attitude of the servants who regularly coddled them. The more possessive mothers felt resentful knowing that their precious babies could grow attached to their *ayahs*, more than to them, because it was the *ayahs* who nursed them and played with them.

This could easily become a source of great anxiety for the memsahibs, and they dreaded leaving their children with Indians for too long. The uneasiness they felt about the intermingling was also due to the belief that their children would quickly pick up local Indian customs and practices, forsaking their own. One of the major fears they had was that their babies' first words might be in an Indian language. It also alarmed them to see their children exhibit typical Indian characteristics as they grew up.

Indeed, the conversations between British-Indian children and their native friends or *ayahs* would be in Indian languages. When Lillian Ashby was a child, during 1870–80, she was unwilling to learn English but was forced to take English lessons by her parents. She spent her days playing hopscotch and marbles and sharing meals with Golab, her Indian friend. Mornings were the best time for play because the elders would be busy with tea, and there would be no one to restrict their games. During hot days, they spent time indoors playing with homemade rag dolls and on the verandas, shielded by the *chiks* or under the shade of trees. When they played dolls, the games were usually re-enactments of weddings, and they dressed their bride and groom dolls for the nuptials. Lillian was a particularly perceptive child and knew that her dear little friend, just a child then, would be married as soon as she hit puberty, according to the Indian custom of child marriages, which during the nineteenth century was widely practised. Golab would begin singing the native songs of weddings:

May you have numerous sons,
And your harvest the best it's ever been.
May your husband never beat you,
And your mother-in-law be kind to you.
May you always wear the best red sari in the village!

The mothers of the *missie babas* (a term of endearment for a young Miss) and *baba logs* (equivalent to 'little master') disapproved of such games. But what could be done? In the isolated postings, where were the children to find their English playmates?

Memsahibs were likewise helpless when they saw their children participating in Indian habits and customs. Lillian Ashby helped another beloved *ayah* of hers in preparing her *paan* (flavoured beetle leaves laced with tobacco that act as stimulants), and Lillian liked to eat one herself (although was forbidden from eating one containing addictive substance). She would squat in the Indian fashion and prepare the sweet and spicy candy-like chewable, which she chewed on for a long time before spitting it out.

Lillian knew that she was the apple of her *ayah's* eye, and her mornings began with being awoken by her (rather than her own mother) as she gently removed the mosquito netting over her bed and while stroking her head affectionately whispered: "Wake up, Lilly-Baba! Morning has *come*!" "Will Golab come to play with me this morning?", she would ask her. "Yes", her ayah would answer. "But she can't stay unless you eat your breakfast, like a good baba". Once, when Lillian's *ayah* unintentionally wrung her arms, causing large red welts, the *ayah* was wracked with guilt and beat her chest in remorse. Then she plastered the red welts with neem leaves, which were supposed to have healing properties, and attempted to draw the evil spirit causing the pain from Lillian's body into hers, to exorcise it. "If my *baba* gets well, I'll feed a beggar; I'll feed two beggars! Allah always hears the cries and blessings of a beggar!" Lillian loved her *ayah* and wrote in her memoirs that it was not possible for a foster mother to remain as loving and affectionate as she was.

For most British-Indian children like Lillian, ideas of fun and enjoyment, taste in foods, and even preferences in stories ended up being influenced by their immediate surroundings. The Goddens wrote: "Our house was English streaked with Indian, or Indian streaked with English. It might have been an uneasy hybrid, but we were completely and happily at home". Indeed, even if their parents had not, the children had grown accustomed to the smells and sounds of a colonial bungalow, which they found comforting. The Indian lullabies that their *ayahs* sang for them soothed them in the long summer nights.

* * *

The deep bonds between children and their ayahs also meant that immense suffering would arise from a separation. *Ayahs*, like other servants, could be removed from their jobs, especially in cases where their employers had to move to another place on a new posting. The tearful farewells on both ends could be extremely moving. And even when the children grew up, they recalled their *ayahs* with fondness.

Lillian Ashby's second *ayah* was extremely dear to her. Even after growing up, she recalled her vividly: she was a twice widowed 19-year-old with perfect chiselled features and smooth olive skin. She applied makeup daily, and her face had a kind of sensuousness. Her long raven hair would be smoothed with *chameli tel* (jasmine oil), and she always smelled fragrant. Little Lillian was fascinated with her, and they spent hours devising fantastic adventures in the countryside, even though her mother was disapproving of their closeness.

Such insecurity on the mother's part could often get more severe. The Godden children had a Eurasian *ayah* who was rather eccentric, which they felt made her a great companion. They were very fond of her and grew extremely attached. This irked their mother, and she enforced strict rules on the woman to trouble her, like making her wear stiff uniforms. When the children wanted to dine with their *ayah*, their mother forbade it.

No matter how jealous memsahibs felt, getting rid of the *ayahs* was out of the question. Beside the difficult conditions of India that they themselves were grappling with, memsahibs did not have sufficient skill to manage their babies in addition to managing the household. Even when their children were in their infancy, they could not escape their other duties, such as towards their husbands whom they had to take care of as they carried out their imperial work. As a result, the torn new mothers could hardly ever invest themselves entirely—or as much as they would have liked—to the rearing of their children. Sometimes, repeated illnesses debilitated their health so much that they were unable to tend to their babies despite wanting to. And so, no matter how uncomfortable they were when they saw their babies clinging to their *ayahs'* sarees all day, they had no choice but to reconcile themselves to the idea that they were not the only 'maternal figures' for them.

Indeed, children valued their bonds with their servants and the attachment could be strong on both sides. And Lillian's attachment with her Indian playmates, *ayahs*, and servants was not unlike that of many other Raj children, who rarely spent long hours with their own parents and lived far away from other British families. These children would be surrounded by Indian domestic servants all the time, who doted on them and pampered them by feeding them by hand or by entertaining them with their own songs and stories. Moreover, they frequently took them to the local marketplaces and fed them Indian treats, which they relished immensely. The richly stocked markets with their brassware, ivory, and silverware were wholly fascinating to them, and they would be badgered by the local traders to purchase their goods and be given 'special treatment' in the shops (for their racial identity). They also enjoyed going down to the *mela* (fair or carnival), to watch the Hindu religious processions and other spectacles.

Sometimes, the servants involuntarily trained their young masters and mistresses in various Indian ways of life, initiating them into Indian customs while enthralling them with a piece of their own culture. During Holi, the festival of spring celebrated by Hindus, the *missie babas and baba logs* liked to join the carousing locals as they smeared powdered colours on each other. Unlike their actual memsahib mothers who abhorred the 'pagan' practices and frequently wrote of the 'barbaric' customs of India, children who were born in India had no such qualms or prejudices. Still innocent of racial arrogance, they would stand amongst hordes of Indian urchins and watch with fascination the sacrificial rituals as the worshippers chanted their mantras. However, the servants could sometimes alienate the sensibilities of their young charges through their tales and fictions. The Godden sisters were told horrific tales of India by their *ayah*. When the sisters saw a deformed boy in the market and asked their *ayah* about him, she told them that Indians sometimes twisted the limbs of babies to deform them in childhood, so that later they could become beggars. Such stories could end up becoming part of the image of India in their impressionable minds—a land of disease, filth, corruption, and grotesque practices.

But for all the harm that some *ayahs* might unintentionally do to their charges, and despite the deep impact they had on the psyche of the children, the *missie babas* and *baba logs* were still sons and daughters of the empire and were often not allowed to forget it.

For instance, having been unable to put a stop to the activities of the children while they were with the Indian servants, memsahibs attempted to at least control their physical appearance and conduct. Even though the climate did not permit it, especially for the naughtier children who liked to run around a lot in the heat and dust, the mothers insisted on keeping their children dressed up presentably at all times. They believed that dressing them up in a European fashion could perhaps mitigate their slowly 'Indianising' conduct, so that they at least looked like they belonged to proper European families. Moreover, it was believed that it was essential to raise children who were born away from home in accordance with English standards of grooming and manners and to instil appropriate habits from a young age. And so, every afternoon, mothers and their *ayahs* brushed and scrubbed down the snot-faced *missie babas* and *baba logs*, then dressed them in clean vests, shirts, shorts, and white suspenders for the boys and white stockings, bodices with buttoned-in drawers, and items with starch-stiffened buttonholes and ruffled lace on the edges for the girls. The little girls' white petticoats would be starched, and over this their clean dresses of white or pale muslin looked pretty and very proper.

Nonetheless, the *missie babas* did not have sustained systematic British training despite their parents' attempts; Lillian Ashby was woefully immune to her mother's instructions in good behaviour and exhibited all signs of being the child of every British mother's nightmare! She spent most of her time gambolling about in the dirt along with her friends, as a result of which she was washed and reclothed multiple times a day, but to no avail. Still, her *ayah* expended all of her energy trying to keep her neat and tidy because for Lillian's mother, like for most British ladies, good English training of their children was non-negotiable. Thus, no matter how freely she played in her childhood, Lillian would have to begin to abide by her mother's rules as she grew older.

In British-Indian families, girls would get their proper training to become wives and mistresses of their homes from an early age, just like they would in Britain. They would be taught proper English etiquette, dressing style, and social talents like dancing, singing, and entertaining guests. Watching their mothers, they would learn how to become the perfect wife to their husbands and be the impeccable hostess during teas and parties. Their steady access to good tailors and seamstresses ensured that their outfits were always prim and beautiful.

As the children grew older, their morality and social conduct also had to be policed, and this became an added cause of concern for their mothers. Chastity was considered particularly important for impressionable young girls, who would normally, back home in England, be trained in all aspects of proper feminine behaviour by the time they were adolescents. However, in India, the older memsahibs were concerned that the conduct of young women of tender age would not be appropriate because in the 'uncontrolled' space of India, lapses and misdemeanours were all too common, as they had seen so many times. Thus, it was not just the Fishing Fleet bachelorettes (who came to India to find husbands) who were surveilled and restricted. Even teenage girls of British families were restricted to keep them from transgressing.

Nonetheless, as the oft-spoilt and immature *missie babas* grew into adolescence, minor lapses here and there did occur. After all, falling in 'love' at that age was almost inevitable. Moreover, children who had grown up in India often tended to be quite precocious as they were all too aware of matters relating to courtship, marriages, and romance. As mentioned before, child marriages were common in India in the nineteenth century, and most of their Indian friends would be married even before they attained puberty. Winsome Ruth Godden, who wrote under the name Jon Godden, remarked, "Girls of our age are married in India".

Fortunately for the British parents, some teenage romances never took flight. When the boy Mervyn fell in love with Jon Godden and constantly sought her out during school dances, he ended up stepping on her toes, making her detest him completely.

Some romances turned out to be ludicrously tragic. Lillian Ashby was sixteen when she fell in love for the first time and had her heart broken. She recalled how "the romantic flame within me burned the stronger for the stifling restrictions of propriety. In our Victorian world, boys were not considered acceptable companions for young girls until both were of marriageable age, and then only under the eagle eyes of watchful chaperones". But in her youthful recklessness, she was willing to gamble her family's honour for her young sweetheart, Cyril, who was a year older than her. Before she was to be sent to school at Nainital in 1893, they arranged a clandestine meeting by exchanging notes during her last day in Alipore. After midnight, there was a low whistle outside her window to signal that her young man was waiting for her. Fully dressed, she tiptoed out of the back door and crept to the rear of her compound, and the lovelorn couple met under a mulberry tree. They planned their future together that night and decided to elope once he had procured work. He gave her a gold ring with the word MIZPAH inscribed on it ('Mizpah' is a token of remembrance, to be worn by lovers as a ring or necklace). Then they kissed before parting. Unfortunately, in a cruel twist of fate, Cyril soon became her brother-in-law. But as it turned out, Lillian knew how to take a romantic knock and get back on her feet. She wrote:

> At nineteen I was enjoying life to the full, in the rapturous transports of a new love affair with every second or third change of the moon. Romantic affairs progressed under difficulties: little

> things—a gesture, a sigh, a flower, or the gift of a book—carried great significance. Mother, permanently confined to her bed after the birth of a sixth child who had not lived to take cognizance of the world, was unable to supervise my goings and comings. My two brothers, Walter, fourteen, and Herbert, twelve, were away at school in Darjeeling; Ethel, fifteen, and Mary, thirteen, attended the Convent School in Bankipur. The making and repairing of their clothes by our *durzee* (tailor) and the supervision of their after-school activities were my principal responsibilities. On the other hand, their nuisance value was such that they were considered sufficiently effective chaperons for their elder sister. William was a handsome young man who gave every sign of being in love with me. Our walks and rides were filled with tender passages, whenever Ethel's or Mary's attention could be diverted.

Although Lillian managed to avoid taking a catastrophic step in her career as a 'lady' in India, youthful indiscretions could sometimes have grave consequences. Memsahibs were acutely conscious of their young daughters' fragile reputation when they came of age. Not policing them adequately could cause them to make serious lapses in judgement or even fall prey to men with ill intentions. They would frequently hear about scandalous affairs and were worried about the fate of their daughters. What kind of women would the little girls grow up to be? How would they become proper English ladies away from Britain, in India? When would they find appropriate suitors? These were some of the questions that haunted the mothers of young girls as they approached the age of becoming memsahibs themselves—no longer the frocked and tanned *missie babas* running amok with the children of the servants.

"Shall I go or shall I stay?": Good Mother, Bad Mother

> *One other point we have decided is that I shall go home every year for three months, to be with him in his summer holidays. We have heard too much of the sad results of divided homes to accept such possibilities, if they can be avoided. One mother told me her boy had ceased to write to her because he said 'he had forgotten what she was like.' And a dear girl said that after dreaming for years of again seeing her mother, something snapped in her heart when her mother came to her school and did not know her, and that the sad fact was she had never loved her again.*

> *Many parents feel as we do, and some mothers, to meet the expenses entailed, remain with their husbands in the plains during the hottest months of the year instead of taking a house in the hills... Anything better than to be told by her child, as one mother was, that 'no one had ever looked as she was looking at him now for three years'.*
>
> – Lady Anne Campbell Wilson, 1911

One of the most poignant moments in almost every memsahib's life in India was when she had to part with her children as they were sent to England to get their education. Parents delayed this event as much as they could, but it was necessary to send them as soon as they were old enough to travel, sometimes as early as the age of six. The parents were convinced that a few years of schooling in their motherland was guaranteed to forge the young ones' identity as British, which was especially crucial because they had never even seen Britain before.

Moreover, proper British education was a matter of great concern because the early years that the child had spent with the *ayahs* and Indian servants and children had already significantly 'Indianised' them. Sun-burnt, dirty, brazen due to neglect by their parents, and overindulged by their *ayahs*, they were hardly the model of good and proper British children, and a far cry from the well-mannered and obedient Victorian schoolboys and girls trained in boarding schools back home. Thus, imparting British education was the necessary measure taken to inculcate a European world-view in them.

Frequently, parents chose not to send their children away if travelling out of India was difficult due to political turbulence, or if there was a shortage of finances, or even if they simply did not wish to part with them. In such cases, they employed European nannies and governesses and made sure the children were trained in the British manner.

India-born Anne Wright, who did not leave even after India gained independence, wrote that she had several governesses while growing up in the Raj. Her last governess was Joan Scott, who was the niece of a tea planter, and whom she described as "delightful" and "very musical" ("The Lost World of the Raj", Ep. 1, 47.00–

49.00). Back then, British families would publish advertisements in newspapers calling for applications, and that was how Joan had come to be employed in the Wright household.

Joan, in her interview, said she had been "floundering" in the plantations for a while, and when she came across the advertisement posted by the Wright family, she was immediately interested. She quickly adapted to the needs of her employers, and Anne later recalled how Joan would always play highbrow music to them, which they loved ("The Lost World of the Raj", Ep. 1, 49.31).

Sometimes, British children in India had Indian teachers called *munshis*, who taught them English and other subjects. Otherwise, they went to English-language convent schools located in nearby hill stations. These were deemed to be better alternatives to Indian schools as the missionary training by the nuns helped instil Christian values in the children. These schools also enforced British-style discipline and could supposedly help curb the 'native'-style delinquency and waywardness in the pupils. The parents were also assured that Western education, and even European styles of extracurricular activities such as theatre, piano lessons, glee clubs, and so on, would be provided.

However, there was a time when the convent schools in the hills were disliked because the children who studied there were mostly of mixed origins. Yet again, British families feared 'contamination' as their children would pick up Indian mannerisms at such establishments, including the so-called '*chee-chee*' accent. And even though the parents partly knew that Indianisation was inevitable in the long run, they wanted their children to avoid it, or hide it underneath an aura of Britishness, as they had themselves.

When parents did send their children to Britain for their schooling, the mothers sometimes accompanied them, either to drop them off, or to be with them as they grew up. But more often than not, the memsahibs' sense of conjugal duty won over, and they stayed back with their husbands in India or left Britain almost immediately after settling their children in. Whatever the case, if children were sent out of India it was usually several years before they got to meet their parents again, by which time they would be all grown up.

Education was not the only reason why the parents parted with their children. Very often, concerns relating to the children's health compelled them to remove them from India at a very tender age. If it was possible, the young mothers went back home where they could care for their children because of the help they received from their relatives. Having physicians who visited their ailing children in the comforts of their homes was a relief.

Sometimes, parents sent their children away because they wanted to give their children a stable home, unlike the situation they had in India where they might have to travel a lot, especially in cases of army families that were given frequent postings. And parents were advised not to take such matters lightly because those who did suffered in the long run. Thus, to tackle this, children were sometimes sent off to live with their grandparents who might be stationed elsewhere in India, like in the case of Lillian Ashby. However, even shuttling between their own homes and those of their grandparents could become overwhelming.

It can be said that no matter what decision was taken, it was always difficult for the children to part with their parents. The condition of the children who were sent away was as pathetic as that of their mothers who would pine for them in the faraway land of India.

The mothers indeed found it difficult to cope with the pain of separation, and their accounts of suffering are extremely evocative. Veronica Bamfield wistfully wrote about how mothers in the empire were doomed to bear the pain of living apart from their children for many years and learning about them only through their brief letters written from school. They would carry their children's photos with them wherever they went. The verandas and large open rooms of their bungalows would echo with the calls of their children long after they left, and they would be constantly haunted by the faces of their babies. Maria Murray Mitchell, who wrote *In India: Sketches of Indian Life and Travels from Letters and Journals*, which her husband, J. Murray Mitchell—a Scottish missionary—called "a woman's book about India", spoke of the heart-wrenching decision to send her daughter to their motherland:

> Home-goings are certainly great drawbacks to Indian life. We were up before daylight to get the party for the steamer under

> way… I was carrying my little pet, Mabel. She would have nothing to say to her new nurse, an Englishwoman, as her beloved *ayah* had to be left behind. It was a bitter parting for both; and the poor old woman has been breaking her heart for her baba ever since. I am nearly as bad as the *ayah:* and the last look I got of the wee darling, as she sat on the new woman's lap, holding up her little arms to me with a wail and such a beseeching look, still haunts me. It is especially hard to pass the nursery door. The scenes on board a homeward-bound ship would need hard hearts to be able to stand them… When we returned from the ship, everything looked so changed and desolate.

Sometimes, the guilt of choosing their husbands over their young ones bothered the memsahibs, but it was not feasible to leave the men behind and live comfortably in Britain amongst friends and family. It was a grave dilemma, and no matter what decision the parents took, it was always difficult and stressful. However, they knew that such acts were simply part of the compromises everyone had to make for the care of children, and almost all families endured it. The only comforting idea for these wretched mothers who were deprived of watching their children grow up was that at least they were being given a proper British education and were away from the harmful effects of India during their growing years.

Still, no matter what the case, the children usually underwent tremendous hardships, either because they were forced to be away from their parents for long stretches of time, or because of the constant moving and travel. Either way, they ended up feeling like exiles. Generations of Raj children grew up believing such was the meaning of life in India.

Some children who suffered more than others ended up feeling deep resentment towards their parents as they recalled how terrible and heart-breaking it was to be removed from their idyllic life in India and put into a boarding school without their families around. Naturally, distance grew between them, and when the children returned to their parents after several years, it could be difficult to re-establish the bond. Anne Wright, who was trained by several governesses at home before being sent back to England to complete her education, was tormented about leaving as she was very attached to her world. She detested the cold European weather and the food, and even got into trouble at school.

Just as some children used to life in India found their British boarding school a horrible shock, others who had been taken out of the colony at an early age struggled to recognise India as their home when they returned. The Godden sisters were sent to London to their grandmother when they were only five and six and a half years old and then suddenly brought back to India while they were still very young, at the start of the First World War. The two sisters were ill-prepared when their aunt arrived to fetch them back and were nothing short of traumatised on the outward journey to India. When they reached their new home in Narayanganj, they were terribly 'homesick' and overwhelmed because of the strange smells of mustard oil and coconuts:

> No answer. No smile. No warmth. An extraordinary stiffness fell on us… two cool, self-restrained girls walked with Fa, Mam, and Aunt Mary up the drive, said, "How do you do," to the governess, Miss Andrews, kissed Rose, and said "Salaam" to the salaaming servants… Our first luncheon, too, was an indication of how different everything was… Over the bowl of pink Sandwich Island creeper Jon looked at Rumer and Rumer looked at Jon. We were ourselves, the same children, but already we were different. Rumer still had her look of alarm.

Luckily for the Godden girls, the Indian way of life was unexpectedly luxurious, and they quickly adapted to it. They liked that they had their own servants who milled around them treating them like royalty, and their mother was able to see that the sudden importance corrupted them quickly. After all, in India, ordinary middle-class families could afford big houses and several servants, and the two girls, whose father worked with a shipping company in India, began to believe that they would have the same in London and move in high circles when they went back later. They even thought that they would dine with the kings and queens. "When I see the King, what shall I call him? Your Majesty or just plain George?", one of the girls asked their mother innocently. When they were transported to London again, it took them a long time to adjust and cope without domestic help.

In reality, however, life for the *missie babas* and *baba logs*, for all their indulgent *ayahs* and servants, was not always as idyllic as was the common belief. Things could change abruptly; they could be made to move without warning and leave friends behind only to move to strange places far away. Very often, children were abruptly left without their beloved *ayahs* and servants. Sometimes, they were separated from their parents all of a sudden because of unexpected circumstances, such as financial troubles or the unplanned pregnancies of their mothers. The latter was a frequent cause, because multiple pregnancies could overburden the mothers, and they would be forced to send some of their children away to take care of the new children, often uprooting very small children from their habitat. In such cases, the children underwent tremendous hardships as they lived amongst strangers for long stretches of time in unfamiliar landscapes, without knowing when and how their parents would send for them.

India-born Harriet Tytler, writer, artist, and an avid photographer, who is most known for her autobiographical account *An Englishwoman in India, 1828–1858* (1864), grew up in this kind of quandary. Her mother had told her that when she was born, in a small station in Oudh in 1828, her *ayah* had spotted a mole on her foot and predicted that she would travel far and wide—a prediction that came true very quickly for her.

Harriet's first journey was when she was a 13-day old infant: her father's regiment had to march from their town to Nusseerabad, and her mother, along with her three siblings, marched with the troops. While she did not remember anything, she realised that it might have been a difficult journey for her nursing mother.

When she was a little over two years of age, her father sent her older siblings to England, and she was left with her uncle and aunt until her parents returned from Calcutta. They did it for the child's good, but it was extremely painful. Then when she was eight, her mother gave birth to another child, and Harriet, although very small, began taking care of the house and the little baby. She learnt embroidery and sewed things for her new sister. She was quite burdened by the domestic responsibilities and resentfully wrote, "Mother used to keep me up till past eleven o'clock at night, mending the little ones' stockings, while she mended her own and father's. It was hard for me considering I used to be dragged out of bed *nolens volens* at four o'clock in the morning… however, it was no use resisting, mother was inexorable when her sense of duty came in the way". Her siblings had already been sent to England or were about to be, and only she was to be left behind in India to support her mother and the new baby. However, at the age of eleven, it was decided that she would be sent to England after all, with her younger brother and sister who were to leave during Christmas. It was an expensive affair, but the parents believed this to be the best course of action for Harriet.

When the three young siblings reached London, there were great ordeals in store for them. They had been placed under the care of their aunt and uncle, Mrs. Raine and Captain Raine, who had recently returned to their home in Birmingham after a posting. Immediately after reaching their home, they were informed that their brother was being sent to a faraway school, to be with his other two brothers. This was hard on him, Harriet wrote later, since he had never been separated from them before.

Moreover, while the Raines had looked pleasant enough at first, they were actually strict and unrelenting. Life with them was sheer torture, and Harriet and her sister lived in terror of them. Her aunt, especially, was a sadistic bully who made a pastime of tormenting them in cruel and arbitrary ways. For instance, they were made to wear summer dresses in the winter and were brutally punished if they dared even to shrug up their flimsy shawls over their shoulders while outdoors in the bitter cold. They were forbidden from speaking to the servants except to greet them formally, and barred from playing outdoors if it did not please their aunt. On most days, they were given stale bread and water to eat.

Perhaps the worst was that they were expected to learn their lessons and do their other chores in the 'schoolroom', which was actually a draughty laundry room without a fire. There they were not even allowed a candle and had to practise on the piano in the pitch-dark room, without a fire, with every finger covered in chilblains so severe that when they struck a chord, the blisters would burst, and they would have to wipe the blood off the keys to proceed. They were even disallowed from heating water and had to break the ice to wash their faces with their frostbitten hands. They were allowed a hot bath only once a week. Once, the young Harriet banged the door after her in anger after an altercation with her aunt and was hit so hard that she thumped down the stairs nearly falling flat on her nose.

Her aunt's viciousness became intolerable when their brother came to visit after a very long time and brought an assortment of goodies for them. Her aunt, suspecting this, stole into the schoolroom, and took all of it without saying anything. They were indignant because she had no right to take away food items that their brother had bought with his own money, but they also could not protest, and had to tolerate everything silently. They could not even write home to their parents to complain about their miseries because the letters were screened.

Desperate and angry, Harriet once considered running away to London and then going to the Pearces, who were old acquaintances of her father, to beg them to send her back to India, but she did not have enough money. She bitterly wrote, "My aunt was horribly strict with us and really cruel in many ways... My poor little sister, having more of a timid nature than myself, was completely crushed by her. We often used to lock ourselves in each other's arms and sob ourselves to sleep."

This kind of abuse may have been an extreme case of suffering on the part of British-Indian children, but it's clear that the families of the British in India always found themselves in a great many difficult situations. Over time, however, this became an accepted truth about parent-child relationships in British-Indian families.

Memsahibs were called upon to do their duty to the empire by supporting their husbands and raising the next generation, but the nature of colonial life set these two priorities against one another. Even in their own homes and families, memsahibs could not escape the political imperatives of their very existence.

No matter what they did, they constantly felt that they were not doing enough for their children, and they knew that in India, they were bound to fail as either a wife or a mother.

9

"NAKED AND BLEEDING, INSULTED AND ABUSED"

THE INDIAN REBELLION OF 1857

Cantonments, Lucknow, May 18, 1857

At Delhi the people rose in the city… murdered every European there, Captain Douglas, Mr. and Miss Jennings, Mr. Fraser (Chief Commissioner), the Judge, the bankers, the post office and newspaper people, shopkeepers, clerks, writers, even women and children, and half-castes—all who had European blood in their veins…

Delhi is in the hands of the insurgents… all we know is from electric telegraph by way of Agra… the dead bodies of our countrymen at Delhi are being exposed to insult in the streets, and there is no one to give them Christian burial. At Meerut last Sunday night the 3rd Cavalry and three native Infantry regiments rose, set fire to the officers' bungalows, and murdered them with their wives and children as they tried to escape… There are rumours of risings all over the country… Almost every hour we hear rumours of fresh horrors… Darling mother, pray that we may be spared to come back and see you.

– Mrs. James P. Harris, 1858

Bloody tales of the great Indian rebellion of 1857–58 haunted generations of sahibs and memsahibs. What had started with a seemingly minor 'spirit of disaffection' amongst the Indian sepoys (infantrymen) had soon spread to different parts of the country. Even the Europeans who were stationed in the hotbeds of violence had not anticipated that it would become as intense as it turned out to be.

Those who lived through the time, like Mrs. Harris, narrated their nightmarish experiences as they sat in wait for further news and instructions, or fled from their homes in the dead of the night with the 'rebels' at their heels. Most had to leave the city entirely and take refuge in nearby towns, with strangers who had also fled their homes. Some were stranded on the way and left to their fate. Those who had delayed their flight were forced to take cover in abandoned buildings or ruins of old structures. They waited, it seemed, for their impending deaths, not knowing if help would arrive before their hideout was discovered. Even if officers were guarding them, they were not safe. Sometimes, musketry and cannonading went on around them all night. If shots cut into the walls in a straight line, the explosions could easily bring down the upper storeys of brick buildings, exposing the whole structure, and the refugees within, to the enemy's firearms.

Adelaide Case, who wrote a journal when she took refuge in the Lucknow Residency—the residence of the British Resident General—noted in June 1857: "I hope few will know how awful it is to wait quietly for death", even as the patrolling sentinels outside cried out every hour through the night, "All's well!"

Those who were unable to escape or chose to stay back, underestimating the gravity of the situation, realised too late that danger was at hand. They could do nothing then but pray they would not be raided, or their servants would not reveal their whereabouts. Often, there was little hope in their hearts as they cowered in darkened chambers, expecting the sepoys to storm in and cut their heads off anytime. Many did not live to tell their stories.

In 1858, following the suppression of the 'mutiny', the direct rule of the Crown began in India. There were brutal anti-insurgency measures employed by the colonial government for the suppression of the sepoys, and it is not known definitively how many Indian civilians and soldiers were killed in the conflict zone or in the backlash due to the paucity of records. Historians have spoken of a range of hundreds of thousands to a million (counting the casualties of the famine and diseases that followed), but these are only estimations.

While the colonial administration did not keep full records of the deaths amongst the Indian populace, they did record that 2,392 British men, women, and children died between 1857 and 1859 (Kohli, 152).

It must be taken into consideration that in the aftermath of the rebellion, there was a profusion of violent images, as the colonial media circulated grisly accounts of the brutalities committed upon Europeans at the hands of the sepoys in order to provoke anger and hatred amongst the British. The detailed newspaper reports, visuals, and hair-raising accounts of abductions, lootings, and murders provoked public fury and fuelled the mass hysteria. These were taken from personal experiences, second-hand experiences, and eyewitness accounts as well as interpretations and analyses of data. Even decades later, there was no repressing the horrific collective memory of the killings. The lurid details were meant to be substantial justification for later, when no mercy would be shown to the 'fiends' sent to the gallows. Moreover, these accounts were to serve as grim reminders of the need to keep the native population suppressed without leniency.

Most of the personal writings about 1857 were a cathartic exercise in remembering, as the constant telling and retelling became a source of comfort to the survivors and escapees. Several such (British) survivors' accounts were dedicated to or were in the memory of so-and-so who passed away during the violence. In some ways, then, these became tools that served to memorialise, preserve, and disseminate the pain and anger. The underlying assumption was that only a rigorous revisitation of the events through a continued writing and rewriting of the revolt could do justice to the casualties, especially in the absence of a normal judicial process whereby the culprit was identified and duly punished. Here, the culprit was a body of people, which was only 'symptomatic' of a larger and more prevalent anti-British sentiment in India. Thus, after the quelling of the uprising, there were impassioned cries for merciless retaliation that echoed back home in Britain.

This thirst for vengeance was mostly motivated by the fear of future attacks on the ascendancy of the empire. Indeed, while it was believed that the uprisings did not indicate an impending end of the empire, there was unease because the very real possibility of it had appeared for the first time.

Thus, memsahibs who wrote their accounts of the violence surrounding 1857 were aware that the need of the hour was an immediate delivery of justice. Their writings were meant to fill the gaps where 'justice', as they needed it, could not be restored. The visceral pain of loss and displacement was therefore a major motif in all the personal recollections of the mutiny that were circulated, as the sahibs and memsahibs both faced the problem of coming to terms with the horrible violence that had occurred. In a way, their narratives were a mode of restoring that sense of reality around them and accepting the tragedies that had taken place. Thus, consistent writing about the revolt, through which a validation of their grief took place, helped in coping with the trauma.

Significantly, the focus of most accounts remained on the attacks of the sepoys on the collective community of colonisers in India, but most British accounts and recollections focused more on the violence against innocent victims: women and children. Clearly, they were determined not to forget the attacks and were keen to sketch out the 'barbarism' of the sepoys who committed gruesome crimes against the defenceless. This was not just done by memsahibs but also by British officers who wrote their own versions of the events around 1857. Colonel A. R. D. Mackenzie of the 3rd Bengal Light Cavalry, who commanded the 8th Irregular Cavalry at Bareilly and was part of the British forces that re-seized Lucknow and Delhi, wrote in his memoirs, *Mutiny Memoirs: Being Personal Reminiscences of the Great Sepoy Revolt of 1857* (1891):

> Two veterinary-surgeons, attached to the regiment, had been killed—one of them with his wife—under circumstances of ghastly horror. They were both sick in bed with small-pox when the uproar of the mob startled them; and they came, in their night clothes, into the verandah, he carrying a gun loaded with shot, which he discharged at the crowd, only further enraging it. He was instantly shot dead. His wife met with a worse fate. The cowardly

> demons, afraid to touch her because of the danger of infection, threw lighted brands at her. Her dress caught fire; and she perished thus miserably (23).

What emerges from the study of the plethora of writings that were thus produced, is that in the wake of the killings of Europeans, there was a ballooning desire for revenge amongst the British. Moreover, the sustained efforts at 'writing the mutiny', by creating its own body of literature, thus not only facilitated the remembering of the 'savagery' of the sepoys but also served as a sign that there was a need for British supremacy in India to control the 'brute' and 'savage' Indian masses and supposedly save them from themselves.

Alongside that, suppressing the rebels and seeking revenge was especially posited as a means for the British to safeguard their own—especially women and children. *The Revolt in Central India 1857–59* (1908), compiled in the Intelligence Branch, Division of the Chief of Staff, stated that "women and children who had been captured were butchered under circumstances of unspeakable horror". Although much of the visual imagery did not focus on the actual death and defilement of their bodies, there was a certain level of voyeurism in the journalistic reportage and primary Company records, which incessantly focused on the ghastly deaths of women and children during the mutiny.

The defilement of British women's bodies also recurred like a trope in almost all the personal accounts from the colonisers' side, although some historians have argued that these ideas were "largely imaginary" (Bates, 55) and stemmed from long-standing fears of interracial sexual violence. W. H. Fitchett categorically mentions in *The Tale of the Great Mutiny*, "English women were outraged", indicating the sexual and physical abuse of women during the mutiny (38). However, Jenny Sharpe, who has studied the deliberate construction of the "dark-skinned rapist" of white women during 1857, has argued that rape figured as a significant and "highly charged trope" that was implicated in the management of the rebellion (2). As she has stated, the so-called unspeakable horrors committed upon women were more in the spheres of literary writing than in reality, since the magistrates commissioned to investigate the so-called eyewitness reports could find no evidence to substantiate the rumours of rebels raping, torturing, and mutilating English women (Sharpe, 2).

While the memsahibs' vivid detailing of the atrocities against them evoked the fear of being brutalised, they also sketched themselves out as heroic and forbearing, which was a contribution to the writing and historicising of the uprising that only British women could make. Yet, the mainstream journalistic accounts dealt with violence against women as a symbolic blow to the 'honour' of the British. In much of popular imagery, women figured as helpless victims, whose abuse was even more appalling because of their steadfast virtue and moral uprightness.

In all this, the white woman emerged as the symbol of the nation and of British bravery as stories of the memsahibs' fearlessness and fortitude circulated amidst news of violence. Although brutalised, they were shown to be unwavering even when faced with the attacking sepoys. One such lady, Miss Margaret Wheeler, daughter of General Hugh Wheeler, who defended herself valiantly and chose to die rather than surrender to the rebels, became something of an icon. *Female Warriors: Memorials of Female Valour and Heroism, from the Mythological Ages to the Present Era* by Ellen Creathorne Clayton (published in London in 1879) called Miss Wheeler "the heroine of Cawnpore". It was said that she was captured by Nana Sahib, an Indian Peshwa of the Maratha Empire. He led the rebellion in Cawnpore and gained control there after capturing the Commander-in-Chief's (General Wheeler's) entrenchment and killing many in June 1857 after supposedly betraying the British Collector whom he had promised he would support. He had promised a safe passage to the Europeans sheltered in the garrison to the docks nearby where he had made arrangements to allow them to escape by boats. However, just as they were leaving the banks, the sepoys who had assembled to witness their escape opened fire.

Miss Wheeler was said to have shot five sepoys with a revolver before being carried off by a trooper. Some versions of the stories about her state that she was taken by a sepoy into his hut, where she cut off his head with a sabre and then flung herself down a well. However, there is much speculation around her, and the exact events surrounding her death are unknown. *The Cawnpore Outbreak and Massacre* (1857), a report published in Calcutta, mentioned her name in the list of "Victims murdered at Cawnpore" of whose "ultimate fate nothing certain is known". Nonetheless, she is hailed as the epitome of British women's courage and patriotism. She was also hailed for her chastity as she chose death over 'dishonour'. An engraving by the London Printing and Publishing Company Limited appeared after 1857, it depicted Miss Wheeler shooting a rebel point blank as he entered her premises, with two rebels lying dead at her feet and another attacking her from behind with a sabre raised. It was titled, "Miss Wheeler Defending Herself Against the Sepoys at Cawnpore".

Suddenly, the victimised Englishwoman was hailed as the symbol of Christian virtue and forbearance as well as imperial strength and superiority. Memsahibs, like Miss Wheeler, were turned into a ferocious retributive force who were going to take revenge upon the rebelling sepoys and preserve the British honour by not surrendering.

It must be noted that rape, and sexual violence in general, have always been used as tools of war to bring shame and fear upon a community. Women are made the custodians of the community or nation's 'honour' and are punished or killed when it is taken away. This cultural currency of 'honour' is disadvantageous to women as they live in the fear of it being lost. Acts of 'self-sacrifice' such as Miss Wheeler's choice of committing suicide in the face of rape is therefore indicative of the problematic nature of female agency in such cases. After all, as women's bodies are turned into sites of nations' identity and 'honour', 'choosing to die' rather than fall into the hands of the enemy is only symptomatic of how women were forced to martyr themselves in battles that were not their own.

Ultimately, the stories about Miss Wheeler's heroism rendered her nothing more than a myth, which was promptly appropriated by British nationalist discourse. The multiple versions of what might have happened to her do not do her justice and merely indicate yet another instance of 'collateral damage' during war violence. The legends about her valour and courage, and her iconisation in British colonial history, do not compensate for the fact that the truth about her death, even now, remains shrouded in speculation and mystery.

Refugee Memsahibs: Mutinies, Massacres, and the Summer of Terror

> *As the Native regiments poured into Delhi the British residents in Meerut left their houses and concentrated in the Infantry and Artillery lines, abandoning the barracks of the Cavalry; and thus the whole force was grouped within a small circle…*
>
> *Outside this busy ring, the country wore the most miserable aspect. The gardens around the desolate houses were hastening to decay; nothing stirred on the roads once so gay with life; here and there the blackened walls of a bungalow… The charred rafters, the black walls, the broken carriage resting on a half-burnt wheel, the skeleton of a bullock lying on a bed of withered flowers… All combined, with the recollection of the fate of the inhabitants…*
>
> *The bazaars were silent as if depopulated by a plague; scarcely a native was to be seen. Trade had ceased; the telegraph-wire lay cut on the ground… no means of communication existed…*
>
> – Elizabeth McMullin Muter, 1911

Mrs. Kate Lindsay, widow of a British civil servant in India, had moved back to Rochester in England after her husband's retirement and might have lived there peacefully, but in the perilous year of 1856, India beckoned to her, luring her back just before the stirrings of the rebellion.

Veronica Bamfield's *On the Strength* (1975) charts out the dreadful turn of events in the lives of the Lindsay women after their fatal decision to return to India. Mrs. Lindsay wanted to be with her son who was stationed in Cawnpore and had no inkling that they would be landing in one of the epicentres of violence. Her daughters, Alice, Caroline, and Fanny, had protested against coming out, and almost every other family member advised her against going, but she was adamant. Eventually, the daughters reluctantly accompanied their mother in 1856, unsuspecting of any political turbulence. It was as if death itself had drawn them out.

When they arrived in India, their landing itself bode ill as there were unusual snags and delays due to poor travel arrangements. But even then, none of them gave up because of these bad omens. The atmosphere of fun and gaiety was at the high point during Christmas when they landed, and they were sucked into the string of balls and parties, even though the daughters were homesick and not particularly happy about being back in India.

The insurrection of the Indian regiments began to be felt just as the weather started to get warm. In May 1857, when the news of court martials of the revolting sepoys came in, especially in Meerut where some sepoys refused to follow orders during a parade, Mrs. Lindsay and her daughters realised that they were in mortal danger. Almost overnight, Mrs. Lindsay concluded that she needed to send her daughters away from Cawnpore, at least to another city where things were more peaceable. But it seemed like it was already too late.

Over the next few days, they wrote letters back home to England recounting the horrors of what was happening around them as several of their friends and acquaintances were murdered. Bamfield describes how on 31 May, they went with other women to take shelter in the barracks, as it was no longer safe to live in their homes. When they reached the barracks, they saw there was complete chaos and confusion at the scene. Some were not able to find beds and had to stay in their carriages, even as a violent thunderstorm hit. Their letters home were filled with despair as they realised death was near. When the sepoys raided their shelter, all were massacred. A note written by Caroline read:

> Entered the barracks May 21st
> Cavalry left June 5th
> First shot fired June 6th
> Aunt Lilly died June 17th
> Uncle Willy died June 18th
> Left barracks June 27th
> George died June 27th
> Alice died July 9th
> Mama died July 12th

The remaining two Lindsay sisters were killed soon after. It came out that they had taken refuge in a *bibighar* (ladies' house), where the walls were completely splattered by blood, and the floor was covered in a blood-stained rubble of personal belongings. The house came to be known as the 'House of the Massacre'.

Usually, the killings were swift. Memsahibs wrote how shells were thrown into shelters and would explode right on the verandas. Bungalows were gutted completely if the sepoys suspected that people were hiding inside. If they managed to break in, they would kill everyone, and then set fire to the buildings so that later it would be difficult to judge how many casualties there were. Men and women were often caught off-guard and killed by their bedsides, and their bodies were found later. Sometimes, the British relief troops chanced upon shelters after the inmates were gone, and they were not able to tell if the women and children had been captured or killed or had managed to escape.

Mrs. Elizabeth McMullin Muter, an officer's wife and a travel enthusiast, wrote how a lady's body lay in a ditch on the side of the embankment and was so disfigured by wounds that she could not be recognised. A track of blood was discernible from the *bazaar*, so it was evident that she had been dragged a long way before being thrown away. Another corpse of an Englishwoman was found in the same ditch. Adelaide Case, wife of Colonel William Case of the 32nd Regiment, who was widowed soon after the uprisings began, wrote of another lady, Mrs. Dorin, who was killed in her sitting room with a bullet that went through the head. She had narrowly escaped from Seetapore (present-day Sitapur in the Uttar Pradesh), where her husband had been killed before her eyes. But it was as if she was fated to die.

In Delhi, there were reports of young women who had jumped down from the fortifications to escape the sepoys, only to be faced with a shower of bullets. Those who managed to escape had then waded through rivers and walked miles in the sun, trying to make an escape without being detected.

Harriet Tytler, who wrote her accounts of surviving the violence of 1857, became known for giving birth to her child in a bullock-cart in Delhi during the high point of the uprising. She was the wife of a Colonel (then Captain) in the 38th Native Infantry and was with his regiment when the 'mutiny' broke out. Two other divisions were also stationed there, and a bullock battery was in the cantonments completing the garrison, which was composed of Indians without any British troops. The garrison was meant to keep an eye out for danger and safeguard against any trouble in the city, which was otherwise secure and strongly fortified. The military cantonments were 3 miles north-west of the city, built on the left bank of the Yamuna and surrounded by a stonewall and broad ditch. When news of Mangal Pandey’s execution reached them in Delhi, stirring up disaffection amongst Captain Tytler’s troops, he told Harriet, “If our natives were to rebel against us, India is lost.”

At that time, it seemed like the prediction would come true because the very next day, Harriet and the other ladies received news that they were to immediately get to the Flagstaff Tower in the ridge near the Civil Lines (‘White Town’) in Delhi. It was a burning hot day in May, and many had no means of travel. But they had to escape immediately or risk being captured by the sepoys.

In the following days while they were at the Flagstaff, stories circulated about how no one was being spared, and even children were being slaughtered mercilessly. Chilling incidents came to be known widely: a lady, Mrs. Beresford, had run down the stairs to the ground floor with a spear, killing three sepoys before she herself was killed; a Lieutenant who was engaged to be married to the chaplain’s daughter wanted to go and rescue her, but she and her friend were dead when he found them. It was later reported that the two girls had hidden themselves under their beds in the upper-floor rooms when the rebels had barged inside. They were then dragged out and flung out of the window onto the pavement below. Harriet gave special attention to this incident because the story of their deaths was one of the ghastliest stories that she had heard.

Harriet’s situation was much more perilous than many others. During the time when uncountable British men and women had been murdered around her, she was in immediate danger because she was in her eighth month of her pregnancy, with two other children to take care of. Although there was no actual mention of rape, Harriet’s writings are testament to the widespread belief that women suffered such tortures as well before being killed. The vial of poison she kept for herself and the children in case the British were defeated speaks for itself. She wrote:

> As you may imagine our hearts were filled more than ever with hopeless dismay and, at the smallest noise, my children would clasp me all the tighter... I thought several times I would try and run over to tell my husband what was occurring in the city, but then the thought of leaving my children to their fate held me back, and the fear that going across those three miles of the ridge to the White House in the burning sun of May with a furnace-like wind would be too much and I might drop down dead with a stroke of the sun, so I had to give up the idea of ever expecting to see my darling husband again and prepare myself for death. I thought they would have shot me or cut me down, but thank God I never supposed that I could have met a worse death which I afterwards learnt was meted out to many poor women.

Soon it became apparent that the help they were expecting from Meerut was not going to come in time, and they would be killed after all. The sepoys had already entered through Cashmere Gate (Kashmiri Gate), which was the gate to the 'walled city' of Delhi, and had met the Mughal Emperor Bahadur Shah Zafar in his court, who gave them his blessings. They had then supposedly massacred every European in sight. Harriet's husband was sure that the remaining sepoys who were protecting them were going to defect soon as well and wanted everyone who was at the Flagstaff Tower to move because they were sitting ducks at that point. The need to flee became clear after a particularly gruesome event took place: a carriage arrived from the city conveying dead bodies of officers piled up on top of each other like ordinary cargo. They were buried quickly behind the tower.

After that, almost everyone fled, but many women and children were caught and taken as prisoners. When the Tytlers were escaping, they saw that the entire cantonment was wrapped in an enormous conflagration. Not knowing which nearby city was safe, they took the chance of Umbala in Haryana (Ambala), where they stayed with friends. If they had chosen Cawnpore instead, they would have been killed by the Nana, along with Miss Wheeler and the others.

After a series of events, Harriet's husband was offered work as a paymaster to the troops in Delhi, which he was obliged to accept as the Tytlers had lost everything in the attacks, including their last month's pay. They returned to the city, and Harriet became the last and only woman to stay in Delhi with the British forces as they took back the city. It was in the middle of all this turmoil that she gave birth to a baby boy.

Up to that point they lived in a cart, near her husband's office tent, but when the monsoons came, they took shelter in an empty bell of arms tent, where they remained until the third week of September. Throughout this time, they did not have sufficient clothes or linen. None of the native shopkeepers were in camp, and they had no bedding and slept on the ground. Harriet noted:

> After such an experience, I quite expected the baby and myself would die, but through God's mercy we were none the worse and I was able to nurse my baby without the usual aid of a bottle of milk, there being neither bottles nor milk to be had for love or money. We slept on the floor with only straw and a *razai* [blanket] under us, with no pillows or sheets to comfort us, till a poor officer who had been killed had his property sold, and my husband bought his sheets. By way of a pillow I used to substitute a few dirty or clean clothes, which we could ill spare, and so make the best of it.

The Tytlers' condition was no worse than that of many others who were likewise on the run or in their own secret hideouts wherever they could find them. Many families had not managed to escape, and news of their killings circulated amongst the survivors.

A British officer, Captain Forrest, was stationed in Delhi with his wife and daughters when the sepoys entered the city. They were hurrying towards Kashmiri Gate with hopes of fleeing the city, but one of the daughters was shot on the way. Somehow, they escaped to Meerut and were rescued on the way by some officers who found them close to death, dressed in tattered clothes, with their feet bleeding through bandages. They relayed how there was a sea of dead bodies at Kashmiri Gate, where the sepoys had slaughtered everyone trying to escape. As they had picked their way through the bodies, they saw that for some bizarre reason, many bodies were covered with beautiful ball gowns, which they understood had been looted from nearby towns and strewn about in the chaos.

Archie and Minnie Wood also had a narrow escape. On 30 May, Archie wrote home to Minnie's mother with the alarming news that the mutiny had spread to Barrackpore, which was just 15 miles from Calcutta, up to their frontier station in Peshawar. About twenty-five regiments had defected. The 9th Native Infantry had joined the rebellion at Delhi and had murdered their European officers. Archie and Minnie were in dire conditions as it was, and if they had had the money, Minnie and the baby would have returned to England, but as we know from the previous chapters, they could not. On 27 May, they wrote with more bad news that the whole country from Calcutta to Peshawar was up in arms, rendering all of them vulnerable to attack. Archie's regiment at that time was loyal, but there was no certainty during such massive bloodshed, and they could not even trust their own servants. Both of them were racked with fear, especially about the safety of the baby, and they began sleeping with a revolver and sword beside them at night.

On 12 July, Archie wrote to Minnie's mother that his regiment had mutinied after all. They somehow escaped just in time after being warned by the Commissioner and galloped away just as the firing started in the cantonments and as cannonballs were fired near them. They had barely been able to dress and pack their things, so they had nothing with them. To add to their troubles, the officers had not been paid since the outbreak of the revolt, and they had lost 50 pounds in the scuffle.

On 22 July, they were the only ones left in Jhelum, besides a doctor and his wife. Minnie was still nursing her baby at that point. She and the other ladies had been sent to a nearby village for shelter, where they were stranded under the sun for hours. Minnie wrote that she was almost naked because she had to put her chemise on the baby to protect it from the unforgiving sun. She had been ill since her confinement, so she was in no condition to trudge through the jungles and to flee from sepoys.

In Gwalior, the situation was equally dangerous for the British. The Raja of Gwalior was loyal to them, so it gave them some comfort in the earliest months of dissent, but danger was imminent. On 19 May, Ruth M. Coopland, who had taken shelter with other women such as Captain Campbell's wife, feared that their *coolies* might cut their throats if they had the chance, and the women slept with loaded pistols next to them. That month, they heard of the 'conspiracy' in Delhi and that the sepoys had taken a large number of British officers into captivity. In her letter dated 23 May, the panic Ruth felt was apparent as she described the ongoing events after Alyghur (Aligarh) was taken and communication with Punjab was stopped. She wrote that the fate of India would be decided in a few days because everything depended on Delhi, and the slightest failure would unleash a chain of massacres across the country.

Ruth's husband wrote in the next letter, dated 2 June, that the troops in Gwalior were planning to burn down all their houses and murder them. They had not received the information on time; they found out just hours before the attack. With so little time, every woman and child fled to the Residency with whatever they could pack. To make matters more difficult, they had to load their carriage and execute the flight with utmost secrecy. The plan was to pretend to go on their usual evening drive and slip off to the Residency. They first drove to the station to avoid suspicion and then drove towards their place of refuge, expecting to be stopped any time. There were several moments where they felt they would be intercepted, especially when they had to pass a long bridge guarded by soldiers, but somehow, they were not stopped. They rode in complete darkness, without knowing the way, and after a long time, reached their shelter. From there, they were moved to the Raja's palace, under whose care they were to stay for the time being. Things seemed to settle down, but some hours later during the night Indians gathered around the palace, excited to see the European 'prisoners' of the Raja. Troops had to be brought in along with a large cannon to guard them in case the crowds tried to break in and lynch them.

Coopland wrote that throughout the year and a half of the revolt, matters were extremely tumultuous across India. In Shimla, many had been captured, and some had escaped on foot in the forests while some had fled to Kasauli where there was a cholera outbreak. In Bareilly, the native troops had mutinied, followed by Ajmere and Nusseerabad (Ajmer and Naseerabad). She recounted that on 11 June, they had received orders from the Lieutenant-

Governor at Agra that women in Gwalior were not to be evacuated and sent to Agra before mutiny broke out. Her husband still wanted to send her, but he could not leave his post and she did not want to abandon him. But if she and the women had been sent away in time, the men could have easily ridden away too when things got out of control on the night of 14 June.

Ruth Coopland's accounts provide a grim picture of the events that transpired thereon. She and some other ladies were trapped in Gwalior with little hope for escape. In the following week, while they were at an officer's house, they were informed that it would be dangerous to stay because the sepoys were coming to butcher them if they did not evacuate immediately. That evening when they were returning home, they passed some sepoys who did not attack them, but did not salute to them either, even though they were with senior officers like Major Blake and the Brigadier—a clear indication that they were soon going to revolt.

As they settled in that same night, uneasy because they could sense that their servants were behaving differently, they kept a bag of essentials ready in case they had to flee. Before they fell asleep, they heard a gunshot, and the alarm bugle rang out in the still night. The servants came running to tell them that the sepoys had arrived and were going to kill them, even as they dressed hurriedly. Fortunately, it was dark so even if the sepoys were nearby, they did not see them rush to their neighbours' house (the Stuarts) where they saw several ladies were huddled together in great distress while their husbands had gone to the lines. News came in that Captain Stuart had been shot, but was not dead, only captured. The women were then asked to go to the artillery lines, and Ruth and her husband decided to leave in a carriage after them, but just as they started out, a young sepoy came riding up declaring that the sahibs were being killed in that direction. Just then they heard the volley of muskets, bugles, and shots that rose up, followed by "terrible shrieks", after which they saw houses burning. They hastily changed direction and went into Major Blake's bungalow, which was nearby, and found some other women, including Mrs. Raikes who was the wife of a medical officer, hiding there.

They were still not safe because the sepoys could barge in at any moment to loot the house, but it was impossible to go anywhere else. Mrs. Raikes and some other women decided to leave to try and get away, and Mrs. Blake and the Cooplands, deciding against it, crept out into the garden to hide behind the trees and lay down in the dark covered with a shawl. As they waited, the Indian guards who were loyal to them kept coming up to give them news about others who had been murdered. Major Blake, the owner of the bungalow, had been killed. Nearby, a lady's house was attacked by a hundred sepoys, and lying there in the dark they could hear them tearing down everything and smashing the glass windows and furniture. By the moonlight, they could see the house burn down and turn into smouldering remains. Huddled in the darkness, they knew they were next.

The sepoys first looked for them inside the house then came out to search the garden. It seemed that they were completely sure that they would find Europeans hidden there and did not want to leave any stone unturned to kill them. In the moonlight, Ruth could spy on them pushing aside the bushes with their bayonets, as they passed very close to where the three lay hidden. When they could not find them, they set fire to Blake's bungalow, and left the premises believing there was no one there. However, the flames spread quickly and were about to reach their hiding place when one of Mrs. Blake's servants offered to give them shelter in his house. They did not have time to think, and ran into the hut in the pitch darkness, stumbling and falling on the uneven ground. Somehow, by then, the sepoys had returned, more furious than ever as they had received news that Europeans were being sheltered by the servants. The Cooplands and Mrs. Blake quickly entered the kitchen of the hut and could hear the sepoys arguing with the servant, trying to see if anyone was hidden inside. The servant tried to convince them that he had not concealed any '*firangees*' (foreigners), but the sepoys were not convinced. Finally, they burst into the room where they sat hidden:

> We saw the moon glistening with their fixed bayonets. We thought they were going to charge in upon us: but no; the hut was so dark that they could not see us. They called for a light; but Muza [the servant] stopped them, and said, "You see they are not here: come, and I will show you where they are". He shut and fastened the door, and they again went away.

After the sepoys left, Muza returned to tell them that they must leave because the other servants were likely to reveal their hide-out. He offered to take them to another servant's house where they would be somewhat safer. Day was beginning to dawn by then, and the horizon was getting bright as they crept out. If the sepoys came back, they would spot them easily. Mrs. Raikes, who had left for another town, returned just then as she had been unable to get away. She had a baby who was crying and fussing. As they hid in the second hut, the sepoys returned, and the baby's crying gave them away. There was no chance of surviving now, and they rushed out, crying "*mut maro, mut maro!*" ("Don't kill, don't kill!") The sepoys shouted, "We will not kill the memsahibs—only the sahib."

Ruth's husband was shot. Another lady with her baby, Mrs. Kirke, who had also been hiding at the Blakes' and had left earlier to escape to another city, was brought over, and they were made to stand together. Mrs. Kirke's husband had been killed before her eyes when they were trying to flee. They were going to kill her 4-year-old boy as well, but the child had golden curls and they thought it was a girl: "Don't kill the *butcha* [child]; it is a missie-baba," one of the men said. The women were then gathered into a room, and "the most insulting remarks" were passed at them, after which they were dragged along, taken from house to house, and then placed under some trees, where hundreds of sepoys mocked and stared at them and passed more insulting comments. After some time, they were told that they were allowed to leave and were reluctantly given a carriage to travel in. Ruth wrote: "How we all got in I can't say: there was Mrs. Blake, Mrs. Raikes, her baby and ayah, Mrs. Kirke and her little boy, Mrs. Campbell and myself, and some sergeants' wives clung to the carriage: how they hung on I don't know."

When they rode out, they came across more ladies, some of whom had just seen their husbands being shot and some of whom were almost naked having been dragged around. It is likely that such narratives added to the belief that memsahibs who fell into the hands of the rebels met a fate worse than death.

Locked Down: The Siege of Lucknow, June–November

Some industrious memsahibs managed to avoid death by constantly moving from one shelter to another, some remained behind in their houses, and some escaped to shelters and refugee sites guarded by British soldiers. In Lucknow, some memsahibs who lived in close proximity to each other were able to plan their flight to safety in a better fashion despite the panic and confusion. But this was also down to regional variations in how quickly and how far in advance news could spread.

Adelaide Case, wife of Colonel William Case of the 32nd Regiment, was awakened in the middle of the night on 17 May with the news that her husband was to leave for the cantonments to check the status there and that all the women in Lucknow were to flee to the Residency before dawn because an attack was likely. But Adelaide and her sister, Caroline, who was living with her, had been warned beforehand. The night before they were to leave, they packed their things with the help of their *ayahs* and servants. They had been told that they would have to mount their horses at 3 am and move with the regiment. Their servants made all the preparations for their journey. The *chowkidars* (guards) went in to take care of the house, the carriages were loaded, and the children were placed inside. Everything was done quietly so as not to rouse the locals and alert them of their flight. While the bravery of the women is commendable, it is incredible how some ladies were still concerned about their belongings even in such tumultuous times. Adelaide and her companions were packing for the whole day before they were to leave, compressing their many things in the carriage: they sewed up their linen in pillowcases and packed their plates in their clothes, and even though death was at hand, they were disappointed that they had to leave their glass and crockery behind!

Due to the shortage of carriages, they started on foot and eventually crammed in to a bullock *gharry* "as closely as a box of sardines". Their journey, although extremely dangerous and difficult, was well executed. Many others were not able to escape to safety in time.

Little did the memsahibs know that merely escaping to safety was not the end of their trials. Securing a good sanctuary itself was of great difficulty, and despite making the best efforts, some were not able to find safe dwellings. Sometimes, people were evacuated without notice and had to seek shelter in other people's homes, which was a great challenge in such chaotic times as most people's homes would already be overcrowded with other refugees. Indeed, upon reaching the Residency, Adelaide and her sister saw that there was a scramble for quarters. They were unable to find a room but chanced upon a spare chamber with no windows that was being used as a storeroom. They had to take it because the houses were all overcrowded, and every hour, fresh arrivals came in.

Adelaide was comparatively better off than many others because she had gained a safe passage to the Residency and had access to provisions during the whole time. She and her sister were even moved to a more comfortable chamber due to her husband's contacts. More importantly, Adelaide was fortunate enough to have her sister by her side, and the company of several women she was already acquainted with.

However, matters got worse as the weeks passed. The condition of the Residency, like in all kinds of refugee camps, became extremely insanitary. Families were grouped together in small spaces, and exhaustion, dehydration, and weakness caused quick deaths. People also died of dysentery and fever. In the garrisons, where people were living in tents in close proximity to each other, cholera, smallpox, and especially scurvy were common and could kill swiftly, due to poor sanitation and ventilation. In fact, scurvy came to be called 'garrison disease' because of the prevalence of it in those congested conditions. Moreover, in the Residency, there was the fear of running out of provisions given that no one knew how long the siege of Lucknow would last.

Adelaide's journal vividly captures the perilous state of affairs in the whole city. They expected bad news to come in at any time; they feared for themselves but feared more for the men who were fighting outside trying to keep them safe. There was an insurmountable feeling of fear and suspicion, and even within the buildings where they had taken refuge, they did not feel safe because of the Indian servants present there. There was also the perennial fear of the building being set on fire or cannonaded. Indeed, the fear of attack was always present, and women kept their things packed at their bedsides at night, ready for instant flight. To make matters worse, while at the Residency women continually received news of officers being killed, and many were widowed while in hiding.

Adelaide had had a terrible premonition even before the defeat of the British during the Battle of Chinhat. They had very little information about which direction the battle was going in, and all they knew was that it was a 'bloody' confrontation. Adelaide's intuition proved to be ultimately correct when the forces were pushed back and the men retreated to the Residency. They brought back the news that Colonel Case, her husband, had been killed.

Lady Inglis, married to Major General Sir John Eardley Inglis of the 32nd Regiment on Foot, was with Adelaide when the men came in one by one "looking more dead than alive", and she described Adelaide standing on the veranda watching the scene as if in a daze. After that, Adelaide fell violently ill, and Caroline filled sections of her journal while she recovered. Even after she got well, her journal entries indicate that she was in a poor state of mind, dealing with the loss of her husband and being suddenly solely responsible for her sister and children with months of a very difficult siege ahead of them. In her journal entry for 27 September, she wrote that like her, several other ladies were contemplating committing suicide.

As the 'mutiny' progressed, the sense of trepidation became overwhelming as they sat together expecting news of infiltration at all hours. Adelaide wrote on Friday 16 October 1857, "I believe an attack was expected to-day, but up to this hour… all has been quiet." The next day she wrote, "No news of any kind today, except that distant guns were heard yesterday."

Lady Julia Inglis, wife of Colonel John Inglis of the 32nd Regiment who took command of the garrison, like Adelaide, experienced great trials and tribulations while they were locked down at the Residency. After the retreat following the defeat at Chinhat, near Lucknow, the Residency was besieged. Julia's husband commanded the Brigade from September until November when they were finally relieved. Her diary provides an exhilarating yet unnerving first-hand account of the fear and delirium experienced by those trapped inside for months, even as heavy musketry and cannonading went on around them at all times. She wrote that every moment was a war-like situation as they could be attacked any time. The Residency was battered after heavy fighting, and many other posts in the garrison were completely damaged. The walls were riddled with round shots. As many as 200 shots were picked up and collected in September after one confrontation. They often had to barricade the windows and abandon the upper storey for fear of shells.

Moreover, she skilfully described the quotidian details of a woman's life as a refugee. Her vivid detailing of the moments of terror when they received information of impending attacks are particularly haunting. She sketched out the miseries they underwent due to the protracted period of the siege as their supply of rations and water began to dwindle.

Another lady, Mrs. Moore, was confined in the Residency after her husband, Captain Moore, was killed. She wrote how the only food the women had while in the shelter was *dal* and rice, and many women died before relief arrived. Sometimes, the rations went out completely, and the sick and the wounded had no provisions or facilities. There were days when there was not enough milk even for dying infants. Lady Inglis wrote:

> The full rations at first starting were a pound of meat and a pound of flour per man; this was reduced to twelve ounces, then to six, and after General Havelock's arrival [25 September] to four ounces. Women got three-quarter rations, children half. Except for hospital comforts, and here and there private stores, there was little else procurable in the garrison—no bread, butter, milk, eggs, vegetables, wines, beer or tobacco. The lack of vegetables was most sorely felt, and was the cause of much illness; and the want of sugar and milk was most trying to the children, amongst whom there was a great mortality.

By August, there was utter despair, and they doubted if relief would ever arrive. The next month, there seemed to be some hope as General Havelock's relief force entered Lucknow. Lady Inglis described 25 September 1857 as "a day never to be forgotten". It was towards the middle of the day when they caught sight of their relieving force. Amidst the turbulence, Mrs. Cowper's son was dying of bronchitis, and she sat with him, uncaring and unafraid of the fear and excitement around. Some hours later, cheering could be heard, and General Havelock came in, congratulating them for the present win. However, many women were too numb with pain to feel the relief of being rescued because their husbands had been mortally wounded in the clashes or their friends or children had died while in hiding.

By October, there were 800 wounded in the garrison as well as 410 women and children. In the hospitals, medicines were fast depleting. It was not only men and women dying, but babies were dying too due to illnesses.

In November, when the clashes were still very intense, Sir Colin Campbell headed the relief of Lucknow. He ordered immediate evacuation after 5 months of siege, and the women, including Katherine Bartrum (wife of Robert Henry Bartrum who died in February 1858), were told to move with nothing except for what they could carry. And they could only carry their infants and children. The evacuation was extremely difficult because everyone, including the sick and injured, had to be moved with only a few hours' notice. They marched several miles from Lucknow to a temporary camp.

In her journal entry for 25 September, Katherine Bartrum had written that she had a terrible sense of foreboding. This proved to be correct because their hardships were not over. They later marched to Cawnpore, reaching it by the end of November, and moved to the artillery barracks there, from where Katherine went to Allahabad in the first week of December.

It was a slow and laborious onward journey to England. From Allahabad, she took a steamer to Benaras, then Ghazeepore, then to Dinapore and Calcutta, where she stayed for a short while. It would be months before they would reach England. Katherine was with Emily Polehampton on the *Himalaya* and landed in Plymouth on 8 June 1858.

Lady Inglis and Adelaide Case's ship was wrecked on the way, but they too eventually reached home safely.

While women like Adelaide Case, Lady Inglis, Emily Polehampton, and Katherine Bartrum were intent on leaving India as quickly as possible, other women, such as Fanny Duberly, were only just arriving. In December 1857, Fanny and her husband, Captain Henry Duberly of the 8 Royal Irish Hussars of the British Light Cavalry, settled into Mazagon near Bombay. The Duberlys had still been at sea near the Cape when the *Himalaya*, carrying Emily Polehampton and Katherine Bartrum back to Britain, brought news of the British recapture of Delhi. They realised that with the reclamation of Delhi, the main mutiny was defeated, and the 'rebels' would not be able to sustain the movement. There was a general sense of jubilation amongst the people on the deck thereafter.

Sometime after the Duberlys had settled into Mazagon, they heard an interesting bit of information: as it happened, the army, which took Delhi after the loss when the city fell, thought that everything would be theirs. They wanted to plunder everything, even though the booty of every man was supposed to be just a few extra rupees each. This gave rise to some dark humour and chalk inscriptions were scrawled all over the town:

"DELHI TAKEN, AND INDIA SAVED,
FOR TWENTY RUPEES"

"*Challo Bahadoor!*": Memsahibs as 'Historians' of the Mutiny

> *In submitting the following pages for public inspection, I have listened to the suggestions of my friends rather than to the dictates of my own judgment. They were written for the perusal of my relatives in England, and with no view whatsoever to publication; and it was not without a struggle in my own mind that I at last complied with their wishes. They represented to me, that but few journals had survived the siege of Lucknow and the wreck of the steamer which conveyed us from India, and that any particulars of that protracted and dreadful beleaguerment would be read with great interest by the friends and relatives of those who fought and bled in that ill-fated city.*
>
> *I have not attempted, by subsequent additions, to produce effect, or to aim at glowing descriptions, but have given it as it was written, in the simple narrative form, which the dangers and privations of the siege alone permitted... It cannot but fail (for no woman is equal to the task)*

> *to do justice to the heroism, or to describe in adequate terms the great sufferings, of the gallant defenders of Lucknow.*
>
> – Adelaide Case, 1858

Nearly all post-facto attempts to account for the broad events of 1857 highlight the inexplicability of the sudden and—to British minds—unwarranted rebellion against the imperial order. Sahibs and memsahibs alike expressed shock and disbelief, and the inability to fully comprehend the "full barbarity of these unprovoked massacres". Ruth M. Coopland, whose account of 1857 was published 2 years later, wrote, "All went on as usual till Sunday (the fatal day), the 10th of May… It burst on us at Gwalior like a thunderclap, paralysing us with horror. We could not help wondering how a plot, known to so many thousands, could so long remain a secret".

Something similar occurred with Elizabeth McMullin Muter, wife of Colonel Dunbar Douglas Muter—a Captain with the 1st Battalion 60th King's Royal Rifles. Elizabeth was stationed in Meerut with her husband at the very start of the insurgency in May 1857. She was at the church in the evening, expecting the men to come parading in that direction as usual, when a gentleman came up to her and gave the news of a "slight disturbance". She was sceptical at first but soon realised that the "slight disturbance" was not only true but also something much graver. As she reached home, her servants immediately came forward to caution her and tell her to hide. And in her panic and confusion she listened to them, but later wrote indignantly in her diary: "to conceal myself in my own house, in the lines of a regiment that had reckoned up a century of renown! And from what?"

Despite knowing that the uprising was against the British, which clearly meant they were all in immediate danger, Mrs. Muter was outraged at the idea of having to hide in her own house. Her reaction showed denial, disbelief, and arrogance, combined with complete faith in the British army, presumably stemming from the common British attitude that the Indians would not dare attempt, or perhaps would not be capable of, a mutiny against the empire. Women in a position of high status within the colony would have indeed found it hard to imagine such a threat, and this feeling of superiority would inform many of their initial reactions to the outbreak of violence as well as the colour of their published accounts in the aftermath.

Like Mrs. Muter, many Brits' sense of surprise and denial was dispelled within days, or even hours, as they became aware of the magnitude of the rebellion. The news spread that the rebels wanted to recapture the cities, eradicate the agents of colonial rule, and reclaim everything. Treasuries were looted, *kutcherries* (courts) were destroyed to remove official records, and the sepoys even released prisoners from the jails. According to Mrs. Muter's account, it was clear that the attack was no ordinary skirmish; it was a matter of "shooting down every European they met", which to her was a serious attempt at revolution.

The extent to which the revolt came as a massive shock to the British is evident in the experiences of women who voluntarily came to India for the first time just before the uprising began. In addition to the Lindsay women we met earlier in the chapter, Madeleine Jackson and her sister Georgina landed in Calcutta at the start of the year in 1857 but ended up being captured in June, then paraded in chains through villages, and ultimately held as hostages in Lucknow during the siege; their brother died in the city before the uprising was quelled.

Some women disobeyed orders out of a misplaced confidence that nothing would happen to the British in India. Believing the British were invincible, they deliberately did not leave the cantonments in time and were killed because of it.

One lady, mentioned in *A Lady's Diary During the Siege of Lucknow* (1870), written by Mrs. R. C. Germon (Maria Germon), remained in her home with her husband despite being aware of the killings. Maria was the wife of one of the officers in Lucknow and wrote in her journal that they too were (initially) in complete denial about the uprisings and did not take any precautions. However, their eyes were opened when Mrs. Brien, who was their friend, told them that she and her husband were caught in the violence within the cantonments and escaped narrowly. On the night of the initial attack, she and her husband had been roused by their servants in the middle of the night as the sepoys stormed into their house demanding to see the sahib and the memsahib. The lady had to take her five children and hide in the servants' quarters. However, the sepoys discovered her hiding place and attacked. While they were under fire, the servants had to cut out a portion of the mud wall to let her escape through the back as there was no other way, even as the bullets went flying by her head. She fled to the nearby village, but the locals threatened to kill her there as well. She had to hide in the *nullah* after sliding down the bank. She was in a terrible state and scared for the life of her children. Her baby was suffering from dysentery and died some days later.

It is evident that the improbability of a revolt against British supremacy had caused complacency amongst the British in India, and memsahibs offering accounts of the uprising did not always shy away from pointing out this fault. In her letter to Lady Stuart de Rothesay, Charlotte (Viscountess Canning) confessed how they had always believed that they were in a secure place in India, although in retrospect she felt that complacency had made them careless. Negligence in defence-related matters became apparent when investigations were undertaken about how security was breached during the uprising.

There are varying historical accounts about the events leading up to the outbreak of the rebellion. In March 1857, one of the most prominent icons of that year, Mangal Pandey, an infantryman in the 34th Bengal Native Infantry stationed in Barrackpore, rebelled against his commander. He was arrested and executed by hanging but not before he had rallied for support amongst his fellow soldiers. This unleashed a series of similar uprisings as entire regiments rebelled after the 34th Bengal Native Infantry was disbanded following Pandey's hanging.

Today, the most cited causes for the rebellion are the 'rumours' that were afloat in 1857; these were rumours about the cartridges of the new Enfield Pritchett Rifle given to the Indian sepoys by the British, which were greased with cow and pig fat. The practice was to bite down on the cartridge to release the gun powder into the barrel, so using those cartridges would have been sacrilegious to the Indian sepoys. There was also a belief that the British had laced edible items in the markets with animal remains. The fear underlying these 'rumours' was that the British wanted to sully the religion of the Indian sepoys and destroy their caste. And although the British denied it completely, there is evidence to suggest that the suspicions about the greased cartridges were not unfounded. In any case, historians have questioned the tendency to reduce the rebellion to a religious conflict, even as the colonialists highlighted the rather limited spread of the 'mutiny' in Northern India.

All of these events were closely linked together, and many amongst the British strongly believed that warnings of the 'mutiny' were there well before the uprising started. Ruth M. Coopland remarked that signs of imminent danger were present at the beginning of 1857 when she and the others heard of the hanging of Mangal Pandey and the matter of the greased cartridges. Several others point to various other errors in judgement committed by the colonial government that had increased the intensity of the attacks. For instance, there were three regiments fewer than before the outbreak, no European regiments in any of the cities or bigger towns, and Allahabad, Cawnpore, Benaras, and Delhi were protected by disaffected regiments. Yet the government in Calcutta had been reticent even when dissent began brewing in early 1857 and merely disbanded regiments thinking this would avert conflict or crisis. This indicates to us that there was some level of laxity in military matters, as well as insufficient media reportage because many were not forewarned of the likelihood of attack. Elisa Greathed, wife of H. H. Greathed who was in the Bengal Civil Service, edited a compilation of her husband's letters that was published in 1858. She wrote in the introduction that even after unrest began, the administration underestimated the severity of the matter, apparently not seeing the signs foreshadowing the disaster.

Therefore, the initial insouciance of the memsahibs could be blamed on this laxity of the government; they were not caught out merely because of imperial arrogance but because they lacked official information or warning by the authorities. Indeed, Ruth M. Coopland wrote about an apparent 'conspiracy' for a general uprising throughout the country on only 16 May, which was almost a week after the start of the revolt. Even then, they only had a vague idea about the sequence of events leading up to the violence. Moreover, as the uprisings continued, the lack of understanding and comprehension of the situation was not because memsahibs were unaware of or uninterested in the political developments but because during the revolt there was a definite breakdown of communication, and hardly anything was conveyed to the civilians officially.

Additionally, due to the lack of information, terrible stories circulated freely giving rise to excessive speculation on what was happening outside the shelters and sending the women into a state of terror and confusion. It was worse that the officers did not divulge much information to them, and when messengers came in with news, they could not trust them entirely because it was simply too difficult to distinguish between reality and rumours. Even when news of deaths created great panic, it was hardly ever possible to get verified information. They would have to send for papers to see the list of those who had been killed or who had escaped, and they would be wracked with suspense over the state of their relatives and friends.

The memsahibs were quite aware that conspiratorial theories, rumours, and hearsay were circulating far more readily than any official updates from the administration, and not everything they heard could be taken as fact. Indeed, Ruth's husband, Reverend George William Coopland, Chaplain to the Honourable East India Company, received news that Delhi had fallen and wrote about it in a letter dated 11 June. However, this was incorrect as they had been misinformed. Ruth clarified in her own diary that they had been misled because of the madness and mayhem: "The day after my husband wrote this letter (the last he ever wrote) the news came that Delhi had not been taken: it was a mistake in the telegram." Sometimes, true events were so horrendous and bizarre that it seemed like exaggeration and could hardly be believed or accepted, and sometimes bizarre news turned out to be true. Ruth was told that Mrs. Campbell had been killed, but later it turned out that she was in hiding, disguised as an Indian *ayah*.

Given the profusion of misinformation, memsahibs were aware that every bit of news needed to be corroborated before relaying it further. Sometimes, in the absence of official updates, they had to observe the varying behaviour of the Indian locals around them to glean information. There were usually signs if they paid attention; for instance, the servants remained faithful to their masters even during attacks and mostly helped them escape, but if they stopped co-operating at any point, it could indicate that they knew about an attack and were hand in glove with the attackers. In any case, the servants always had more information about the plans of the 'mutineers' than the women of the empire did. In early June, when Mrs. Muter's *ayah* became concerned about her employment "when the ladies and children are murdered", she knew that an attack on the area was coming, and they needed to evacuate immediately.

However dissatisfied the memsahibs may have been with the government's handling of the uprising, the wrath in their accounts was of course almost entirely reserved for the Indians. It has to be considered that official narratives as well as private accounts of the revolt that deliberated on the issue of caste and religion labelled it unjustified, superfluous, and simply farcical.

Memsahibs even wrote that the uprising was not a struggle for political freedom but an issue of caste and religion, if not a random expression of generalised insubordination. Indeed, even as they wrote about the extremity of attacks, memsahibs, like their sahibs, were simultaneously dismissive of the uprising. They painted the controversy about greased cartridges in Meerut, which lit the fuse of the whole uprising, as either an excuse used by irresponsible soldiers or else as a mistaken expression of strong cultural feeling based on a 'misunderstanding'. If only the rumour about the animal fat had never started, these accounts seemed to imply, there would never have been any dissent from the natives to disturb the empire's functioning.

For instance, Mrs. Muter's accounts clearly reveal that she had known about the matter of the cartridges seemingly in depth, but ultimately informed her readers that: "it appears that the movement on the part of the Sepoys was more a revolt—with much of panic in it—against a suspected attack on their religion and caste, than as we all at first thought, a struggle for Empire." Viscountess Charlotte Canning went a step further and categorically wrote in a letter written from Calcutta on 18 May 1857 (Mangal Pandey had been executed by then) that "the cartridges had no grease at all on them, and the men were to put on what they pleased, and to tear them with their hands. Either they misunderstood this when it was told to them, or it was merely a pretext." Either way, she seemed to suggest, the uprising was not to be taken seriously.

However, such statements do not mean that memsahibs were unaware of the various diplomatic and military disputes between the coloniser and colonised. Their writings reveal an insight into the important administrative and political events that had culminated in the revolt. But it was not in the interests of anyone with a stake in the continuation of British India, the memsahibs included, to publicise or dwell on the actions of the British themselves that may have led to the uprisings.

It is perhaps expected that after the rebellion, there was a sustained vilification and trivialisation of the sepoys. This entailed a definitive diminution of the revolt and the rebelling forces, as it was described as a mere 'disobedience'—a nuisance or inconvenience to the British—and not so much a significant political and military event in the history of imperial rule in India. Some memsahibs' accounts consistently downplayed the 'rebels' as mere 'mutineers' who were nothing more than turncoats and who were going to be brought back to servility after proper retribution. Mrs. Muter was of the opinion that "Sepoy Revolt" would be a more accurate term than "Indian Mutiny". She declared, "This war was begun by the Sepoys in treachery, ingratitude and cruelty; was continued in ignorance and incapacity, without energy and without courage".

It was also suggested that the violence of 1857 had exposed the Indians' true intentions towards the British as well as their basic 'treacherousness' of character. Mrs. Muter categorically mentioned that amongst the rebels were their own known employees, including butchers, tailors, servants, carpenters, and masons, who had turned against them. Furthermore, most of the events recorded by memsahibs promoted the belief that the killing of British civilians was not only inhuman but also dishonourable. And Mrs. Harris bitterly wrote, "I expect they are much too cowardly to make any attempt on a place so well prepared: it is only while they can take you by surprise and murder defenceless women and children that they dare attack Europeans."

With this narrative of duplicity came a steady promulgation of the notion that even though the uprising had been put down, the British were no longer safe in India. To tackle this feeling of threat, there was an aggressive attempt to efface the idea that the end of the empire in India was near: the immediate response was to unleash a barrage of patriotic imperial discourses within official, military, and personal records of the time to declare the threat on the empire to be fake or mythical. The revolt was thus projected as a temporary disorder that had dissipated in the face of the British imperial might. It was treated as a grotesque but temporary 'saturnalia'—a momentary barbarian frenzy of the power dynamics—which had finally purged the natives. Ultimately, in popular perception, the British forces had restored the 'natural' colonial status quo after suppressing the sepoys.

Be that as it may, the cumulative impact of the numerous indigenous and peasant movements in the subcontinent, in addition to the rising discontentment amongst the *zamindar* (feudal) classes, which took place throughout the imperial expansion in the subcontinent, cannot be glossed over. Biswamoy Pati, a historian of colonial India, has said that historians like Tapti Roy, Rudrangshu Mukherjee, and Eric Stokes, amongst others, have deliberated on issues such as caste mobilisation, economic dislocation, peasant protests, territoriality, and anger of the commoners including the elites and business class (5–8), which were all significant factors at the beginning of the rebellion in 1857.

Clearly, the 'rebels' who had dared to oppose the British were not only not limited to the sepoys of the army but were a rather heterogenous mix of people. In any case, although it was not the first uprising against the British at the time, it was a defining point in the history of the colonial presence in India and certainly a momentous point in Indian military activities because of the challenge to the British forces who had been present in India for over a century. Indeed, the 'mutiny' was a significant confrontation to the British imperial order, and nationalist historiographers have even attempted to read the events of 1857 as possibly the 'First War of Independence' (although 'nationalism' itself was nebulous at the time). But it was psychologically and politically all but impossible for British colonials to concede to this without admitting to their vulnerability or limitations.

Returning to the issue of memsahibs as 'historiographers' of the 'mutiny', it must be highlighted that some of their writings explicitly stated that they were written to 'inform' people back home about the atrocities committed upon them. It is likely that the women of British India wanted to ensure that their experiences would feature prominently amongst the stories emerging from the ashes of the uprising. Ruth M. Coopland wrote:

> Some men may think that women are weak and only fitted to do trivial things, and endure petty troubles; and there are women who deserve no higher opinion: such as faint at the sight of blood, are terrified at a harmless cow, or make themselves miserable by imagining terrors and unreal sorrows; but there are many who can endure with fortitude and patience what even soldiers shrink from.

Memsahibs, who were not at the forefront of the battle but were more vulnerable, wrote extensively about their courage and fortitude in the ghastliest of situations. Apart from the subtle glorification of the British woman as mentioned earlier, there was also a kind of stubborn racial pride and self-confidence in their writings, especially in those writings compiled after some time had passed since the uprising. While they certainly lauded the brave British officers, many of whom were martyred while defending their people, there was a tone of pride as they detailed their own trials and triumphs. In this, there was a marked self-congratulatory attitude in their expressions of disdain towards the 'enemy' as well. Mrs. Leopold Paget rejoiced when she heard of rebels being killed; she wrote: "One never heard of a more arrant set of cowards than the rebels proved themselves, and they were butchered like sheep by the Sepoys of the 28th, who, when their blood is up, are wonderfully cruel."

Several records by memsahibs were deliberately fashioned as imprisonment-and-escape stories, and they projected women as heroes in their own right who overcame paralysing fear and anxiety and displayed great adaptability and astuteness. They highlighted how the memsahibs' quick responses and willingness to co-operate showed their strength and valour as British women in the Raj. Some such writings are *Our Escape from Gwalior* by Mrs. Blake, *Our Escape in June 1857* by Mrs. Irwin, *A Lady's Escape from Gwalior* by Ruth Coopland, *The Story of Our Escape from Delhi* by Julia Haldane, and *Ten Months in Captivity* by Amelia Bennett. As we have seen, such terrifying yet exhilarating narratives did take hold in the British press back home.

Some recollections, such as *The Siege of Lucknow: A Diary* (1892) by Lady Julia Inglis, were written after long stretches of time—more than three decades in her case—and represented a clear attempt by a memsahib at writing a serious history. In her preface, Inglis wrote explicitly that although there had been several writings in the form of reminiscences and historical facts about the mutiny in Lucknow, which was a site of "grand struggle" where valiant men fought tirelessly to "defend the lives and honour of their wives and children", enough had not been written as a "clear and accurate account". She explained that her work, which contained "a simple account of each day's events", was aimed at giving an idea of what transpired within the garrison during the siege—so it was a woman's version of events. In her words:

> My object in writing this little book will be attained if it gives the present generation a clearer knowledge of the defence of Lucknow, and greater appreciation of the services of those engaged in it. I have added my diary of the events that happened subsequent to the reinforcement by Generals Havelock and Outram, and to the relief by Lord Clyde, and have wound up the narrative by an account of my journey down country and voyage home and shipwreck, as being a curious sequence to the horrors of the Mutiny.

In fact, both during and after the mutiny, memsahibs wrote with the specific intention of providing information and documenting events but also wrote because there was an urgent need to stir patriotic zeal. When it came to manufacturing public opinion, both back home in Britain and in the British quarters within India, such individual recollections of the revolt played a major role in generating anger and outrage towards the "treacherous" sepoys. In other words, these women were not just recording their experiences, they were consciously participating in the process of history-writing and by extension in the broader colonial project in India. Moreover, the idea of recording first-hand accounts and relaying them back home was to ensure the transmission of correct information given the profusion of rumours. This was because even in confinement, they were reading the newspapers that were being read back home or they at least knew what kind of official narratives were being circulated amongst their family and friends. They realised that such accounts could not give a true idea of the complexity of the situation and of the great variety in experience from place to place.

Thus, their accounts contain elaborate descriptions of the clashes between the sepoys and the British troops, portraying the natives as monsters that the officers had to fight against to defend not just the Europeans in India but the India of the empire herself.

Memsahibs did not shrink from elaborating on the scenes of destruction that they had witnessed. Their accounts contain spine-chilling descriptions of escapes, evacuations, and time spent in refugee sites, which for some lasted months. With immense alacrity, they wrote the gory details of how the remains of murdered people had been pulled from the smoking ruins of houses, the streets, and ditches or how the mangled bodies of women were found lying naked and hacked with sabres. They wrote how, in Setapore, a whole heap of babies was found; they had been bayonetted and thrown together. Another account mentioned how a woman's leg was blown up by a round shot and she died soon after. They wrote how the deaths were sometimes so great in number inside the shelters that each corpse was sewn into his or her own bedding, and those who died during the day were put into the same grave at night. There could be as many as nine funerals in one day near a single shelter. Mrs. Harris wrote that one pretty lady was shot down as she tried to wade through a river. A Sergeant, his wife and their two children, who happened to be in cantonments, were stabbed and hacked to death on the road.

Memsahibs' accounts of the abuse of women's bodies significantly intensified the public rage. But more importantly, their writings humanised women's suffering, which was not brought out fully in official accounts since women's ordeals were relayed in official discourses as facts and figures. Women's personal accounts of their experiences enabled them to give a narrative to the horrors they were put through, which were specific to their gender and which were all the more horrible because of the attacks on their modesty.

In her diary, Mrs. Germon wrote that the sepoys bayonetted women and children, then selected fifteen to eighteen young ladies and took them off to their camps. The purpose of stating these occurrences, despite the great Victorian taboo on discussing sexual matters, was to provoke anger, induce shock, and document women-specific personal experiences.

Ruth Coopland wrote: "it must be obvious to all that I cannot do so without great pain; but I think that Englishmen ought to know what their own countrywomen have endured at the hands of the sepoys". Mrs. Henry Duberly also wrote with the same intention to put forward a "faithful record" of the events that transpired during the mutiny while touching upon points that "may seem beyond a woman's province".

In all this, there was the constant reliving of the violent events that surrounded the supposedly unprecedented 'insubordination' of the Indian troops. Heinous tales of the horrors also continued to be circulated orally. These were relayed repeatedly alongside official data on killings and abductions.

Moreover, some included events too traumatising to state even in private letters or journals. Mrs. Germon, in her preface to her diary published in 1870, highlighted that her account contained original wording as it was written by her day by day at Lucknow, without any embellishment. But out of a feeling of delicacy, she omitted the names of some people who suffered through frightening incidents. This indicates that even while memsahibs attempted to write and circulate every horror of the rebellion, they did practise a kind of self-censorship in some cases.

Ultimately, the dominant discourse was completely tilted against the rebels without addressing the main issue of India's desire for liberation. The fault of the colonial governance was mostly passed over, and the counterinsurgency and retaliatory violence was mostly unrecorded. But historians have commented on how the average British soldier and civilian official remained completely against pardoning the rebels. Biswamoy Pati writes: "A harsh ignorance could be noticed among the commanding officers for the dreadful conduct of a British or European soldier towards the Indians. When a British soldier kicked a native and left him almost half dead, no one was accused. But being two minutes late for parade or failing to polish up one's cap or collar badges were considered serious offences in the army" (92).

Memsahibs were also not willing to explicitly accept the abuse by the British that had directly caused unrest amongst the native subordinates. Their writings simply seem to establish that women played their part in the resistance to the mutineers, if not by actively fighting then by keeping their faith in the Crown. In other words, they too had defended the empire, and by publishing their accounts of their resilience during those hard months, they staked their claim in the post-mutiny posterity. The argument was that they, like the men, had made personal sacrifices and paid the price of war. Even though they could not take up arms themselves, it was their husbands who died fighting against the rebels, leaving them widowed. Mrs. Harris wrote: "The ladies were equally calm and heroic; they knelt down with their little ones, under a tree praying, and as soon as their husbands were slaughtered their turn came". Some volunteered in the hospitals and took care of the injured. Lady Inglis wrote: "Mrs. Polehampton was very indefatigable in her labours at the hospital; she went daily and seldom empty-handed, and at this time one could not give away without self-denial. I have since heard how much the soldiers loved her. Mrs. Gall and Mrs. Barber also worked most indefatigably amongst them."

Having asserted their right to be recognised both as victims and warriors of the clashes, memsahibs also served as commentators on thier brutal conclusion as the trials, and hangings of the captured sepoys are given great attention in some of their writings. In some cases, they also contained extensive dialogue about the period following the revolt with regard to the colonial government's responses, investigations, trials and court proceedings, the Indian monarchs, and the overall political status of India. Moreover, there were common threads on the themes of British identity, Christianity, and humanity throughout their writings. In fact, duty to the monarch and sacrifice for the empire were ubiquitous in all writing about the events of 1857.

There would be almost a century of Crown rule before the British would ultimately be forced out of India, but with the uprising came a realisation of the need to defer that moment was necessary. And the memsahibs of the new Raj were there to live through it all.

It must be kept in mind that the post-traumatic writings about the revolt demonstrate a negotiation with reality but also indicate that every writer and recorder's representation of the reality was filtered through their unique level of comprehension, memory, and political insight. The mutiny literature and, in particular, recollections should be read as products of a 'memory' impacted by physical and psychological trauma, containing varied and individualised meaning but always imbued with a fear that was both intensely personal, and inherently political.

10

"WE ARE NOT WANTED IN INDIA"

GOING BACK 'HOME', OR STAYING ON?

We sailed for England from Calcutta in March that year. It was a grey chill rainy spring morning when the ship berthed at Plymouth. Everything was grey, wet, colourless, as we stood by the rail watching the luggage being unloaded into the customs sheds... A cold realisation was creeping over us...

"Where are we going?" asked Rose for perhaps the hundredth and ninety-ninth time since we had left Calcutta.

"To Randolph Gardens first", Mam told her.

"Home", said Fa.

"Our home is Narayangunji," but nobody said it; nobody could, because it was no longer true.

– Jon and Rumer Godden, 1966

Even after two centuries of British presence in India, many amongst the sahibs and memsahibs felt like exiles from their homeland. India was their place of domicile, perhaps even their birthplace, but it still wasn't what they identified as their 'motherland'. Many of them felt a keen sense of alienation, as they constantly yearned to 'go back'.

On the other hand, a great portion of the British elite had grown accustomed to India and could not imagine leaving. Several memsahibs who had set up their 'little Britains' in the vast spaces of the subcontinent felt quite settled in their 'second home'. Even in the mid-twentieth century, as Indian independence movements grew stronger, they did not consider leaving. Finally, as the 1940s rolled in, they had to weigh up their attachments. The Japanese attack on Pearl Harbour had jolted them out of their complacency, and by the end of the Second World War, many of their friends and relations had already left. They were forced to accept the reality of India's imminent independence, and the question before them was whether to stay on or to leave.

Indeed, in the final decade of the colonial rule in India, the fate of the last generation of colonists seemed uncertain. Were they destined to become part of independent India? Or would they have to pack up and go home, leaving behind the country and a way of life they had grown to love?

While there were some who chose to leave, many felt torn and expressed great regret at having to leave. Ursula Graham Bower, who lived in north-east India for several years, said in the early 1940s "I don't know what's going to happen… But my home's here, in Laisong [in Assam], and I'm coming back to it whatever happens." Alice Reading, the Vicereine of India and wife of Lord Reading, wrote in 1925 that despite the jubilation she felt about going back home, she felt saddened at the prospect of leaving India as she had felt quite at home. She wrote that she had given the country her heart, and "may have left some of it behind as many of us have done before and since. The gift of the heart is one that India never refuses or denies". A similarly strong sense of association with India as home existed for several others. And yet, the inexorable drive for India's freedom from the Crown rule signalled the end of the Raj era, and their impending exodus to Britain.

Thus, amidst the socio-political disturbance in the subcontinent, the remaining British-Indian families, knowing the world around them was going to change soon, were intent on making the most of the numbered days in the Raj. They were determined to take back memories of their part in the glorious empire and wanted to record and preserve as much as they could of their own golden days as sahibs and memsahibs—an era which would soon be lost.

Writing accounts of their travels in journals and letters had always been a practice amongst the British in India, but as technological developments increased, letter writing and journalling gave way to a more visual form of archiving, and they passionately captured the fast-changing landscapes around them, along with sundry vignettes of their glamorous lives in the outposts. Photography had become popular amongst Westerners as portable cameras became easily available, and videography became a favourite for those in India wishing to record snippets of ordinary activities in the 'exotic East'. Like their predecessors, these sahibs and memsahibs were self-styled modern ethnographers wanting to record the 'oriental' scenes and themselves within them. Over the years, they created a substantial number of cine films, video clips, and home videos to take back home with them. This was not just their attempt at memorialising the past; these were their personal keepsakes of a glorious time in their lives in a period that was a 'gilded age' in its own right.

It must be noted that the most common subject for the amateur Raj filmmakers was mundane domestic affairs and quotidian aspects of Raj life. India had always been something of a romantic enigma for people back home who had never witnessed the luxurious life of the sahibs and memsahibs living in sprawling bungalows with their army of servants serving them day and night. In fact, throughout the period of British rule in India there had been a great curiosity about the famous yet quite mysterious Raj lifestyle. The British-Indian families knew that even the most ordinary scenes would be a novelty for people back home, and they took innumerable photos and videos of their children playing with the *ayahs* and being carried in baskets on the backs of their servants, of them feeding cattle or riding elephants or rolling around in the sun in the vast backyards of their bungalows. They photographed themselves walking around in the countryside in their outdoorsy outfits of *jodhpurs* (trousers) and *sola topees*, sipping drinks at their campsites, or picnicking in picturesque corners of the country. Today, a rich body of archived material, in the form of photographs and videos, is available and shows the sahibs and memsahibs' grand luncheons in hill stations, their hunting expeditions, and even the interiors of their bungalows. There are also sepia-tinged videos of the sahibs dispensing their daily duties in their offices, very much looking the part of British-Indian Civil Service officers in the Far East. Videos of memsahibs walking around in their manly trousers and hats or posing in the wild grass while their *ayahs* took care of their children are also available.

Although monochromatic, these visuals give an insight into the vibrant lives of the last of the British in India. Jocelyn Abbott, who kept a cine film of her early years in India during the 1930s as a young woman, recorded scenes from her daily life as she played with her newborn outside her home. She also had videos of her wedding—she was married to an Indian Civil Service officer in India in 1936, and her uncle had recorded the wedding on his video camera. She was dressed in a chiffon dress which was suitable for the hot weather. Apart from that she also had videos of her socialising with her neighbours in the classic memsahib fashion. One of the clips featured her sipping tea with a friend on the veranda of her house.

Abbott, in an interview for the BBC, appeared exceedingly nostalgic for her life in India. There were many others like her who could not forget the wonderful luxuries of the Raj lifestyle, unique as they were to that time. During her interview for the BBC, Anne Wright, having grown up in India, recalled fondly her favourite head servant, Kali Khan, who lived with her family for two decades and who every year got larger and larger and so had to use two belts to wrap around his enormous belly. She said nostalgically that the Raj children were always spoiled because all the bearers and gardeners were there to take care of their needs. "We could get on a pony and ride straight out in the jungle… nothing to stop us from doing anything we wanted… we had a wonderful time…" ("The Lost World of the Raj", Ep. 1, 33.00–34.00).

Joan Scott, who came to India in 1939 and lived on a tea plantation run by her uncle, also recalled wistfully the last days of Raj luxury, when everything would be done for them. They had eighteen domestic servants, *ayahs*, and multiple gardeners. Labour was readily available and cheap. She said that servants were so plentiful that there would be two to polish one pair of shoes. She also remembered the lovely sounds around her home as Indian women in the gardens usually sang together while plucking and pruning the shrubs. She still associated the sounds with 'Home' ("The Lost World of the Raj", Ep. 1, 26.25–27.50).

Iris Butler, born in Shimla in 1905, who became a journalist and historian, summed up the sentiment quite well when she said, "We took our life in India for granted, it was home."

An Unstable World

> *In 1945, with the end of hostilities in Europe, I was offered a two year assignment in connection with service clubs in India. I sailed almost immediately for Bombay. Before I left, friends asked me why I had chosen to go back. It is difficult to put the intangible into words... Most of all I wanted to see for myself the great progress already made by India in forging her own destiny.*
>
> – Monica Campbell Martin, 1951

Even at the beginning of the twentieth century, it seemed unlikely to the average European in India that the Raj would come to an end any time soon. There was a popular belief that Indians needed the British for effective governance, so the slowly fermenting desire for 'home rule' seemed incongruous to most. "What is going to happen when the British leave India?" they asked each other, sceptical of India's ability to be a sovereign state.

However, even to the most politically challenged memsahibs living in obscure towns, the calls for liberation clearly spelled the inevitability of their withdrawal. Papers contained news of daily political demonstrations, and the waves of rebellion were beginning to be felt strongly, especially since the division of Bengal in 1905. An attempt to assassinate the Viceroy, Charles Hardinge, in 1912, in what came to be known as the "Delhi-Lahore conspiracy", added to the highly charged atmosphere in the nation. Stray incidents of violence on the streets also became frequent. But this also meant that in some cases, the authorities cracked down on protestors with greater vehemence if they could.

By the 1920s, Gandhi became an icon for the masses. There were widespread protests across the nation, and even Indian women began discarding the orthodox *purdah* system of gender segregation to join the freedom movement. Courting arrest was common, and sustained political demonstrations and civil disobedience acts were executed based on Gandhian principles of *satyagraha*, which meant 'passive resistance'. In Patna, women laid on the ground across the street during a protest, holding up traffic. No one was afraid of the British anymore, and in those days "everybody wanted to get a gaol ticket", as it became a symbol of nationalistic fervour (Allen, 248).

The discontentment with British rule only increased with time, and the pressure for liberation was beginning to get stronger. India was fast modernising, and with the beginning of the twentieth century, it was a country of a heterogeneous group of educated elite and professional individuals, as well as thriving businessmen and merchants, many of whom were campaigning for political representation. By the turn of the century, Indians began to enter the civil service and their number grew steadily—by the 1930s, Indians occupied high ranks in the Indian Civil Service. Furthermore, an increasing number of Indians, as part of the Indian National Congress, demanded radical changes to the political system of India, vociferously advocating for India's liberty and sovereignty.

India was the 'jewel in the crown' of the British Empire in the East, and her fate was something all were concerned about. Almost every prestigious and affluent family in England knew or were related to someone stationed in the Raj. They waited with bated breath to see the outcome of a rule that had lasted about two centuries, especially when it was believed that the 'sun would never set on the empire'. But with the Japanese advancement, it was proved to the world that the empire was no longer invincible.

The risk of being ousted began to loom large as Gandhi-led mass campaigns animated the minds of Indians. Educated elites like Nehru and Gandhi were rallying to end the British rule as strikes were called against the British and even small shops refused to serve them. In 1942, the Quit India Movement demanded immediate independence from the British. The British were not used to such open hostility and humiliation but were helpless in the face of it. When Iris Portal (néeButler) encountered a group of boys shouting "Quit India" while she was bicycling, she felt a slight twinge of apprehension as she went past.

Furthermore, even when the leaders of the peaceful political resistance, including Gandhi, had been imprisoned early in the war for protesting against the British control of India, some of those left at liberty had chosen another path: forming an army to collaborate with Britain's enemies in the hope of gaining independence after an Axis victory. For those memsahibs who had not even known of the existence of such an army until the press declared that the leaders were going to be tried for treason, this information came as a rude jolt. They were told that four main figures of the Indian National Army were charged with being false to their oath of loyalty to the King Emperor, fighting with the enemy against the Allies in Burma, and being guilty of grave crimes in torturing their fellow Indians and forcing them to join their movement.

The British were painfully aware that the Indian National Army was symptomatic of the expanding hunger for freedom and self-rule amongst those they had governed for so long. The leaders who had been tried were revered heroes of the nation in the eyes of the Indian public, and even the most subservient of Indian employees worshipped them. These leaders attained the reputation of saviours and martyrs in the public eye. As the trial against the Indian National Army progressed, it became apparent that while they had to be tried for treason for joining Japan against Burma, they also could not be sentenced. Convicting them could provoke the entire nation to rise up as they were already brimming with anti-British sentiment.

For Enid Saunders Candlin, this information came as a sudden awakening, and she conceded that there was a good reason for the Indian National Army becoming revered. They had been forced by British conscription to take up arms in a war which they did not wish to fight, and it was natural for them to gravitate instead towards their compatriots in the resistance, offering an alternative with the slogan "Asia for the Asiatics". In her writing, she mentioned Subhas Chandra Bose, the Congress leader who had lived in Tokyo and was killed in a plane crash at the end of the war, and how he still exerted a certain influence over the psyche of Indians. Bose had travelled extensively in Europe advocating for India's independence and had found sympathy from the Axis powers; most Indians believed that he was still alive and would return soon to reinvigorate the anti-British movement. Her husband's faithful clerks venerated Subhas Chandra Bose and hung his picture in their houses.

Despite the growing strain, the Conservative Party was in power in England and did not favour withdrawal from the subcontinent. The Indian princes favoured the Raj for their own vested interests, giving grand and verbose speeches in favour of the empire, meaning that the British could at least sigh with relief saying "the Princes are loyal". Nonetheless, the country was in the grip of passionate calls for independence. Politicians, activists, and orators violently denounced the British and demanded their immediate withdrawal of sovereignty. Valentine Chirol, a historian and journalist who published a 1910 account of the burgeoning independence movement in *India Unrest*, later added to his preface:

> It is little more than ten years since I wrote my *Indian Unrest*. But they have been years that may well count for decades in the history of the world, and not least in the history of India. Much has happened in India to confirm many of the views which I then expressed. Much has happened also to lead me to modify others, and to recognise more clearly today the shortcomings of a system of government, in many ways unrivalled, but subject to the inevitable limitations of alien rule.
>
> At the very early stage of the Great War the Prime Minister warned the British people that, after the splendid demonstration India was already giving of her loyalty to the cause for which the whole Empire was then in arms, our relations with her would have henceforth to be approached from "a new angle of vision".
>
> A century is but a short moment of time in the long span of Indian history, and the antagonism between two different types of civilization cannot be easily or swiftly lived down. It would be a folly to underrate forces of resistance which are by no means altogether ignoble... I have studied their origin and their vitality because they underlie the strange "Non-cooperation" movement... not merely

> against British rule, but against the progressive forces which contact with Western civilization has slowly brought into existence under British rule in India itself… Once placed in its proper perspective, this great experiment though fraught with many dangers and difficulties, is one of which is the ultimate issue can be looked forward to hopefully as the not unworthy consequence to the long series of bold and on the whole wonderfully successful experiments that make up the unique story of British rule in India.

Most British observers, however, were not satisfied with the progress they had made in India and were wary of the agitations for political autonomy as they were concerned about their personal safety as well as their future in India if the Crown rule ended. The Ilbert Bill of 1883 had already created a sense of apprehension amongst the British as the bill sought to allow Indian magistrates to judge cases in relation to British Indians. Memsahibs, especially, were increasingly wary of all Indians in the volatile political climate of the last few years of the Raj.

Communal violence further added to the turmoil. The provincial elections of 1946 reflected the growing division between the Indian National Congress and the Muslim League, which were the two major political parties of the time, with the latter strongly advocating a separate Muslim-majority nation state, Pakistan. The Muslim League emerged as the second-ranking party in the nationwide elections, paving the way for the creation of Pakistan on 14 August 1947. But in the years leading up to the actual event of independence, there was mob violence almost every other day in Calcutta, Bombay, Allahabad, and other major cities. Communal riots occurred frequently amidst demonstrations against the British. But even those who were suspicious of Gandhi conceded at that time that it was he who played a major role in tempering the spirits of the revolutionaries. Enid Saunders Candlin wrote that "It was he who now restrained them, and had he not been on the scene, affairs would undoubtedly have been much worse… It is true that in spite of his past trickery there was something of the saint in him".

When the Indian Naval Mutiny broke loose in Bombay and Karachi in February of 1946, the Candlins were in Bombay and went about their daily activities unaware of the risk since they had not read the morning papers and did not know of the violence that had occurred the previous night. Later that day, they were shocked to see the Victoria Station full of protestors shouting "*Jai Hind!*" ("Hail Hindustan"; an ostensibly pan-Indian slogan used widely during the nationalist protests, although there has been criticism about its exclusionary nature for assuming the land belongs to only Hindus), moving along the platforms, and spilling into the squares and streets of the city. It was unsafe to go anywhere with this happening: shops had closed down and the protestors were moving through the streets, fierce and angry. Enid, who was deeply disturbed by the widespread and repeated *hartals*—protests and boycotting—wrote miserably, "Everywhere we went we saw chalked on the walls 'Quit India'—and we longed to do so."

When Mountbatten became the Viceroy, he admitted that administration had broken down in India. Indeed, by the 1940s, especially with the end of the war, there were not enough police personnel to maintain order in the streets, nor troops who could be called in to help. The British were completely vulnerable on the streets, and many wrote with horror that it had become common for Indians to "pass remarks" as Europeans passed through villages, especially at memsahibs if they happened to be travelling alone. Sometimes the stares and glares were enough to make them feel disconcerted. Mostly, the British were incensed by the blatant attacks against them and claimed that the Indians had grown ungrateful for the good things the colonial rule had introduced into the country. It was truly the end of an era for the British who had grown accustomed to being exalted by Indians. However, it was the sudden 'insolence' and insubordinate behaviour from the Indians within their own houses and offices that really put them on the edge. It was too frightful to contemplate the full extent of an all-out rebellion. Given such a situation, Candlin wrote:

> Even in our little station there was a series of incidents, which were multiplied a thousand times all over the country. Bricks were thrown at Europeans in the dark, windows were smashed, women's handbags snatched and thrown away, and most of these acts were unpunished. In the military hospital which belonged to our transit camp an English nurse had her face slapped by a sweeper in

full view of an Indian ward—and the authorities dared do nothing. Any spark, it was thought, might start a conflagration.

It must be mentioned that there was not any level of unawareness amongst the British in India regarding the callousness of the colonial administration, which regularly used excessive force in restraining and punishing the Indian masses. A small case in point is the so-called 'avenging' of Miss Sherwood, a missionary who was attacked by a mob and almost killed due to her injuries. In 1919, in the days after the attack, General Dyer issued the infamous "crawling order" which ordered every Indian to crawl along the street on their hands and knees (Macmillan, 225). Dyer also committed a heinous atrocity at Jallianwala Bagh in 1919 when he ordered British troops to open fire at a peaceful gathering, killing Indian men, women, and children indiscriminately.

Still, the British argued that despite everything the Crown rule had actually advantaged India in many ways. Many were also outraged by the growing leniency of the government towards the agitating Indians. This could have been a direct consequence of the Indian National Army trial, where the leaders were not penalised, leaving many within Europe feeling betrayed by their own government. They squirmed uncomfortably when the leaders of the Indian independence movement toured the nation, giving speeches and 'inciting' the masses. Millions would assemble at such gatherings where the general theme was freedom from Britain. As a result, the overall respect for the authorities quickly dissipated.

However, by this point, criticism of the Raj had begun to come from within British quarters, and there were obvious signs of these fissures. Memsahibs, who had often cast a critical eye on the behaviour of the British towards the natives, were well aware that the colonial masters had been exploitative, and many of them were inclined to the cause of India's freedom. They criticised the insensitivity and racial arrogance displayed by the Europeans towards Indians, citing various occasions on which the British had deliberately demeaned and denigrated Indian customs and practices. The British were, in fact, also conscious of the glaring gap between the colonists and the colonised, which had not reduced even after more than two centuries. Emma Roberts, who was a travel writer and toured India extensively in the first half of the nineteenth century, had observed this tendency, arguing that the Europeans seldom entered native towns in their neighbourhood, either out of contempt or out of apathy. Even on occasions when the natives behaved poorly towards Europeans, it was usually found that they were not the first aggressors and were acting on provocation. The real problem was that the Europeans were so officious that they interpreted lack of absolute servility as impertinence. Their racial arrogance made them vainglorious as they required constant subservience and homage, and when they did not receive it, they believed it to be the sign of insubordination.

It must be highlighted that several memsahibs posited anti-colonial sentiments as they challenged the hegemonic discourse of the 'white man's burden'. Radical views about the entire colonial project in India were also heard from them. Even though it was believed for the longest time that the British influence in India was to the advantage of Indians, this notion came under direct scrutiny from memsahibs who were aware of political and trade-related matters.

In fact, even before the rise of nationalism in India, when the colonialist views were staunch and largely unrivalled, radical thinkers like Christina S. Bremner asserted that British rule had impoverished the country. Bremner wrote in 1891 that even though the British had managed to bring in certain scientific and technological advancements, the price that Indians were made to pay to their colonial rulers was too high. She also took a close look at the economic performance of the country and the so-called 'development' that had taken place because of British initiatives. She pointed out that while some large towns had grown, it did not seem that people such as local traders, bankers, and merchants profited because of British rule. Even if some did, the proportion of the people who benefitted was too low. Bremner even highlighted the 'proofs' of how fallacious the argument in favour of colonialism was. She elaborated on how the increase of Indian exports and imports, while positive on the outside, was actually deceptive because it did not indicate the prosperity of India and was merely profitable to Britain. Her writing clearly shows that the empire exploited India for raw materials, "draining India of her resources" and causing severe debts. She wrote, "No one can deny that capital thus renders an immense service, but it can also be maintained that a foreign nation sweeping into her coffers interest that might assist to collect native capital for future use, is a condition likely to produce morbid results." Needless to say, such a scathing critique of imperial activities emerged from a deep awareness of the administration.

Bremner was not the only one to speak against the British rule in India. Emily Eden did not mince her words when she was visiting her brother, the Governor-General, in 1867 and commented how horribly a certain class of Europeans oppressed the natives. Constance F. G. Cumming admitted that the British did not even understand the natives due to the diversity of languages. Given the nature of imperialistic ideologies, such counter-imperialist discourses coming from memsahibs were nothing less than revolutionary, especially at a time when women were relegated to the domestic sphere and disallowed from participating in governance.

Notwithstanding these unconventional opinions, many of the memsahibs' writings did pander to the popular perception that the Europeans were engaged in a noble cause of uplifting the 'heathen' races. British women usually supported the Raj, and most of their memoirs and journals record their staunch belief in the supremacy of the white race and therefore the inferiority of the natives. Some expressed disdain towards the native culture openly and projected Indians as 'little children' who needed to be guided and controlled by the Europeans. Their perspectives towards Indian religions were similar, and they often wrote elaborate descriptions of the 'pagan' gods, strange religious practices, rituals, and festivals. Many even wrote long defences of British rule in India in the nineteenth century, categorically justifying the British dominance over the land and people.

"It Was the Time to Endure": Wartime and Independence in the "Land of Regrets"

Having put our names down in all the requisite places and visited all the harassed gentlemen who were trying to control this vast exodus, we settled down to that winter of '45–'46 to possess our souls in patience. It seemed then... as though the country would burst into flames, so great was the political pressure, the public unease. It was a hard period to sit through quietly. The fierce impatience of the Indian to be freed... and the intensity of their apprehension that even now Whitehall might not honour its promises gave cause for constant demonstrations... The Muslim-Hindu impasse seemed as insoluble as ever... While feeling great sympathy for everyone concerned, it was impossible for the transient not to wish that he could be safely out of the way before the balloon went up...

We then had three or four months to pass in an almost empty bungalow... Here in sort of suspended animation we read, talked, and observed through the long days of uncertainty, rising passion and near mutiny.

– Enid Saunders Candlin, 1974

In June 1947, as the last Viceroy, Lord Mountbatten, formally (and apparently prematurely) announced the so-called 'transfer of power' to two dominions, it was finally confirmed that the British would have to pack up and leave—and fast. However, even before that the British middle class that had spent most of their lives in the colony and had been there for the heyday of the Raj could feel the marked difference in the cultural dynamics of the country. No matter how uncomfortable it made them feel, the remaining Raj families braced for the massive transformations that took place right before their eyes. Most had not anticipated the scale of change or the speed at which it took place.

If they had been brought up in India, they felt the change in their lifestyle much more intensely. Even the mood of their beloved hill stations where they escaped every summer during their childhoods felt different as many houses were left empty during the holiday season. It meant that families preferred to go back home rather than travel to hill stations. Perhaps what made them uneasy was that at the cusp of political change, the country that they had to struggle to make their own was, yet again, beginning to feel unfamiliar, only this time they wanted to belong.

This was a grave quandary because most of the Raj families 'out in India' had come to believe that India was their home but also believed there was a home in Britain as well that was waiting to embrace them. This, as they found out, proved to be incorrect as the connection with Britain was neither so natural nor so easily forged. Even memsahibs who regularly visited their families and relatives in Britain often felt out of place or alienated amongst them, even though they had always claimed to want to return when they were 'away' in India.

The lack of connection with Britain was perhaps because of their long absences, and their inability to visit as frequently as they would have liked to. This was because travelling to Britain for short durations before the First World War was an expensive affair, and sometimes it would be over a decade before memsahibs would see their friends and family. Eventually, it was officially recognised that the British in India were often unable to return to Britain for protracted periods because of financial problems. It was only in 1925 that changes were made to regulations, and each officer and his family was allowed to return home more frequently than before. A system of loans also became available, which enabled some to send their family members back home with relative financial ease (Gowans, 430). Additionally, all officers of European backgrounds who were of the superior ranks were granted four standard first-class return passages during the course of their service. Moreover, an officer's wife was allowed an equal number of passages, and one single passage was granted to each child. This significantly reduced the major hurdle of travelling to Britain, and 'home' finally seemed more accessible.

This also encouraged those born in India to discover their roots, and those who had made the crossing from Britain to make more regular visits back. Making journeys back home could be quite delightful for all members of the family, especially the men, because it would be a long break from duty after many years. Ruth Donnison was in Burma with her husband for 6 years before they made their first journey back home to England. She wrote how excited she was to return and how England, which had earlier seemed remote and difficult to travel back to, did not seem very far away anymore. Enid Dawkins, who lived in India for about 25 years, made several trips to England while her children were growing up.

Such developments in transcontinental sea travel certainly made the departure of the British from India easier than it had been a century ago when memsahibs began arriving in great numbers. And while some British families were reluctant to quit India even at the cusp of independence, most knew they should not delay in preparing for leaving. Enid Saunders Candlin began contemplating departure in the year 1945, 2 years before India gained independence, because she knew that the process would not be an easy or quick one, and she was keen to exit at the earliest opportunity. She had come to India in 1941 after her husband was sent to work there in the Inspectorate of a Metal and Steel Factory, escaping the Japanese invasion in China. In India, they had not found the Raj to be a good employer and believed that the Indianised service would not benefit them in any way.

The Candlins started their preparations for leaving well in advance, but they found that repatriation was cumbersome and daunting. People had to wait for their turn to travel, which took place according to government lists. Enid wrote in annoyance how the sick and VIPs wanted to leave first, followed by those who were longest overdue to return. Nearly everyone wanted special treatment, and it was nothing short of a scramble.

This 'scramble' worsened as 1947 drew nearer, and utter chaos was unleashed. The last of the British struggled under pressure as almost any government procedure suddenly became impossible. Sometimes, there could be disputes about payment because passages were being handed out by, as Candlin says, "tens of thousands", and sometimes there were errors. This was also the time when armies were being moved from India, and troop ships, which would be absolutely packed, would go out of Bombay every week, but these were never suitable for families. However, refusing passages could be risky as alternatives would sometimes not be available and nobody knew when they would get another chance. Many civilians left the country on troop ships for this reason and later wrote about the horrible conditions on-board in the communal cabins. Families had to be prepared well in advance so that they would not be caught in a last-minute scrimmage when the summons came. But even then, many families were given passage without prior notice.

One of the greater challenges of moving away was the challenge of taking all their belongings with them to Britain. These last generations of the Raj families had accumulated enormous quantities of belongings in the years they spent in India, and they wanted to hold onto these remnants of their past if they could. In a way, they were holding onto their nostalgia for the Raj era. But dismantling everything for their departure was extremely painful. Memsahibs who had carefully arranged their household had to take apart everything and sell or discard a majority of their items. Their furniture, rugs, paintings, china, and other items that they had carefully collected over many years were thus given away or simply left behind. It made matters complicated that every family was desperate to sell their belongings at a time when no one wanted to purchase household items. They had not expected this because earlier on, when officers' families moved from post to post, it was quite easy to sell household items before moving.

Moreover, even packing what they could take with them was difficult as there were hardly any servants or labourers to engage for the work. Besides, transporting items by road was tricky, and transporting items overseas, with other people's luggage, was sure to damage their belongings. Enid was horrified to see how the packers, who were handling her crockery, put the plates and glass into crates without any stuffing. She tried to scold them, as it was the custom of memsahibs to scold their servants during the Raj, but things had changed and the men knew the *firangees* were leaving for good. They remained adamant and did not help. She wrote that they gave her a volley of promises and guarantees that nothing would be damaged, but seeing the work, she did not believe them. She added, "We were fairly sure we would have long sea voyages and many changes, we did not want to lose our Chinese treasures through breakages." Miraculously, a year later when she opened her luggage after many journeys, she found only one plate broken.

Jocelyn Abbott, who had preserved cine films of herself and her family members in the Raj, had also brought back huge quantities of large furniture, such as chairs and side tables. These were the pieces that could be assembled and disassembled, and which even after many years still carried the old embossing of makers like

"HAKIMDIN & BR., CABINET MAKER, SIALKOT". Like many other ladies of her time, she had also diligently packed as many of her household items as she could and brought them across the seas. Amongst the items that had survived over the years was the same tea set that was seen in one of her cine films, in which she was sipping tea with her friend on her veranda many years ago in India. That set had been with her for 70 years, and she even remembered how she had come to purchase it in her younger days as a new memsahib in 1935. The pattern had been trendy in those days, and the whole set had survived more than a dozen moves on bumpy roads ("The Lost World of the Raj", Ep. 1, 10.47–10.50). It was her own personal relic of the Raj days.

However, planning and packing were just the beginning of the troubles for the families leaving India. Much to the chagrin of the sahibs and memsahibs who were already flustered because of all the overwhelming processes surrounding their homeward migration, the post-World War period had brought in various arbitrary government rules and regulations. They strained under the tremendous amounts of paperwork and had to make prior arrangements for the minutest of activities. Even random matters, like the government houses they were leaving behind, became the subject of great tedium as all sorts of rules were enforced with regards to their maintenance.

Enid Saunders Candlin was greatly perplexed to find that while the Japanese war was going on in 1945, someone high up in the administration had decided that two rooms of every bungalow in Ambernath were to be distempered and plastered by the families occupying them. They said that this was being done because every house was in a state of disrepair and in desperate need of refurbishment. This mandate came at a time when there were much more serious matters that required urgent attention. The costs involved were being borne by the government, but the families were greatly inconvenienced as the task was quite cumbersome. Besides the trouble of emptying the rooms, the preparation involved in plastering walls required 6 weeks during which time the furniture remained piled on the verandas, exposed to the elements and being damaged more with each passing day. The Candlins did their best to avoid this 'amenity' and even wrote letters to be excused, but these letters were received with indignation. It was wartime, and complaints were not being entertained. Candlin wrote, "It was the time to endure" things including mandatory domestic refurbishment.

This was indeed true for them as they had a particularly tough time in the last 2 years of their stay in India. After a long and suspenseful wait, they were finally granted passage in a civilian packet, the *City of Exeter*, which had carried the British delegates to Russia in 1939 to attain agreements preventing the rapport between Nazi Germany and the Soviet Union. Before they departed, the Inspectorate at Ambernath had given them farewell parties where they were presented with garlands, brass vases, and books about Gandhi.

The Candlins were touched when the Indian clerks who had worked under them said goodbye, some with tears in their eyes. Enid had given them her precious lily plants and other supplies and household items that they were not taking with them as parting gifts. When they reached the docks on the morning of their departure, they found their servants were there to say goodbye one final time. Enid was extremely moved to see this. It was an emotional moment for all of them, and she wrote the final lines of her book in the following manner:

> Let us go. Come;
> Our separation so abides, and flies,
> That thou, residing here, go'st yet with me,
> And I, hence fleeting, here remain with thee.
> Away!

It was a stroke of luck that the Candlins were given two cabins, amidships, on the starboard side. They were pleased with the sleeping arrangements, the good food, and the excellent service of stewardesses.

The 'return' was, however, not always as smooth for some women. Moreover, unlike what people expected, reaching Britain felt more like being displaced from India than a homecoming. Most families did not have any wealth or property to go back to, and life after India was not always how these memsahibs, so eager to 'return', had imagined. For many, the prospect of a less prosperous life in Britain was very real. Some were driven to extreme measures: Nelly Price got into the company of bad people, and when they docked at Portsmouth she decided that a certain way of life was better than poverty in England. In fact, ironically, several families that were returning to their homeland after years of yearning for it landed there in a pathetic state. They had spent all their savings in India and, lost a lot over the years, and when they arrived in England "in white muslin gowns, coloured shoes" they hardly had any comforts to look forward to (Bamfield, 80).

Even those who were better off were disappointed when they started their new lives. The first thing they were dismayed by was the homes they had to live in, which were absolutely unlike the large sprawling bungalows they had grown accustomed to. Moreover, many wrote that they felt out of place or ill at ease in whichever place they went after they quit India and had to struggle to adapt. It seemed that while time had frozen in the Raj, things had changed significantly in the West.

Lillian Ashby and her husband left for America in 1928. Before finally leaving the country, she had visited her children in California, during which time the political climate of India was quite perilous. When her ship was passing through Penang and Singapore, and through the China Sea, she received an alarming telegram from her husband informing her about the strained political climate she had left behind: "ANOTHER STRIKE DAY AFTER YOUR DEPARTURE I AM WELL BUT ANXIOUS". She dreaded that her husband would be injured like he had been once before when there was a strike. But she couldn't turn back and returned only when her husband's health began failing. It turned out that he would have to retire early, and both of them decided to leave for California.

In America, the challenges of settling included a number of cultural shocks. Lillian was amazed to see her children's neighbours engaged in tasks like taking out garbage and washing diapers. Much to her amusement at the irony, she had to learn how to sweep now—something for which there would always be a *jharuwallah* (sweeper) back home in India. Even though she was happy to adapt and assimilate into the new culture, memories of India haunted her frequently, and she wrote her final lines in her memoir with a note of wistful longing for the country she had left behind:

> To the north, back of our tiny garden, we see the Santa Monica and Hollywood Hills. In the moonlight they resemble the Singhbhum Hills hard by Jamshedpur. In the real, unreal world of mind, memory, and affection, India is not far away; it is ever with us.

Nostalgia for India was not uncommon in memsahibs' accounts of their past lives after they had left. Nancy Vernede spoke about her wonderful and idyllic childhood in India, saying that she was "very happy, I loved it… Completely happy… Completely happy, when I was a child—I often think back—complete happiness, security" ("The Lost World of the Raj", Ep. 1, 36.29–36.41) while thinking back on the days of her childhood. Those days were exceedingly memorable because they had all felt so content and secure while growing up in India: "You just had India, and the sort of smells and sounds and servants and my pony and few little friends" ("The Lost World of the Raj", Ep. 1, 36.40–36.52). She especially loved Lucknow as it was her "dream home" ("The Lost World of the Raj", Ep. 1, 38.52). She added, "I loved India… miserable when I came home" ("The Lost World of the Raj", Ep. 1, 54.03–54.07), and was recorded saying "It's in my blood" ("The Lost World of the Raj", Ep. 1, 2.50–2.54). Indeed, the last of the British families that had left India had left behind friends, faithful servants, and subordinates as well as a part of themselves. Lady Pamela Hicks, who had left India with her parents, the Mountbattens, wistfully wrote:

> I missed India… I missed the noise and chaos of the clinic, and I even missed the long marble corridors of the Governor-General's House. I was finding it difficult to adapt to life back at Broadlands, roaming around the house moodily or standing in the schoolroom twiddling the knobs on the wireless in search of the faint crackle of Indian music. It was some compensation that we had brought Neola with us—he didn't seem to mind which continent he made mischief in, and spent his days turning my bedroom into a mongoose stronghold. Downstairs there was a little more to remind me of India as my parents had brought their bearers, Wahid Beg

> and Abdul Hamid, to Broadlands. Both were Muslim and it was thought they might fare better away from Delhi when we left. To me they seemed rather lost in England, shivering in the navy-blue waistcoats they had worn in Simla. Seeing them in their uniform brought on a wave of nostalgia, but these small touches of India did not make me feel that I belonged back in England.

It is perhaps not surprising that some British families could never bring themselves to leave India. Anne Wright decided to stay on because of her love of and attachment to the country and recalled the earlier days of her wonderful childhood spent in different parts of India where she and her siblings grew up. In her family home movies, there are clips of her playing with her pet goats and three elephants (Rupkali, Motipyari, and Phulmati), along with the other children, looking happy and gay. She had many little friends of her age, and they spent their time cycling out in the open, playing on the veranda, and simply gambolling around, while being vigilantly watched over by the *ayahs*.

Some who left returned to revisit their youthful days. A Raj couple who were married out in India, Brian and Margaret Williams, had to return to England. However, they missed India so much that they came back to Rawalpindi, 60 years later, to revisit their old haunts. They also went to see the hospital where their son was born and saw that it had been turned into a school for children. They visited the Lahore cathedral as well as it was the place where they were married.

Mark Tully, author and former Bureau Chief of BBC, New Delhi, who was born in India in 1935, went to revisit the Himalayas with his sister, Prue Swindells, many years after India's independence. They went to visit his old school and recalled the carefree days of their childhood when they were sent to the hills by their parents to keep them away from the heat of the plains ("The Lost World of the Raj", Ep. 1, 51.33–53.00). In their home videos, they had recorded their childhood games of golf at the clubs and running around freely in the open gardens.

Indeed, many believed that their time in India was unparalleled and felt the difference most keenly after returning to England. While most of them associated the Raj with comforts and luxuries, there was no doubt that they had formed deep emotional bonds with the land and its people. Many of them were not able to forget their ties with India and expressed a deep sense of loss as they realised that this wonderful world of theirs had disintegrated and remained just in their memories. Indeed, the Raj was a time to remember, and the nostalgia for it haunted those who left it behind. And while it had taken a long time for India to feel like 'home', once it did, it remained so even after they had left.

Ironically then, the former sahibs and memsahibs who left India to return 'home', very often wanted to make another 'return'—this time, to India.

EPILOGUE

It is perhaps fitting to end this book with the extraordinary and action-packed life and career of the 'Naga Queen', Ursula Violet Graham Bower, whose tale I did not quite get to tell in full over the course of the chapters. She was one of the more audacious memsahibs, and her memoirs, I must say, I personally found most exhilarating.

Ursula came to India in 1937 and stayed until after its independence. At the mere age of twenty-three, she fell irrevocably in love with the Naga Hills during the turbulent period of the Second World War and wrote how she had felt an instant connection with the land the first time she explored the hilly regions of the North-East. She had an anthropological bent of mind, and when she first came across the indigenous tribal community of the Nagas, it was as if she had understood her life's purpose. She later documented it in her book, *Naga Path* (1952):

> It's twelve years now since that moment, and I still don't know what happened. There was a sudden surge of recognition. I must have sat there like a fool, gaping. Nagas!—of course!—illumination so plain, so known and obvious, that I was speechless at my own stupidity in not remembering sooner… The landscape drew me as I had never known anything to do before, with a power transcending the body, a force not of this world at all.

In the initial years, Bower enjoyed her time in the "neat Imphal cantonments" where there was beautiful foliage, sprawling lawns, and the Manipur River running by. There was golf at the club, tennis at the residency, and duck shooting on the lakes—life for memsahibs was enjoyable. She shopped, dined, visited museums, ambled through the *bazaars*, and went to watch the polo. It was when she went on tour to Ukhrul in Tangkhul Naga country and began her anthropological photography that she realised the full extent and potential of her affinity for the hills and the people.

When she returned to England shortly after, she had a substantial collection of photographs, which had turned out to be more professional than she had expected. During this visit, a family friend introduced her to the Royal Geographical and Royal Central Asian Societies, and some professional anthropologists, quite by chance. And while she had originally wanted to study archaeology, things changed after her trip to Assam, and the prospect of going back and conducting anthropological research amongst the Nagas, even though she had no training, seemed like an exciting idea. Besides, she had a verve for adventure, and she knew that the hills were calling: "It was as though I had re-discovered a world to which I had belonged the whole time; from which, by some accident, I had been estranged… I had to go back."

And go back she did. She wrote to professors at Oxford and Cambridge, and found that there was interest in the work she was proposing. They wanted still photographs and cine films of the indigenous culture. Around that time, by another coincidence, she was invited by a friend to go out with her and stay in Manipur, where she was keeping house for her brother who worked in the Indian Civil Service. It was a splendid opportunity and she accepted gladly. And thus, even with no money or financial support, she began her pioneering work in the Naga Hills in 1938.

It was a great challenge to tread in a man's world. Ursula was a young and single white woman, with just a guide, a translator, and a bodyguard named Namkia to accompany her on her journeys. The work was demanding and often risky as she toured extensively for long stretches of time and lived amongst people who did not speak the same language as her. Her memoirs give an insight into the challenges she faced, such as sexism, superstition, prejudice, disease, sexual harassment, injuries, jungle animals, and even grass fires, but no matter what the situation, she dealt with all this with extreme alacrity. She was even undaunted in the face of inexplicable phenomena like *jaadu* (magic) and hauntings. At one point, due to a misunderstanding, she was hailed as a goddess in a Naga village as they mistook her for Gaidinliu (a revered Naga spiritual and political leader).

However, despite her popularity amongst the people she began living with, political disturbances caused significant setbacks to her work in 1939, and at one point she almost had a mental breakdown. Still, she had enough sense to maintain control and went to North Cachar to continue her studies. There, she found the Kacharis, the major indigenous tribal community, whom she found to be complex and whose heritage she found fascinating and suitable for her work. The Kachari kingdom had a tumultuous political history, and it was in the nineteenth century that the regions came under the British rule. To her great fascination, they rebelled against the British rule in 1918 as well as against the neighbouring Nagas.

Ursula's years in the Naga villages were marked with the most perilous adventures. Moreover, the political climate of India was unstable. In 1941, when she was in Laisong, she went to Calcutta for a holiday and was detained on government orders as an invasion by the Japanese was imminent. Soon, Ursula and those in the Naga villages heard about the bombing at Pearl Harbour. Then followed the blow of losing Singapore and the invasion of Burma. It did not reach the Naga villages at that point, but the rumblings were felt where they were. When Ursula went to the plains to visit her friends, she found everything prepared for evacuation at 24 hours' notice. She wrote:

> The war was on us. There was one thing I didn't intend to do, despite the general confusion, and that was to leave Assam—whether there was a general evacuation or not. Returning to Laisong, I recruited, not without difficulty, a team of Zemi volunteers, and offered our services to the Government on any of the refugee routes where we could be of use. Our luck was out. They had stopped sending women workers up the roads, because the conditions there were so appalling.

At the end of March 1942, they received orders to go to Lumding Junction to run a refugee canteen. When they got there, they saw it was in utter chaos. The yards were choked with wagons, massive consignments were lying about, and mail trains were delayed. There was no shed, store, hut, space, cook shed, food, or fuel, and not even a place to sleep. Everyone was in panic. Every day in the morning, trains rolled in completely loaded with refugees who were tired, hungry, and numb with shock.

Ursula and the volunteers slaved day and night trying to help, exhausted and afraid of attack. In the morning, someone would come in to inform her about the number of people to be fed—there were enormous quantities of food to be prepared for the Indians as well as for the Europeans. At 3 am, she would wake the men, who would work in the dark to be ready for breakfast. She wrote, "there were sixty gallons of water to carry, at eight gallons a trip, the fires to light and the water to boil, and while it heated, we cut the sandwiches and set out the mugs."

It was dirty, sweaty work, something that could make the strongest weaken before the sheer human suffering of the hundreds of crying and despairing displaced people; but Ursula was made of stronger stuff, and in the midst of all the trouble, had true comrades to rely on. She wrote:

> This abrupt upheaval, involving myself at least in the fringes of world catastrophe, threw sudden strain on relations with the Zemi... One couldn't expect too much; but, though the others remained behind with the house and dogs, Namkia, Haichangnang, Ramgakpa and Dinekamba were all going with me.
>
> "If you people won't come, it's my bad luck—I've had the orders, not you."
>
> Namkia got off his perch and wiped his eyes. "*Asipui-ghao*," he said. "Dear elder sister—don't be afraid, we're all in it together."

In 1942, Ursula and her helpers went back to Laisong again when the Burma army was falling back. Imphal was bombed and the Japanese invasion was imminent. Evacuations were in full swing. Then the rains arrived and stayed for weeks, and when they ended it was discovered that an epidemic had started. Moreover, people were starving due to shortages and so a famine was underway. The epidemic resulted in many deaths.

At that time in Manipur, the Kabui, Zemi, and Lyeng people held a meeting to decide on a joint action if the administration withdrew, and they asked Ursula to be their leader. The Japanese were at the Burma border by then and were likely to attack India. In India, the Congress Party had stirred internal unrest. A Colonel belonging to a guerrilla organisation called 'V Force' that recruited from the locals for service as scouts came to meet Ursula, and asked her to join them. They were interested in the border areas, especially in North Cachar and Manipur.

There was no time to lose. Ursula began recruiting in Hangrum, which was a tough zone. The men were reluctant to fight for the sahibs because they thought they would be taken away and die like the Zemi porters had died during the Lushai War. Ursula managed to recruit a few, nonetheless.

With this, Ursula's research became more entwined with political work. Far from what she had planned for her anthropological studies, to "potter about with a few cameras", she actively became involved in guerrilla warfare against the "Japs". But the work seemed to come to her naturally, and this could either be because she belonged to a military and Indian Civil Service family and it was in her blood or because of her loyalty to her adopted family of Nagas.

By December, their "Watch and Ward" were in operation. The scouts were supposed to scour the areas to keep an eye on people, report any men who were not from the hills, and report any crashed aircrafts. They wanted to stay alert in case of infiltration because the Japanese spies could already be within borders.

Times were precarious. While Ursula and her helpers were in the remote village of Khangnam, in a camp that stood on the ridge beyond the village, they were bombed but could not tell if it was the enemy. In March 1944, the Japanese attack along Manipur was heightening. Their defences were down. The Japanese had crossed Imphal Road. The frontline lay on the railway, 20 miles behind them, and that was the only thing between them and the Japanese. It came down to defending the village with whatever they had.

Ursula was asked to mobilise the locals. She had a force of 150 Indian scouts then, one service rifle, one single-barrelled shotgun, and seventy muzzle-loaders. They had to be quick. The camp was a perfect trap, but she could not move into the jungles or it would start a panic. She had to stay where she was and maintain a cool air. There was no wireless communication, not enough troops to protect them, and no way of knowing which direction the Japanese were coming in from. They used the railway telephone with code words: one elephant meant ten Japanese (then because of the confusion, some turned up at the Silchar border with forty elephants). They had to find the fifty Japanese quickly. The V Force was to comb the jungles for them, and patrolling began with Ursula leading the scouts. She had asked for thirty rifles:

> At night we left the camp, and slept out in the thick, low scrub to the north, in shelters hollowed out below foliage-level. One man was left as sentry in the camp, to fire a shot and bolt if the Japs appeared, and the rest slept in holes in the jungle warren. We honeycombed the scrub with tunnels and little chambers beaten and cut out, and every night changed rounds from one group to another, so that no outsider ever knew where exactly in the wide spread of bushes we were hidden.

What's more, the heroine of this story, now hailed as a warrior princess of the Nagas, found love in the middle of all this turmoil.

It was May of 1945. A certain Colonel Betts, who Ursula described as "tall and strong", came to visit her in Laisong, requesting her company on a butterfly-catching expedition. For four days he hung around, looking very much uninterested in butterflies and behaving peculiarly around everybody. Then on the fourth day, he proposed to her abruptly while she was taking her tea. They kissed, and within moments, they were engaged. He later told her that he came to meet her because he had heard of the "Naga Queen" when he first joined the V Force and was intrigued by the idea of a lady guerrilla. When the Japanese invasion occurred, his camp was overrun and he walked for 3 weeks, right through the Japanese army, and came to Kohima starving, where he was sent off to a hospital. He intended to meet Ursula in Calcutta, but that never happened. A year later, the unit was in Shillong. But with the war over, and the V Force about to be disbanded, the Colonel believed that it was time like no other to get married. He told her that he believed he had more in common with her than anyone else he had met. Bower wrote:

> On July 7th, we were married. Cake, wine, wedding-dress, reception—Mrs Mills, by some unfathomed miracle, produced them all. Namkia and Haichangnang stood picturesquely on either side of the church door—Namkia with his well-deserved British Empire Medal just gazetted. There was a guard of honour of Assam Rifles. We came out under an arch of kukries, and the last little rifleman on my side, who was more than usually pint sized, had to raise his weapon at the last moment to avoid beheading the bride.

Apart from her adventurous life events, Bower's subtle humour and nonchalant 'story-telling' appealed to me immensely. In fact, it is precisely her writing style that sets her apart from her predecessors.

Be that as it may, almost every work of the memsahibs that I have read has had its own unique narrative. In fact, I have not found a single work that looked too much like another. There were overlaps and similarities, and there were some patterns here and there, but no two memsahibs experienced India in the same way, as stereotypes would have us believe.

Due to the sheer variety, it may be said that understanding the entirety of memsahibs' experiences in India is challenging. Although this is always a risk with facets of marginalised histories, it seems accurate to say this especially for memsahibs because a myriad of voices was subdued in the hustle and bustle of life in the Raj. Many of them left no records of the years they spent in India or wrote privately so their work was passed around between friends and family, until it was finally locked away in old trunks and forgotten. Some such writings resurfaced decades later when members of their families became curious about their family history and dug them up. Sometimes, the stories came out if a journalist or researcher, wanting to interview the last generation of Raj sahibs and memsahibs, came knocking at their doors.

The writings that are available to us now allow us a glimpse, at best, into this still enigmatic aspect of British colonial history—the life and works of the contested rulers of India: the memsahibs. Studies on the memsahibs must act self-consciously as a necessary retrieval of their lost voices, as it is only through a sustained scrutiny of the variety of their activities in the Raj that we can finally understand them. The clichés, therefore, entertaining as they may be, threaten to obfuscate historical realities of the Raj. They also become impediments to feminist understandings of women's role and place in British imperial history, and effectively downplay how women had to elbow their way into the largely masculine enterprise of running an empire, as Bower did.

SELECT BIBLIOGRAPHY

Primary Texts:

A Lady Resident. *The Englishwoman in India*. Smith, Elder and Co., 1864.

Allen, Charles. *Plain Tales from the Raj*. Abacus, 1975.

An Old Resident. *Real Life in India: Embracing a View of the Requirements of Individuals Appointed to Any Branch of the Indian Public Service* (1847). Houston and Stoneman, 1847.

Ashby, Lillian Luker and Roger Whatley. *My India*. Michael Joseph Ltd., 1938.

Baillie, Mrs. W. W. *Days and Nights of Shikar*. John Lane and Bodley Head Ltd., 1921.

Bamfield, Veronica. *On the Strength: The Story of the British Army Wife*. Charles Knight & Company Ltd., 1974.

Bartrum, Katherine. *A Widow's Reminiscences of the Siege of Lucknow*. James Nisbet & Co., 1858.

Beames, James. *Memoirs of a Bengal Civilian: The Lively Narrative of a Victorian District-Officer*. Eland Books, 1984.

Billington, Mary Frances. *Woman in India*. Chapman & Hall, 1895.

Birch, Edward A. *The Management and Medical Treatment of Children in India*. Thacker, Spink & Co., 1879.

Blunt, Edward. *The I.C.S.: The Indian Civil Service*. Faber and Faber Ltd., 1937.

Bower, Ursula Graham. *Naga Path*. John Murray, 1950.

Bremner, Christina Sinclair. *A Month in a Dandi: A Woman's Wanderings in Northern India*. Simpkin, Marshall, Hamilton, Kent & Co., Ltd., 1891.

British Government of India. *Allen's Indian Mail and Official Gazette*. Vol. xxxvi. No. 1339, 1878.

———. *The Revolt in Central India 1857–59: Compiled in the Intelligence Branch*. Government Monotype P, 1908.

SELECT BIBLIOGRAPHY

Butler, Iris. *The Viceroy's Wife: Letters of Alice, Countess of Reading, from India, 1921–1925*. Hodder and Stoughton, 1969.

Candlin, Enid Saunders. *A Traveler's Tale: Memories of India*. Macmillan, 1974.

Carpenter, Mary. *Six Months in India*. Vol. 1. Longmans, Green & Co., 1868.

Case, Adelaide. *Day by Day at Lucknow: A Journal of the Siege of Lucknow*. R. Bentley, 1858.

Cheem, Aliph. *Lays of Ind*. Thacker, Spink and Co., 1883.

Chirol, Valentine. *Indian Unrest*. Macmillan and Co., Ltd., 1930.

Clayton, Ellen Creathorne. *Female Warriors: Memorials of Female Valour and Heroism, from the Mythological Ages to the Present Era*. Vol. ii. Tinsley Brothers, 1879.

Clemons, Mrs. Major. *The Manners and Customs of Society in India; Including Scenes in the Mofussil Stations*. Smith, Elder and Co., 1841.

Clive, Henrietta. *Travels in South India, 1798–1801*. Nancy K. Shields, ed. Speaking Tiger, 2009.

Clive Bayley, Emily (Lady). *The Golden Calm: An English Lady's Life in Moghul Delhi*. Webb & Bower Publishers, 1980.

Coopland, R. M. *A Lady's Escape from Gwalior and Life in the Fort of Agra During the Mutinies of 1857*. Smith, Elder, and Co., 1859.

Diver, Maud. *The Englishwoman in India*. William Blackwood & Sons, 1909.

———. *Honoria Lawrence: A Fragment of Indian History*. John Murray, 1936.

Duberly, Frances Isabella. *Campaigning Experiences in Rajpootana and Central India*. Smith, Elder, & Co., 1859.

Dufferin, Helen Blackwood (Lady). *Our Viceregal Life in India*. Vol. i. John Murray, 1889.

Duncan, Sara Jeannette. *The Simple Adventures of a Memsahib*. New York: D. Appleton and Company, 1893.

Eden, Emily. *Up the Country: Letters Written to her Sister from the Upper Provinces of India*. Vol. i. Richard Bentley, 1866.

———. *Letters from India*. Vol. i. Richard Bentley, 1872.

Elwood, Anne Katherine Curteis. *Narrative of a Journey Overland from England by the Continent of Europe, Egypt, and the Red Sea to India Including a Residence There, and Voyage Home in the Years 1825, 1826, 1827, and 1828*. Henry Colburn and Richard Bentley, 1830.

Falkland, Amelia Cary. *Chow-Chow; Being Selections from a Journal Kept in India, Egypt, and Syria*. Hurst and Blackett, 1857.

Fay, Eliza. *The Original Letters from India*. Thacker, Spink & Co., 1908.

Frederica Gordon Cumming, Constance. *In the Himalayas and on the Indian Plains*. Chatto and Windus, 1884.

SELECT BIBLIOGRAPHY

Gardner, Nora. *Rifle and Spear with the Rajpoots: Being the Narrative of a Winter's Travel and Sport in Northern India*. Chatto and Windus, 1895.

Godden, Rumer and Jon Godden. *Two Under the Indian Sun*. Alfred A. Knopf, 1966.

Graham, Maria. *Journal of a Residence in India*. George Ramsay and Company, 1812.

Greathed, H. H. *Letters Written During the Siege of Delhi*. Longman, Brown, Green, Longmans, & Roberts, 1858.

Griffin, Z. F. *India: and Daily Life in Bengal*. Buffalo, 1896.

Hare, Augustus J. C., The *Story of Two Noble Lives, Being Memorials of Charlotte, Countess Canning, and Louisa, Marchioness of Waterford*. Vol. ii. George Allan, 1893.

Harris, G. *A Lady's Diary of the Siege of Lucknow, Written for the Perusal of Friends at Home*. John Murray, 1858.

Harris, G. and Adelaide Case. *Ladies of Lucknow: The Experiences of Two British Women During the Indian Mutiny*. Leonaur Ltd., 2010.

Hicks, Pamela. *India Remembered: A Personal Account of the Mountbattens During the Transfer of Power*. Pavilion Books, 2008.

———. *Daughter of Empire: My Life as a Mountbatten*. Simon & Schuster, 2012.

Inglis, Julia Selina, Lady. *The Siege of Lucknow: A Diary*. James R. Osgood, McIlvaine & Co., 1892.

Jacob, Violet. *Diaries and Letters from India*, 1895–1900. Carol Anderson, ed. Canongate, 1990.

King, E. Augusta. *Diary of a Civilian's Wife, 1877–1882*. Richard Bentley, 1884.

Kingscote, Adeline Georgina Isabella. *The English Baby in India and How to Rear It*. J. & Churchill, 1893.

Lang, John. *Wanderings in India: And Other Sketches of Life in Hindostan*. Routledge, Warne, and Routledge, 1861.

Lang, Monica. *Invitation to Tea*. The World Publishing Company, 1952.

Leonowens, Anna Harriette. *Life and Travel in India: Being Recollections of a Journey Before the Days of Railroads*. Porter & Coates, 1884.

Lownie, Andrew. *The Mountbattens: Their Lives and Loves*. Blink Publishing, 2019.

Mackenzie, A. R. D. *Mutiny Memoirs: Being Personal Reminiscences of the Great Sepoy Revolt of 1857*. Pioneer Press, 1891.

Mackenzie, Helen Douglas Catherine (Mrs. Colin). *Life in the Mission, the Camp, and the Zenana Or Six Years in India*. Vol. ii. Redfield, 1853.

Maitland, Julia Charlotte. *Letters from Madras During the Years 1836–1839*. John Murray, 1946.

Marryat, Florence. *Gup: Sketches of Anglo-Indian Life and Character*. Richard Bentley, 1868.

Martin, Monica Campbell. *Out in the Midday Sun*. Casell & Company Ltd., 1951.

Mitchell, Maria (Mrs. Murray). *In India: Sketches of Indian Life and Travel from Letters and Journals*. T. Nelson and Sons, Paternoster Row, 1876.

Moore, W. J. *Health in the Tropics; or, Sanitary Art Applied to Europeans in India*. John Churchill, 1862.

Muter, Elizabeth McMullin. *My Recollections of the Sepoy Mutiny*. John Long Limited, 1911.

Nugent, Maria. *A Journal From the Year 1811 Till the Year 1815*. Vol ii. T. and W. Boone, 1839.

Ouvry, M. H. *A Lady's Diary: Before and During the Indian Mutiny*. Chas. T. King, 1892.

Paget, Mrs. Leopold Grimstone. *Camp and Cantonment: A Journal of Life in India in 1857–1859*. Longman, Green, Longman, Roberts, & Green, 1865.

Parkes, Fanny. *Wanderings of a Pilgrim in Search of the Picturesque During Four and Twenty Years in the East with Revelations of Life in the Zenana*. Vol i. Pelham Richardson, 1850.

Postans, Marianne. *Western India in 1838*. Vol i. Saunders and Otley, 1839.

Riddell, Elizabeth and Yvonne Cramer. *With Fond Regards. Private Lives Through Letters*. National Library of Australia, 1995.

Roberts, Emma. *Scenes and Characteristics Hindostan, with Sketches of Anglo-Indian Society*. Vol. 1. W. H. Allen & Co., 1895.

———. *Scenes and Characteristics Hindostan, with Sketches of Anglo-Indian Society*. Vol. 2., W. H. Allen & Co., 1895.

———. *Scenes and Characteristics Hindostan, with Sketches of Anglo-Indian Society*. Vol. 3., W. H. Allen & Co., 1895.

Savory, Isabel. *A Sportswoman in India*. Hutchinson & Co., 1900.

Shepherd, W. J. *A Personal Narrative of the Outbreak and Massacre at Cawnpore, During the Sepoy Revolt of 1857*. London Printing Press, 1879.

Sherwood, Mary Martha. *The Life of Mrs. Sherwood*. Presbyterian Road of Publication, n.d.

Simpson, William John. *The Maintenance of Health in the Tropics*. William Wood and Company, 1905.

Steel, Flora Annie. *The Garden of Fidelity: Being the Autobiography of Flora Annie Steel 1847–1929*. Macmillan and Co., Ltd., 1930.

———. *Tales of the Punjab: Told by the People*. Asian Educational Services, 1989.

Steel, Flora Annie and Grace Gardiner. *The Complete Indian Housekeeper and Cook*. The Edinburgh Press, 1893.

Symonds, David and Gurdip Bhangoo, BBC. "The Lost World of the Raj", Episode 1. Andrew Muggleston, Vimeo, 2020.

———. "The Lost World of the Raj", Episode 2. Andrew Muggleston, Vimeo, 2020.

———. "The Lost World of the Raj", Episode 3. Andrew Muggleston, Vimeo, 2020.

Tilt, Edward John. *Elements of Health, and Principles of Female Hygiene*. Lindsay and Blakiston, 1853.

———. *Influence of India on the Health of British Women, and on the Prevention of Uterine Affections*. John Churchill and Sons, 1868.

———. *The Change of Life in Health and Disease*. John Churchill and Sons, 1870.

———. *Health in India for British Women and the Prevention of Disease in Tropical Climates*. John Churchill and Sons, 1875.

———. *A Handbook of Uterine Therapeutics and Diseases of Women*. J. & A. Churchill, 1878.

Tytler, Harriet. *An Englishwoman in India: The Memoirs of Harriet Tytler*. Oxford University Press, 1986.

Vansittart, Jane, editor. *From Minnie, with Love: The Letters of a Victorian Lady 1849–1861*. Peter Davies, 1974.

Waghorn, Thomas. *Messrs. Waghorn & Co.'s Overland Guide to India: By Three Routes to Egypt*. Smith, Elder and Co., 1846.

Waring, Edward John. *Remarks on the Uses of Some of the Bazaar Medicines and Common Medical Plants of India*. John Churchill & Sons, 1883.

Wilson, Anne Campbell (Lady). *Letters from India*. William Blackwood and Sons, 1911.

Secondary Sources:

Agnew, Eadaoin. *Imperial Women Writing in Victorian India: Representing Colonial Life, 1850–1910*. Palgrave Macmillan, 2017.

Andrews, Robyn. "Being Anglo-Indian: Practices and Stories from Calcutta". Diss. Massey U, 2005. The Engine of New New Zealand, mro.massey.ac.nz/handle/10179/959. Accessed 12 June 2019.

Aronderkar, Anjali. *For the Record: On Sexuality and the Colonial Archive in India*. Duke UP, 2009.

Athanasiades, Andreas. "Re-visiting the Raj Revival Genre: Expressions of Masculinity in *The Best Exotic Marigold Hotel*". *Revisiting Sexualities in the 21st Century*, edited by Constantinos N. Phellas, Cambridge Scholars Publishing, 2015.

Ballantyne, Tony, and Antoinette Burton, eds. *Bodies in Contact: Rethinking Colonial Encounters in World History*. Duke UP, 2005.

Ballhatchet, Kenneth. *Race, Sex, and Class under the Raj*. Weidenfeld and Nicholson, 1980.

SELECT BIBLIOGRAPHY

Barr, Pat. *The Memsahibs: The Women of Victorian India*. Faber and Faber, 1976.

Bates, Crispin. *Mutiny at the Margins: New Perspectives on the Indian Uprising of 1857*. Sage Publications, 2013.

Bhandari, Rajika. *The Raj on the Move: Story of the Dak Bungalow*. Roli Books, 2012.

Bhattacharya, Nandini. "The Sanatorium Enclave: Climate and Class in Colonial Darjeeling". *Contagion and Enclaves: Tropical Medicine in Colonial India*. Liverpool University Press, 2012, pp. 84–98.

Bhattacharyya, Sujata. "Professor B.B. Chaudhari Prize: Encounters in the Zenana: Representations of Indian Women in 19th Century Travelogues of English Women". *Proceedings of the Indian History Congress*, vol. 70, 2009, pp. 649–56.

Bissell, William Cunningham. "Engaging Colonial Nostalgia". *Cultural Anthropology*, vol. 20, no. 2, 2005, pp. 215–48.

Blunt, Alison. *Domicile and Diaspora: Anglo-Indian Women and the Spatial Politics of Home*. Blackwell Publishing, 2005.

Blunt, Alison, and Gillian Blunt, eds. *Writing Women and Space: Colonial and Postcolonial Geographies*. The Guilford Press, 1994.

Boehmer, Elleke, ed. *empire Writing: An Anthology of Colonial Literature 1870–1918*. Oxford UP, 1998.

Buettner, Elizabeth. *Empire Families: Britons and Later Imperial India*. Oxford UP, 2004.

Burton, Antoinette. *At the Heart of the Empire: Indians and the Colonial Encounter in Later-Victorian Britain*. U of California P, 1998.

———. *Empire in Question: Reading, Writing, and Teaching British Imperialism*. Duke UP, 2011.

Butler, Judith. *Gender Trouble: Feminism and the Subversion of Identity*. Routledge, 1990.

Caplan, Lionel. "Iconographies of Anglo-Indian Women: Gender Constructs and Contrasts in a Changing Society". *Modern Asian Studies*, vol. 34, no. 4, 2000, pp. 863–92.

———. *Children of Colonialism: Indians in a Postcolonial World*. Berg Publishers, 2003.

Chanana, Karuna. "Hinduism and Female Sexuality: Social Control and Education of Girls in India". *Sociological Bulletin*, vol. 50, no. 1, 2001, pp. 37–63.

———. "Women's Education in India". *Sociological Bulletin*, vol. 39, no. 1/2, 1990, pp. 75–91.

Chaudhuri, Nupur. "Memsahibs and Motherhood in Nineteenth-Century Colonial India". *Victorian Studies*, vol. 31, no. 4, 1988, pp. 517–35.

———. "Memsahibs and their Servants in Nineteenth-Century India". *Women's History Review*, vol. 3, no. 4, 1994, pp. 549–62.

Chaudhuri, Nupur, and Margaret Strobel, eds. *Western Women and Imperialism: Complicity and Resistance*. Indiana United Press, 1992.

Chitra, Sinha. *Debating Patriarchy: The Hindu Code Bill Controversy*. Oxford UP, 2012.

Clive, Henrietta. *Birds of Passage*. Eland Publishing Limited, 2016.

Codell, Julie F., ed. *Imperial Co-Histories: National Identities and the British and Colonial Press*. Rosemont Publishing & Printing, 2003.

Cornwell, Gareth. "George Webb Hardy's *The Black Peril* and the Social Meaning of 'Black Peril' in Early Twentieth-Century South Africa". *Journal of Southern African Studies*, vol. 22, no. 3, 1996, pp. 441–53.

Cramer, Yvonne. *With Fond Regards: Private Lives Through Letters*. Canberra, National Library of Australia, 1995.

Crane, Ralph, and Radhika Mohanram. "The Laws of Desire: Intimacy and Agency in Anglo-India". *Imperialism as Diaspora: Race, Sexuality, and History in Anglo-India*. Liverpool UP, 2013, pp. 108–35.

Dalrymple, William. *Begums Thugs and White Mughals*. Sickle Moon Books, 2012.

———. *The Anarchy: The Relentless Rise of the East India Company*. Bloomsbury Publishing, 2019.

David, Deirdre. *Rule Britannia: Women, Empire, and Victorian Writing*. Cornell UP, 1995.

David, Deirdre, et al. "Imperial Chintz: Domesticity and Empire". *Victorian Literature and Culture*, vol. 27, no. 2, 1999, pp. 569–77.

Davis, Nira-Yuval, and Flora Anthias. *Woman-Nation-State*. Palgrave Macmillan, 1989.

———. *Gender and Nation*. SAGE Publications, 1997.

Dean, Carolyn J. "The Productive Hypothesis: Foucault, Gender, and the History of Sexuality". *History and Theory*, vol. 33, no. 3, 1994, pp. 271–96.

De Courcy, Anne. *The Fishing Fleet: Husband-Hunting in the Raj*. Orion, 2012.

De Gruyther, Leslie. "Mixed Marriages". *Journal of Comparative Legislation and International Law*, vol. 11, no. 1, 1929, pp. 34–41.

Dohmen, Renate. "Memsahibs and the 'Sunny East': Representations of British India by Millicent Douglas Pilkington and Beryl White". *Victorian Literature and Culture*, vol. 40, no. 1, 2012, pp. 153–77.

Douglas, Jessica. *A Glimpse of Empire*. Rupa, 2012.

Duncan, Nancy. *BodySpace: Destabilizing Geographies of Gender and Sexuality*. Routledge, 1996.

Dutta, Sutapa. *British Women Missionaries in Bengal, 1793–1861*. Anthem Press, 2017.

SELECT BIBLIOGRAPHY

Fitchett, W. H. *The Tale of the Great Mutiny*. Charles Scribner's Sons, 1901.

Forbes, Geraldine Hancock. *Women in Colonial India: Essays on Politics, Medicine, and Historiography*. Orient Longman, 2005.

Forster, E. M. *A Passage to India*. Dover Publications, 2020.

Foster, William. *The Embassy of Sir Thomas Roe to India: 1615–19*. Oxford UP, 1926.

George, Rosemary Marangoly. "Homes in the Empire, Empires in the Home". *Cultural Critique*, no. 26, 1993, pp. 95–127.

———. *The Politics of Home: Postcolonial Relocations and Twentieth-Century Fiction*. U of California P, 1999.

Ghose, Indira. *Women Travelers in Colonial India: The Power of the Female Gaze*. Oxford UP, 1998.

———. "The Memsahib Myth: Englishwomen in Colonial India". Women and Others: Perspectives on Race, Gender, and Empire, edited by C. Daileader et al., Palgrave Macmillan, 2007.

Ghosh, Durba. "Gender and Colonialism: Expansion or Marginalisation?" *The Historical Journal*, vol. 47, no. 3, 2004, pp. 737–55.

———. *Sex and the Family in Colonial India: The Making of Empire*. Cambridge UP, 2008.

Gillis, John R. *For Better, For Worse: British Marriages, 1600 to the present*. Oxford UP, 1985.

Goodman, Sam. "Lady Amateurs and Gentleman Professionals: Emergency Nursing in the Indian Mutiny". *Colonial Caring: A History of Colonial and Post-Colonial Nursing*, edited by Helen Sweet and Sue Hawkins, Manchester UP, 2015, pp. 18–40.

Gowans, Georgina. "Imperial Geographies of Home: Memsahibs and Miss-Sahibs in India and Britain, 1915–1947". *Cultural Geographies*, vol. 10, no. 4, 2003, pp. 424–41.

Grewal, Inderpal. *Home and Harem: Nation, Gender, Empire and the Cultures of Travel*. Duke UP, 1996.

Grossman, Joyce. "Ayahs, Dhayes, and Bearers: Mary Sherwood's Indian Experience and 'Constructions of Subordinated Others.'" *South Atlantic Review*, vol. 66, no. 2, 2001, pp. 14–44.

Hammerton, A. James. *Emigrant Gentlewomen: Genteel Poverty and Emigration, 1830–1914*. Taylor & Francis, 2016.

Harrison, Mark. *Public Health in British India: Anglo-Indian Preventive Medicine 1859–1914*. Cambridge UP, 1994.

Hasan, Narin. *Diagnosing the Empire: Women, Medical Knowledge, and Colonial Mobility*. Taylor & Francis, 2011.

Hickman, Katie. *She-Merchants, Buccaneers & Gentlewomen: British Women in India*. Virago P, 2019.

SELECT BIBLIOGRAPHY

Hoch, Paula. *White Hero, Black Beast: Racism, Sexism, and the Mask of Masculinity*. Pluto P, 1979.

Hyam, Ronald. *Empire and Sexuality: The British Experience*. Manchester UP, 1990.

———. *Understanding the British Empire*. Cambridge UP, 2010.

Illbruck, Helmut. *Nostalgia: Origins and Ends of an Unenlightened Disease*. Northwestern UP, 2012.

Khair, Tabish. "Introduction: The Gothic, Postcolonialism and Otherness". *The Gothic, Postcolonialism and Otherness: Ghosts from Elsewhere*. Palgrave Macmillan, 2009.

Kohli, Atul. *Imperialism and the Developing World: How Britain and the United States Shaped the Global Periphery*. Oxford University Press, 2020.

Kukla, Rebecca. *Mass Hysteria: Medicine, Culture, and Mothers' Bodies*. Rowman and Letterfield, 2005.

Kumari, Jayawardena. *The White Woman's Burden: Western Women and South Asia during British Colonial Rule*. Psychology P, 1995.

Levine, Philippa, editor. "White Women's Sexuality in Colonial Settings". *Prostitution, Race and Politics*. Routledge, 2003.

———. *Gender and Empire*. Oxford UP, 2007.

Lind, Mary Ann. *The Compassionate Memsahibs: Welfare Activities of British Women in India, 1900–1947*. Greenwood P, 1998.

Loomba, Ania. *Colonialism/Postcolonialism*. Routledge, 1998.

Looser, Devoney. *British Women Writers and the Writing of History 1670–1820*. John Hopkins UP, 2000.

Macmillan, Margaret. *Women of the Raj*. Thames and Hudson, 1988.

Marshall, P. J. "British Society in India under the East India Company". *Modern Asian Studies*, vol. 31, no. 1, 1997, pp. 89–108.

Masters, John. *Bhowani Junction*. Bantam Fifty World Books, 1955.

McCabe, Jane. *Race, Tea and Colonial Resettlement: Imperial Families, Interrupted*. Bloomsbury, 2017.

McClintock, Anne. "The Angel of Progress: Pitfalls of the Term 'Post-Colonialism'". *Social Text*, no. 31/32, 1992, pp. 84–98.

———. *Imperial Leather: Race, Gender, and Sexuality in the Colonial Conquest*. Routledge, 1995.

———. "British Cinema and Raj Revival". *Hybrid Heritage on Screen: The 'Raj Revival' in the Thatcher Era*. Palgrave Macmillan, 2015.

Meyer, Susan. *Imperialism at Home: Race and Victorian Women's Fiction*. Cornell UP, 1996.

Mezey, Jason Howard. "Mourning the Death of the Raj? Melancholia as Historical Engagement in Paul Scott's Raj Quartet". *Studies in the Novel*, vol. 38, no. 3, 2006, pp. 327–352.

Midgley, Clare, ed. *Gender and Imperialism*. Manchester UP, 1998.

Millet, Kate. "Instances of Sexual Politics". *Sexual Politics*. U of Illinois P, 2000.

Mills, Sara. "Constraints on Production and Reception". *Discourses of Differences: An Analysis of Women's Travel Writing and Colonialism*. Routledge, 1991.

———. *Gender and Colonial Space*. Manchester UP, 2005.

———. "Indigenous Spatiality within the Colonial Sphere". *Gender and Colonial Space*. Manchester UP, 2005, pp. 136–57.

Misra, Geetanjali, and Radhika Chandiramani, editors. *Sexuality, Gender and Rights: Exploring Theory and Practice*. SAGE Publications, 2005.

Mitchinson, Wendy. *The Nature of their Bodies: Women and their Doctors in Victorian Canada*. U of Toronto P, 1991.

Mizutani, Santoshi. *The Meaning of White: Race, Class, and the 'Domiciled Community' in British India 1858–1930*. Oxford UP, 2012.

Naiyer, Promod K. *Colonial Voices: The Discourses of Empire*. John Wiley & Sons, 2012.

Nelson, Claudia. *Family Ties in Victorian England*. Praeger Publishers, 2007.

Nevile, Pran. *Rare Glimpses of the Raj*. Somaiya Publications, 1998.

———. *Stories from the Raj: Sahibs, Memsahibs and Others*. Indialog Publishing, 2004.

———. *Sahibs' India: Vignettes from the Raj*. Penguin Books, 2010.

Nicholson, Nigel. *Mary Curzon*. Harper & Row, 1977.

O'Riley, Michael F. "Postcolonial Haunting: Anxiety, Affect, and the Situated Encounter". *Postcolonial Text*, vol. 3, no. 4. Ohio State U, 2007, https://www.postcolonial.org/index.php/pct/article/view/728/0. Accessed 20 March 2019.

Pal-Lapinski, Piya. "Infection as Resistance: Exoticised Memsahibs and Native Courtesans in Colonial India". *The Exotic Woman in Nineteenth-Century British Fiction and Culture: A Reconsideration*. U of New Hampshire P, 2005.

Parry, Benita. *Delusions and Discoveries: India in the British Imagination, 1880–1930*. Verso, 1972.

Pati, Biswamoy. *The Great Rebellion of 1857 in India: Exploring Transgressions, Contests and Diversities*. Taylor & Francis, 2010.

Paxton, Nancy. "Feminism under the Raj: Complicity and Resistance in the Writings of Flora Annie Steel and Annie Besant". *Women's Studies International Forum*, vol. 13, no. 4, 1990, pp. 333–46.

Peppin, Brian. *Black and White: The Anglo-Indian Identity in Recent English Fiction*. AuthorHouse, 2012.

Phegley, Jennifer. *Courtship and Marriage in Victorian England*. Praeger, 2012.

Pratt, Marie Louise. *Imperial Eyes: Travel Writing and Transculturalism*. Routledge, 1992.

Procida, Mary A. "'The Greater Part of My Life Has Been Spent in India': Autobiography and the Crisis of Empire in the Twentieth Century". *Biography*, vol. 25, no. 1, 2002, pp. 130–50.

———. *Married to the Empire: Gender, Politics and Imperialism in India 1883–1984*. Manchester UP, 2003.

Procter, James, and Angela Smith. "Gothic and Empire". *The Routledge Companion to Gothic*, edited by Catherine Spooner and Emma McEvoy, Routledge, 2007.

Purcell, Hugh. *After the Raj: The Last Stayers-On and the Legacy of British India*. History P, 2008.

Ramusack, Barbara N., and Antoinette Burton. "Feminism, Imperialism and Race: A Dialogue Between India and Britain". *Women's History Review*, vol. 3, no. 4.

Regaignon, Dara Rossman. "Intimacy's Empire: Children, Servants and Missionaries in Mary Martha Sherwood's 'Little Henry and his Bearer'". *Children's Literature Association Quarterly*, vol. 26, no. 2, 2001.

Rege, Sharmila. *Sociology of Gender*. SAGE Publications, 2003.

Roye, Susmita, and Rajeswar Mittapalli. *The Male Empire under the Female Gaze: The British Raj and the Memsahib*. Cambria P, 2013.

Rubenstein, Roberta. *Home Matters: Longing and Belonging, Nostalgia and Mourning in Women's Fiction*. Palgrave Macmillan, 2011.

Rushdie, Salman. "Imaginary Homelands". *Imaginary Homelands: Essays and Criticism*. Granta, 1991.

———. "Outside the Whale". Granta Magazine, 1984, https://granta.com/outside-the-whale/. Accessed 20 March 2020.

Schroeder, Janice. "Strangers in Every Port: Stereotypes of Women Travelers". *Victorian Review*, vol. 24, no. 2, 1998, pp. 118–129.

Scott, Paul. *The Raj Quartet: Jewel in the Crown*. Alfred A. Knopf, 2007.

Sen, Indrani. *Women and the Empire: Representations in the Writings of India (1858–1900)*. Orient Longman, 2002.

———. "The Memsahib's 'Madness': The European Woman's Mental Health in Late Nineteenth-Century India". *Social Scientist*, vol. 33, no. 5/6, 2005, pp. 26–48.

———. "Looking through the Purdah". *Economic and Political Weekly*, vol. 41, no. 18, 2006, pp. 1775–1777.

Sen, Samita. *Women and Labour in Late Colonial India: The Bengal Jute Industry*. Cambridge UP, 2004.

Sen, Samita et al. *Intimate Others: Marriage and Sexualities in India*. Stree, 2011.

Sharpe, Jenny. *Allegories of Empire: The Figure of Woman in the Colonial Text*. U of Minnesota P, 1993.

Sinha, Mrinalini. *Colonial Masculinity: The 'Manly Englishman' and the 'Effeminate Bengali' in the Late Nineteenth Century*. Manchester UP, 1995.

Sreenivas, Mytheli. *Wives, Widows and Concubines: The Conjugal Family Ideal in Colonial India*. Indiana UP, 2008.

Stanford, J. K., ed. *Ladies in the Sun: The Memsahibs' India 1790–1860*. The Galley P, 1962.

Stoler, Ann Laura. *Carnal Knowledge and Imperial Power: Race and the Intimate in Colonial Rule*. U of California P, 2002.

Strobel, Margaret. *European Women and the Second British Empire*. The Association of American UP, 1991.

———. *Married to the Empire; Gender, Politics, and Imperialism in India, 1883–1947*. Manchester UP, 2002.

Victoria, Margree. "The Good Memsahib? Marriage, Infidelity and Empire in Alice Perrin's Anglo-Indian Tales". *British Women's Short Supernatural Fiction, 1860–1930*. Palgrave Macmillan, 2019.

Tunzelmann, Alex von. *Indian Summer: The Secret History of the End of an Empire*. Simon & Schuster, 2008.

Walder, Dennis. *Postcolonial Nostalgias: Writing, Representation and Memory*. Taylor & Francis, 2011.

Watt, Cary Anthony, and Michael Mann, editors. *Civilizing Missions in Colonial and Postcolonial South Asia: From Improvement to Development*. Anthem P, 2011.

Younger, Coralie. *Wicked Women of the Raj: European Women Who Broke Society's Rules and Married Indian Princes*. HarperCollins Publishers India, 2013.

Zahid, R. Chaudhary. *Afterimage of Empire: Photography in Nineteenth-Century India*. U of Minnesota P, 2005.

Zlotnick, Susan. "Domesticating Imperialism: Curry and Cookbooks in Victorian England". *Frontiers: A Journal of Women Studies*, vol. 16, no. 2/3, 1996, pp. 51–68.

INDEX

INDEX

INDEX

INDEX

INDEX

ABOUT THE AUTHOR

IPSHITA NATH has a Ph.D. in English literature and was formerly an Assistant Professor at the University of Delhi. She is currently a Postdoctoral Research Fellow working in the area of health and medicine in colonial India at the Department of History, University of Saskatchewan. Her short story collection, *The Rickshaw Reveries*, was published in 2020.